# Conference Season

## Steve Leach

Published by Bennion Kearny Limited
6 Woodside, Churnet View Road
Oakamoor, ST10 3AE

*www.BennionKearny.com*

Steve Leach is Emeritus Professor of Local Government at De Montfort University, Leicester. He has published (singly or jointly) twelve books about local politics and local government, including 'Managing in a Political World' (Palgrave/Macmillan, 2010.), 'Local Political Leadership' (Policy Press, 2000; with David Wilson.), and 'Botched Business; the Damaging Process of Local Government Reorganisation 2006-2008' (Douglas McLean, 2008; with Michael Chisholm.). Conference Season stems from a lifelong interest in professional football at all levels, and an enthusiasm for visiting and commenting on the kind of medium-sized towns in which most of the clubs in the Football Conference are based.

## Acknowledgements

I would like to express my gratitude to the various people who have helped me get this book into a publishable form.

First, I would  like to acknowledge those who read earlier drafts of chapters, and made helpful comments which invariably improved their quality. So grateful thanks to John Davies, Anna Levin, Eleanor Levin, Karen Lloyd, and Dennis Reed.

In particular, in this connection, I would like to thank Michael Crick for volunteering to read through all twenty-six chapters, in the gaps in his busy work schedule for Channel Four News. His feedback, sometimes critical but always constructive was invaluable in enabling me to transform something that was almost certainly not of publishable standard into a version which a publisher was prepared to accept.

Which brings me to my publisher, James Lumsden-Cook of Bennion Kearny. Many thanks to James, for seeing enough quality in the draft chapters I sent him to agree to publish 'Conference Season' and then for his many helpful suggestions on ways in which each chapter could be improved. The book has benefitted greatly from his refreshingly proactive attitude to the work of the authors he deals with.

I would also like to thank Harry Pearson, for providing a key inspiration for my book. His football classic 'The Far Corner', first published in 1994, is one of my favourite books about the beautiful game, which convinced me that a book with the same kind of structure as his - a series of visits to football matches in a range of different places (in his case the North-East, in mine the Conference) - might just be a viable proposition.

Next, grateful thanks to Karen for supporting the project, even though it involved a series of often inconvenient absences from home, as I made my way to Braintree, Kidderminster, Woking and other faraway places, often necessitating overnight stops. Thanks too to Callum and Fergus for showing genuine interest in my accounts of visits to these places, even though (despite my best endeavours) neither is particularly interested in football.

Thanks again to Aileen Kowal who typed up the first draft of all the chapters, displaying her customary skill in translating my scruffy handwritten versions into coherent prose.

Finally, I would like to thank all those supporters at the twenty-four Conference venues who were prepared to talk to me in nearby pubs, supporters clubs bars, and on the terraces or in the stands, and share their thoughts about their teams' recent fortunes, prospects and idiosyncrasies. The book has benefitted greatly from their input.

# Table of Contents

# Introduction

As a schoolboy in Manchester, it is not surprising that my first experience of watching professional football was with one of the two famous Manchester clubs. I was first taken to Maine Road, in 1950, when City were emerging from a brief spell in Division Two, and where they beat Barnsley 6-0. The match generated expectations, in seven-year-old me, of goal feasts which have rarely happened since!

Like many youngsters, I immediately fell in love with the game. I'd never before experienced anything like the feeling of being part of a large excited crowd that roared with one mighty voice every time City scored. In the early 1950s, Britain was still emerging from the austerity years after the Second World War; the traditional reserve of its middle classes had not yet been diluted by the changes in attitudes to sex, which didn't develop momentum until the early 1960s. Maybe watching football was one of the few outlets which allowed us to transcend this reserve and express emotions overtly and joyfully.

I loved the fact that the game of football involved both competition and co-operation. However talented your individual players, you had to operate effectively as a team to beat your opponents. I loved the intricate patterns of play: the sequence of passes which split open a defence; the tricky winger with the ability to dribble past a series of opponents and put over a dangerous cross; the stalwart defender whose headed goal-line clearance prevented a certain goal.

I enjoyed the journeys to and from the Maine Road: walking with my dad through the terraced streets of Moss Side which surrounded the ground, which seemed so different

## Introduction

from, and much more interesting than, the rows of semi-detached houses in the Manchester suburb where I grew up. Later I cycled to the ground with my friend John Davies, where we parked our bikes in the back yard of one of the many terraced houses which permitted you to do so (for the charge of three pence, old money).

These qualities – the emotional outlet, the euphoria of a goal scored, the individual artistry, the momentum of a well-worked passing sequence, and the heady atmosphere of the journey to (and from) the football ground in the company of countless others – have continued to delight me over the subsequent sixty years.

I also played football in my younger years, but my career as a midfield dynamo with Parrswood Athletic, St Theresa's F.C. (Chester), and Cheshire County Planners need not detain us here.

In the early 1950s I was taken three or four times a year to either Maine Road or Old Trafford by my dad and my Uncle Arthur, neither of whom, untypically, had developed a strong allegiance to one club or the other. I suspect that there was a degree of opportunism about these visits; they went when domestic responsibilities permitted, on a Saturday when either City or United might be at home. Old Trafford had only recently been renovated after considerable war damage. For four seasons after the war, United had played their home games at Maine Road. At both grounds, it was not uncommon for the turnstile attendant to let my dad lift me over the turnstile (thus distorting the accuracy of the published attendance figure!).

I remember, too, the crush of people leaving Old Trafford after a match. There were a couple of pedestrian bridges over the railway which ran alongside the ground, which had to cater for large numbers of supporters on their way back to Stretford or Chorlton. The proximity of existing bodies was such that it was not uncommon for me to be carried along with my feet off the ground. Looking back, it's surprising that no one was ever crushed to death. At the time it seemed great fun!

By the mid-1950s I had identified with City rather than United. I can't quite remember why - maybe it was a preference for the underdog? By the time City reached the Cup Final in 1955, John Davies and I were committed supporters. Dad and Uncle Arthur both went to the final, where City lost 3-1 to Newcastle United, but not to the final in 1956 which City did win, and which was memorable for the heroics of Bert Trautmann, who played on after breaking his neck (though he didn't know it at the time).

Although Manchester City was my main football interest throughout the 1950s and '60s (and indeed, remained so until the first decade of the new millennium) two visits to other clubs led to the development of a parallel interest in league football at lower levels, an interest which later eclipsed my focus on the big clubs and the Premiership. The first took place in 1953; a visit to watch Accrington Stanley play Chesterfield at Peel Park in the old Third Division North when Accrington were struggling near the bottom of the league[*]. Chesterfield played the better football, as befitted their position in the upper reaches of the league but one had the impression that a team of real quality (by Division Three North standards) would have made mincemeat of Stanley that particular afternoon. As it was, Chesterfield scored before the interval, and after a good deal of honest endeavour, Accrington managed to equalise towards the end of the second half.

---

[*] Indeed they finished next to the bottom at the end of the season.

## Introduction

In reality, with the benefit of hindsight, it was a rather ordinary game between two undistinguished teams. At the time, however, I was transported. It was different from my previous visits to Maine Road or Old Trafford, but equally compelling. What fascinated me was the immediacy of the experience: being close to the pitch, seeing the expressions on the faces of players, observing the crunching tackles up close, and hearing the individual comments (including a good deal of abuse) of the spectators.

Football was still packing in the crowds, in the euphoric period following the end of the Second World War. There were around 7,000 people at Peel Park that day; the ground seemed full, and the atmosphere (to a ten year-old) was one of great excitement. I remember in particular the unenviable experience of Accrington's outside-right, whose name was Collins. In those days right-wingers were expected to run with the ball towards their opposing full-backs, neatly sidestep their tackles, and create space to dispatch dangerous crosses into the penalty area. Collins was manifestly incapable of making any progress beyond the approaching run. Time after time the full-back blocked his progress. As the game went on, Collins's confidence fell lower and lower. The home supporters' reaction moved from frustration to abuse to ridicule. Even as a ten year-old, I felt sorry for the poor bloke. I wonder if he ever played for Accrington Stanley again.

The second game involved a visit in the spring of 1957 to watch Stockport County play Workington at Edgeley Park, with John Davies (whose family had moved to Stockport the previous year). Again it was a memorable experience. Again there was the proximity to the pitch and the teams, the intimacy of the atmosphere, the closeness of the contact between spectators and players. It was an important game; both Stockport and Workington had an outside chance of

promotion from Division Three (North) to Division Two.
Stockport's centre-forward was a young goal-scoring
prodigy called Ray Drake, whose growing reputation was
such that rumours had been heard of an exchange deal with
the venerable Nat Lofthouse, the famous Bolton Wanderers
centre-forward. It was probably as well for Bolton that they
did not pursue the deal, because a year later, Lofthouse
scored twice for Bolton in the FA Cup Final against
Manchester United, whilst Ray Drake, having failed to fulfil
his early promise, was turning out for Cheadle Rovers in a
local semi-professional league.

On the day, Stockport could not continue what had been a
very successful run; Workington won 1-0, and Stockport's
hopes of promotion evaporated. But I had developed a taste
for football in the lower divisions, which was rewarded the
next season, when Stockport had a famous cup run, which
included 3-0 victory over Luton Town (then fourth in
Division One) before they lost unluckily 3-2 to West Ham
United in East London.

That experience was the start of a 56-year (and still
counting) attachment to Stockport County, which operated
in parallel for half a century with an attachment (recently
terminated; see below) to Manchester City. In May 2011, to
my dismay, County were relegated from Division Two of
the Football League to what used to be called the (Vauxhall)
Conference, but which is now, for the time being anyway,
the Blue Square Bet Premier League. After 55 years of ups
and downs – mostly downs, but some notable ups, such as a
five year sojourn in the Championship between 1996 and
2001, and reaching the League Cup semi-final in 1996 -
Stockport County, my local club, had finally fallen out of
the League into the uncertain world of non-league football.

In the Blue Square Bet Premier League (which from now on
I'm going to refer to as the Conference, because the term is

## Introduction

still widely used and it enables me to devise a clever title for this book) they encountered many old friends. The Conference in 2011-12 comprised a mixture of other giants (by non-league standards) who have fallen on hard times, such as Wrexham and Mansfield Town; long-term Conference stalwarts such as Forest Green Rovers and Kettering Town; and new recruits who would either find themselves struggling (such as Alfreton Town) or would move up to higher things (as did Crawley Town in 2011, and Fleetwood Town in 2012).

Despite losing all but three of their 2010-11 playing staff, Stockport County were expected to be amongst the leaders in this new (and unwelcome) world. A new manager – Dietmar Haaman – had been appointed (the former Liverpool and Germany international whose goal at Wembley in 2000 triggered the resignation of Kevin Keegan as England manager). A new set of players with impressive (by non-league standards) credentials had been recruited. Surely we would be back where we belonged by May 2012, or at the very least, contesting the play-offs?

Sadly, it didn't work out like that. After a mediocre start involving several 1-1 draws, interspersed with the occasional victory (or defeat), things went downhill. Dietmar Haaman resigned, having demonstrated, as had Bobby Charlton and Roy Keane (amongst others) before him, that an impressive playing record is no guarantee of managerial effectiveness. County slumped into one of the four relegation places, where they kept company with Bath City, Alfreton Town, and Hayes and Yeading. The spectre loomed of a further relegation into the Blue Square Bet North, where they would be facing Guiseley (where?), Solihull Moors, and Vauxhall Motors (a factory team?). Could this really be the same club which I had seen, as recently as 2009, holding moneybags Leicester City to a 1-1 draw at the Walker Stadium?

The one ray of hope was the managerial appointment in December 2011 of Jim Gannon, the former player and manager, who had saved County from an earlier exit to the Conference in 2006, and then inspired them to promotion to Division One, after a memorable play-off final against Rochdale in 2008. But results continued to be disappointing, and by the end of February, County were a mere four points above the relegation zone, and had played a couple of games more than most of their fellow-strugglers.

This perilous situation inspired me to make a decision. During the previous 3-4 years, I had considered from time to time the idea of writing a book called 'Conference Season' which would involve a visit to each of the twenty-four towns in which the Conference clubs were based. The intention would not only be to attend and report on 24 matches, but also to research and explore the towns themselves, observing how they were coping with the impact of the economic recession, from which there seemed no sign of recovery in 2012. So the book would not only be about football, although my love of football would be its main inspiration.

If County survived, I vowed to myself that I would put this plan into action. I would bear witness to a season in which their fortunes would surely improve, and hopefully result in the team returning to their rightful place (the Football League), and me with a best-selling book on my hands! In the event, survival was ensured on Saturday April 14th when Stockport managed a 1-1 draw at Edgeley Park with Braintree Town (a result which itself illustrates how far the once-mighty County have fallen) whilst Hayes and Yeading (average home gate 300) obligingly lost 3-1 at home to

## Introduction

Mansfield. It was still possible for Hayes and Yeading to overtake AFC Telford United or Newport County, but not Stockport, who were seven points better off with two games each left to play. Who else went down didn't concern me. It wasn't going to be Stockport; and my book was about to become a reality.

The Conference was already familiar territory. My family moved from Gateshead to Kendal, in Cumbria, in 1995. The nearest Football League clubs were Carlisle United and Preston North End, both 45 miles away. But I noted with interest at the end of the 1996 season that Morecambe, a mere twenty miles from where we lived had been promoted to the Conference. I began to watch them intermittently, typically in crowds of between 1,000 and 1,500. They prospered under the astute managership of Jim Harvey, and after a couple of near misses, finally gained promotion to the Football League in 2007, after a 2-1 play-off win at Wembley against Exeter City. I was impressed by the quality of football I saw at Morecambe, which seemed to me as good as anything you'd see in Division Two, a judgement supported by the fact that clubs promoted from the Conference typically prospered in these more illustrious circles. I looked forward to the prospect of exploring the world of the Conference beyond the games I'd seen at Christie Park (Morecambe's home ground)[*] between 1996 and 2007. Indeed my involvement with the club will be reflected in the indulgence of commenting from time to time on ex-Morecambe players who appear in the games I attend.

The decision to invest a season of football-watching in the Conference was strengthened by a growing sense of

---

[*] Since redeveloped as a supermarket, with Morecambe moving to a new stadium – the Globe Arena in 2011

disillusionment with the over-commercialised world of the
Premiership, with its plethora of over-paid prima-donnas.
Admittedly the quality of football there was, at its best, in a
different class from that of Division Two and the
Conference. But there was a sense in which links between
club and local community had been weakened not least in
the make-up of most of the teams concerned, with a high
quota of overseas imports and the dearth of players who
had been discovered and nurtured in the locality. The last
straw (for me) came in 2010 when Manchester City were
taken over by a group of Middle-Eastern oil sheikhs with
apparently limitless resources to pump into the club. As a
result City could (and did) attract high profile targets from
other clubs, by the simple process of offering them (much)
more money than they could hope to get at Everton (Joleon
Lescott) or Arsenal (Sammi Nasri). I really didn't want to be
associated with this world. So I detached myself from a club
I'd supported since the 1950s, and happily focused my
attention on the Conference, where the link between club
and local community remained strong. I began to see my
book as a quest to rediscover the soul of professional
football, by focusing on a level far removed from this
commercialised circus, where local teams were supported by
local people.

It was thus with a greater than customary interest that I
followed the various play-off results from the top of the
Blue Square Bet North and South Divisions, as well as the
Conference itself, and the relegations from Division Two of
the Football League. Who would join Fleetwood Town in
the League and (more importantly for me) who would it
leave behind? The answers were York City, who were
promoted, and Luton Town, Wrexham and Mansfield
Town who stayed down. A pity in a way because I would
have enjoyed a visit to York rather more than to any of the

## Introduction

other three. And who would join Hyde and Woking in being promoted to the Conference? The answer was Nuneaton Town (the recently re-born successor to Nuneaton Borough) and Dartford.

The resulting composition of the Conference for the 2012-13 season contained the usual diverse mixture of clubs. I identified four categories; first, the 'fallen giants'. It may seem something of an exaggeration to regard the likes of Lincoln City and Grimsby Town as giants, but by non-league standards they are. However, not all clubs who have been in the Football League merited this epithet. For example Kidderminster Harriers had enjoyed half-a-dozen seasons in Division Two of the Football League relatively recently, but their previous (and subsequent) experience has been that of 'Conference regulars', a category which also includes AFC Telford United and Forest Green Rovers. Third, there are clubs currently in the Conference who once graced the lower reaches of the Football League (in the days of Division Three (North and South) and later Divisions Three and Four, but who failed to be re-elected at some point in their history and have (so far) never returned. So whilst I remember the days when Southport and Barrow were regular visitors to Stockport's Edgeley Park in the 1950s and 1960s, many younger readers will be unaware of their long-departed glory days. These clubs have the achievement of Accrington Stanley (ejected from the Football League in 1962; back in 2007) and Aldershot as an inspiration. And there are several others in this 'blasts from the past' category waiting lower down the pyramid: FC Halifax and Bradford Park Avenue to name but two.

Finally there is a category which brings to mind the derisory chant which often greets the introduction of a substitute of the visiting team whom none of the home supporters have ever heard of …'ooo are yer?' (a taunt sometimes applied to

the away team per se). Some of the clubs now in the
Conference will not even be familiar to Conference
aficionados. Amongst such newcomers in 2011-12 were
Alfreton Town and Braintree Town. It is unlikely many
supporters of other clubs will have the foggiest idea where
Alfreton, in particular, is (in fact it's in south Derbyshire).
The 2012-13 'ooo are yers' included Hyde and Dartford.

So, at the start of my journey to the 24 Conference venues I
was faced with the usual mixture of has-beens, never-wases
and young upstarts; clubs as big as one-time FA Cup
finalists Luton Town, and as small as Forest Green Rovers
(located in Nailsworth, Gloucestershire, population 6,600)
and Alfreton Town. I had no journeys of more than 230
miles to undertake; fortuitously none of Truro City, Dover,
Eastbourne Borough or Weymouth had been promoted in
2011-12.

Football teams express and inspire a sense of identity with
particular places. Despite the fact that we live in a more
mobile society than our parents did, a sense of place still
matters to most of us, either because we've lived there most
or all of our lives, or because we've made a positive choice
to move there. Because place still matters, we find ways of
expressing its significance for us: we join a local society, we
do voluntary work (for agencies such as the WRVS) which
contribute to the local community; or we support the local
football team, actively or passively. If the team does well, we
are pleased. It puts our settlement on the map, and makes
other people more aware of it. Who would know that
Forest Green was a suburb of Nailsworth in the Cotswolds,
if Forest Green Rovers hadn't won promotion to the
Conference in 1989 (and stayed there ever since)? Who
would ever have heard of Alfreton if they hadn't done
likewise in 2011? When a Conference team (e.g. Morecambe
in 2007) or a Division Two side (e.g. Stockport County in

## Introduction

2008) competes in a play-off final at Wembley, a crowd of supporters up to ten times their average home gate typically makes the trip to London, to demonstrate the fact that living in Morecambe (or Stockport) means something to them. So, throughout the book, I'll be emphasising and illustrating the importance of the relationship between place and football team.

My professional career has been focused on local politics and local government. One of the constant threads in the series of local government reorganisations in recent years has been the decoupling of real places, with which people continue to identify, from the councils which represent them. Some of the Conference venues I visited still have a council where there remains a connection (e.g. Tamworth, Nuneaton, Braintree, Woking). Others, however, 'have lost that link' and become subsumed in larger amorphous councils whose names mean little to residents or outsiders (Hyde in Tameside; Macclesfield in East Cheshire; and Southport in Sefton). I make no apologies for drawing readers' attention to anomalies in the relationships between football club, community identity, and local politics and government when to do so aids an understanding of the context in which the club operates.

My first visit would be to Barrow. I couldn't wait for the season to start!

# Submarines, Screamers and Savage Dogs

Barrow vs AFC Telford United

Saturday 11th August 2012

Barrow: the end of the road, the end of the line. A one-horse town at the dead end of what has been described as 'the longest cul-de-sac in England' (the A590). A town like Hull or Margate that you would go to only if you chose to, or had to; you don't pass through it on the way to anywhere (apart from the nature reserve on Walney Island).

Or at least that's the popular misconception of Barrow from those who don't really know the town. To those who live there or those (like me) who regularly visit it, it's a unique friendly place, full of character. If you don't believe me, check out Nella Last's heart-warming accounts of life in Barrow during, and after, World War Two ('Nella Last's War' and 'Nella Last's Peace', Profile Books, 2006 and 2008).

Barrow is a 'company town', dependent on its shipyards, and in particular one firm - BAE Systems - for its economic viability and its economic future. If BAE Systems went out of business, Barrow would become a ghost town. There is precious little else in the way of non-service industry. There is a sizeable toilet-roll manufacturing concern (Kimberley-Clark) but that doesn't have the same status as shipbuilding, does it? It's reminiscent of what happened to Consett in County Durham – it used to manufacture steel, now it manufactures potato crisps.

Barrow is the nearest conference venue to Kendal, where I live. In its heyday (up until the 1990s) the physical, economic, and psychological dominance of the shipyards was transparent. My wife's father used to work at Vickers shipyards and Karen remembers watching in awe as the flood of workers poured out of the factory gates – on foot or on bicycle – at clocking-off time. In 1990, one in five of the population of the town and its catchment area were employed at Vickers. It remains the best surviving example in Britain of the company town. My first visit to Barrow in the early 1980s was to take part in a mass protest against the Trident programme. At an appointed hour, we protesters all simulated death and lay prone on the cold road surfaces of Barrow. I don't suppose the shipyard workers (or the government) lost much sleep as a result of our play-acting (or indeed presence).

Barrow remains a compact isolated town, once a northern outpost of Lancashire, now a southern outpost of Cumbria. It has spread inland from its historic fishing village core, adjacent to Barrow Island, where the shipyard is located. No resident of Barrow lives more than three miles from the town centre. It is unlikely that many people would choose to live in Barrow and work elsewhere (although the reverse doesn't hold true; the senior executives of BAE Systems are highly unlikely to be found living in Barrow itself!). Because of its isolation, Barrow is probably as close to a real community as you will find nowadays; a place where people live, work, and pursue leisure activities together. To be a 'Barrovion' still has a real meaning.

Barrow is a town with a tradition of civic enterprise, epitomised by its impressive town hall; once a proud county borough responsible for all the local services within its boundaries. A town where the local captains of industry, including the founding fathers of industrial Barrow - James Ramsden and Henry Schneider (see below) - played a leading role on the town council. Sadly those qualities of local status and independence disappeared long ago. In 1974's local government reorganisation, Barrow was demoted to district council status, with many key services, including education, social services and highways transferred to the newly-created Cumbria County Council and administered from Carlisle, 90 miles and a two-hour journey away. Given Barrow's isolation and strong community identity, this change seemed a retrograde step. And unlike Ramsden and Schneider, BAE executives would not dream of involving themselves in local council affairs.

Although the shipyard now demonstrates Barrow's economy, it was not always so. Barrow's transformation from a small fishing village in 1840 to a smoky industrial town within 30 years was inspired by the two aforementioned men. James Ramsden was the managing director of the Furness Railway, and masterminded its development in the 1840's and 50's, largely to facilitate the movement of iron ore around the Furness area, where there were plentiful deposits. Only in 1857 was this self-contained little railway network linked to the outside world. Henry Schneider, on the other hand, established an ironworks at Hindpool in 1859, a venture which in 1866 merged with a recently-established steelworks to become the Barrow Haematite Steel Company, 'the engine which was to drive Barrow's growth for the next thirty years'[*]. Also influential at the time was William Cavendish, the seventh Duke of Devonshire, who had an estate at Holker Hall, fifteen or so miles away, and who provided much of the investment finance behind the establishment of these various ventures (and later the Docks and the juteworks).

Until the turn of the century, Barrow was a one-horse town, dominated by iron and steel-making. It then changed

---

[*] 'The Barrow Story' p6

horses. Steelworking in Barrow declined significantly in the first decade of the 20th century, and continued to decline with an ever-reduced workforce until 1963, when the venture closed permanently. Fortunately for the town, this decline was balanced by a rapid growth in shipbuilding. In the 1890s, the relatively small shipyard which had begun to build and launch ships in the 1870s, was taken over by Vickers. By 1914 Barrow had been transformed from a steel town to a shipyard town, and that has been its dominant economic identity ever since.

Like many shipyard-based towns its economic fortunes have fluctuated over time. By 1910, the shipyard was employing 10,500 workers. During the First World War, the figure rose to an amazing 31,000. In the inter-war years, Barrow's shipyard workers became accustomed to protracted periods of unemployment, and either dug their heels in and waited for better times, or left the area to seek work elsewhere. The approach of the Second World War revived the shipyards' fortunes, and the Trident nuclear submarine programme provided a post-war boost, with employment peaking at 16,000 in the 1990's. Currently the workforce has stabilised at around 5,000, but the future remains uncertain.

In an attempt to broaden its appeal and economic base, Barrow now proclaims itself, in publicity material, as being 'where the Lakes meet the sea'. That claim is something of an exaggeration. The boundary of the Lake District National Park is not reached until one has travelled a dozen miles north of Barrow. Still, it's worth a try. Certainly you can readily see the Lake District's mountains from many parts of the town. The excellence of the 'view out' across to these mountains is a feature the town shares with Morecambe on the other side of the bay.

It was the first day of the new season, and I had come to watch Barrow play AFC Telford United. Walking into

Barrow town centre from the railway station is like walking back 50 years in time. The place has the feel of the 1960's about it. There are areas of tightly-packed terraced housing, and small shops selling a variety of unlikely products. Some time ago I came across a newsagent where the whole of the shop window frontage had been covered inside with yellow cellophane paper, presumably to reduce the likelihood of sunlight causing the colours to fade on the range of out-of-date magazines displayed therein. That's not a sight you see very often in the 21$^{st}$ Century! Over on the Barrow Island, where the shipyards are located, there are examples of the kind of 4-5 storey tenements found in Glasgow, with inner courtyards full of drying washing – a relic, I suppose, of the influx of Scottish workers in the late nineteenth century.

To be fair, the main shopping area in the town centre is more pleasant than many examples of the genre; a lively pedestrianized area, containing a range of smaller local shops as well as the inevitable and familiar 'see them wherever you go' high street stores. There's a Debenhams which was quite a catch for Barrow. The only other Debenhams in Cumbria are in Carlisle and Workington. The traditional street pattern in the central shopping area has been retained, mercifully avoiding the rigid geometry of many shopping malls and centres. There was an air of vitality about the place with children skipping around and a hubbub of street conversation. I was struck, as I had so often been recently, by the prevalence of adult and child obesity, but it was no worse than anywhere else (now there's a good slogan: 'come to Barrow; it's no worse than anywhere else'). On a warm Saturday morning in August, it was a pleasant place to be.

The placards for the North-West Evening Mail (Barrow edition) told us of a 'Barrow puppy attack horror'. A vision was evoked of a rabid Barrow puppy running amok through

the town, attacking passers-by at random. But no; the reality
was that the puppy 'had been mauled by an out-of-control
(adult) dog, suffering horrific injuries' from which, I'm
delighted to say, it appeared to be recovering. Headlines in
local newspapers are often worth perusing; my all-time
favourite is 'Budgie dies in Wilmslow house blaze'.

Elsewhere in the local paper were other intriguing headlines.
'Beckhams' beefy boost for butchers top steak'. 'Driver
aged 90 went south on north lane' and 'Our street is no
war-zone; it's really lovely' (I bet!).

The feeling of moving back into earlier times continued as I
walked to Barrow FC's ground through an area known as
Hindpool, which was built in the late nineteenth century to
house workers at the steelworks nearby. It has survived
more or less intact, a reticule of streets of well-maintained
terraced houses, with their front doors opening onto the
street (and you can buy one for £60,000; Barrow is a
bargain for houses of all shapes and sizes).

Barrow town council, in the 1960s had decided to retain as
many as possible of the traditional terraces, and to resist the
conventional wisdom of the time that the best thing to do
with such areas was to raze them to the ground and replace
them with blocks of high-rise flats. The council showed
good judgement here; tower blocks proved unpopular with
their residents wherever they were built, with 'streets in the
sky' proving no substitute for the social cohesion of the
terraced streets they replaced.

It is refreshing that Hindpool still exists in its original form,
an outcome aided by the fact that despite the area's
proximity to the shipyards, the German bombers in the
Second World War were singularly unsuccessful in their
attempts to bomb Barrow. I enjoyed a lunchtime pint at the
'Furness Arms', on one of the street corners (a couple of

dozen patrons, mostly elderly, and a relaxed, friendly atmosphere) before walking on to Barrow's stadium, which is right on the edge of Hindpool.

In theory, Barrow's Holker Street ground is no more. It is now the Furness Building Society Stadium, Wilkie Road. But on emerging through the turnstiles onto the terraces, it is difficult to see what substantive changes the Furness Building Society have actually made, beyond financing a new mundane rectangular administrative block at one end of the ground, from which the teams later came out. In the remainder of the ground, you really felt you could have been back in the 1950s. There was the original main stand, painted in blue and white, on one side. There was a covered area, similarly painted, on the other. Elsewhere there was open terracing (with barriers) which looked like absolutely nothing had been modified for at least half a century. The gents' toilets consisted solely of a long channel at ground level, in a dilapidated shed.

In a sense, the ground is a historic relic, a veritable unreconstructed delight. It was definitely still 'Holker Street', whatever it now chooses to call itself. In the 1950s and 60s, I used to 'collect' league football grounds. I think I reached a total of around 60 by the early 1970s. Holker Street could now be (retrospectively) added to the list.

Barrow FC's time in the Football League was briefer than I'd thought. They were admitted in 1921, and failed to gain re-election in 1972, which means that, allowing for the intervention of World War Two, they enjoyed a total of only 44 seasons in the Football League. Actually 'enjoyed' is perhaps a misleading term to use. The club achieved little during this period, only once (in 1967) gaining promotion from the old Division Four to Division Three. By 1970, they were back in the basement of the League, and in 1972, out of it altogether. From 1921 onwards, they typically finished in the lower half of Division Three North, often at or near the bottom. It is not a distinguished history. Nor were there any major giant-killing achievements in the FA Cup. Indeed during much of Barrow's time in the Football League, Rugby League football played as high a profile role as soccer, sometimes more so. Barrow RFC reached the final of the Challenge Cup at Wembley in 1955. Sadly, since the 1970s the economic decline, not just of Barrow but of the whole West Cumbria coast (Sellafield excepted) has been matched by the decline of its football and rugby league clubs. Workington lost its league status in 1978, and Barrow, Workington Town and Whitehaven rugby league clubs now play in ramshackle grounds in front of less than a thousand diehards in Rugby League's Division Two.

Since 1972 Barrow FC have oscillated between the Conference and the next division down the pyramid, and have survived periodic financial crises. In 1990 they enjoyed their greatest glory, winning the FA Trophy Final at Wembley. 2012-13 represented their fifth consecutive season in the Conference.

The match I was attending was Barrow against Telford, and I looked though the programme to see who I recognised. Garry Hunter, a Morecombe midfield stalwart for the previous seven or eight seasons, was making his debut for Barrow having been (surprisingly) released by Morecombe in the summer at the age of 27. In the previous Sunday's 'Non-League Paper' Stuart Hammonds had identified his 'trump cards' from the new signings made by each of the 24 Conference clubs. His choice for Barrow was Hunter... 'A midfielder who came through the ranks at Morecombe under Jim Harvey, so knows only one way to play... with the ball on the deck'.

On the Telford side was Chris Blackburn a 'vastly experienced' central defender who had helped Morecombe

gain promotion to the Football League in 2008. AFC
Telford's trump card Michael Briscoe, a 'vastly-experienced'
central defender signed from Kidderminster Harriers, was
not playing, but Danny Rowe, Stockport County's 'trump
card' (a former Manchester United youngster) was in the
Barrow line-up, having apparently migrated from Stockport
to Barrow some time during the previous week. I saw
Danny Rowe a couple of seasons ago, during a brief spell
with Kendal Town, where his talent stood out in the murky
depths of the Evo-Stik Northern Premier League, before he
was signed by Fleetwood Town. So with Telford's 'trump
card' absent, and the home side fielding two of them, how
could Barrow fail to win! Otherwise both teams were the
usual mixture of promising youngsters (i.e. on the way up,
possibly) and their 'vastly experienced' teammates (i.e. on
the way down, probably) with a handful of intermediaries
who might go in either direction.

AFC Telford are the reincarnation of Telford United, long-
time Conference stalwarts who went bust in 2004, but who
fought their way back up the non-league Pyramid to their
familiar milieu in 2011. In their first season back they just
survived, finishing in 20$^{th}$ position, six points above
relegated Hayes and Yeading. They operate on a part-time
basis, unlike the majority of Conference clubs (including
Barrow) and so looked likely to face another uphill struggle
this season.

Barrow's manager, Dave Bayliss, struck a somewhat
defensive note in his 'View from the dugout' column – 'You
might have got a little anxious when you heard of other
clubs making signings, and no news of a boost to our squad.
Well I can assure you that I was not sat on a sunny beach
and forgetting all about Barrow AFC. I have been on the go
all the time....' I hope the Barrow fans were satisfied with
these reassurances. I must admit I wasn't. To update

## Chapter 1

Shakespeare, 'the manager doth protest too much, methinks'.

The two teams duly emerged from the modern block at 2.55 pm to sporadic applause. Barrow are known as the 'Bluebirds', but appeared in a black-and-white striped Newcastle United kit. Their new 2012/13 strip was 'not yet available' according to the Evening Mail. It's hard to imagine that happening in the Premiership! So, for today, the Bluebirds were the Blackbirds. Telford appeared in shirts which can be described as a 'lighter shade of purple' (with white sleeves) and matching shorts. Hard to imagine that colour scheme anywhere in the Football League! Telford's unusual strip reminded me of the equally unconventional shirts in which my Manchester primary school side turned out back in the 1950s – yellow shirts with brown sleeves ('play up, play up, play up the yellow and brown. There ain't no team in the Football League can beat the yellow and brown' our supporters used to sing). Telford's Chris Blackburn, I noted, still sported a pony-tail, something that Karen considers should be made an offence for men (a capital offence if sported by elderly men with beards and thinning hair).

The first game of the season always starts in an atmosphere of optimism. All teams as yet unbeaten. Anyone could win the league, a possibility which has all but disappeared for some clubs a month into the season. Some papers now publish 'league tables' on the day the season starts, before kick-off; they consist of a listing of the teams in alphabetical order. On this basis, we were about to witness a top-of-the-table tussle between Barrow (third in the League) and AFC Telford (top). In both cases it was probably the highest position they would reach all season. Downhill all the way from now on.

In the decrepit corner of the ground reserved for visiting supporters, I counted a mere 25 people. No great expectations in Telford regarding the 2012/13 season then. However soon after the game began, a raucous chant of 'Telford, Telford…' could be heard, further along the terrace from where I was standing. On closer inspection, a group of around 20 young Telford supporters, resplendent in their purple replica shirts could be seen. Either Barrow FC was fairly relaxed about its segregation policy, or the bloke on the turnstiles, through which they came, hadn't had his mind on the job.

The game started uneventfully and continued that way. The Conference is often an arena for some excellent football, but not today. We had to wait around 15 minutes for the first clear-cut chance (for Telford) and a further 15 for the second (also for Telford). Barrow just didn't threaten; but then Telford, with a greater share of possession was only marginally more penetrative.

Both sides relied on a lofted long-ball game. Clearly Garry Hunter's reported preference for 'keeping the ball on the deck' was not part of Barrow's game plan that day. Some of the sequences of misplaced passes or headers reminded me of tennis rallies. The number of 'passes completed' must have been derisory compared with the games in the recent European Championship finals. The teams left the field at half-time to a totally undeserved smattering of applause.

Towards the end of the first half, I became aware of the presence of a 'screamer'. A screamer is a spectator who sees his attendance at the game as an opportunity to launch a tirade of invective at the officials, typically the nearest linesman who, unlike the referee, is rooted to his line and hence cannot escape (from the proximity of the screamer). Screamers are usually middle-aged men, full of pent-up aggression which suggests a less than idyllic domestic life.

# Chapter 1

The Barrow example of the genre took great exception (amongst other things) to the linesman's failure to spot a clear case of obstruction perpetrated by Chris Blackburn on a Barrow forward. He raced down to the wall separating the terraces from the pitch and told the linesman what he thought of him. Wisely the linesman didn't turn around to confront his vociferous critic. The same sequence was repeated on two more occasions, before the screamer, having screamed himself out, went off for an early cup of tea.

Sadly, the second half was no better. Two well-organised defences dealt competently with two unimaginative attacks. Two 4-4-2 systems cancelled each other out. Barrow were more dominant in the second half than they had been in the first, without ever looking as if they would find the net. Telford continued to look (marginally) the more likely team to break the deadlock. With fifteen minutes remaining, Barrow sent on their second substitute, one Vinny Mukendi, who had apparently once played under-19 international football for the Congo. Standing six foot four and sporting orange boots, he did briefly suggest that he might liven up the game, with his speed and his untypical (in this match) ability to take on and slip past opposing defenders. But, apart from a flurry of late Barrovian corner kicks, the game ended as it had started: a dull stalemate. Neither of Barrow's 'trump cards' had delivered, nor indeed particularly impressed.

It had not proved an inspired choice for my first visit of the Conference season. Elsewhere the goals had come thick and fast; 42 in 12 games – that's nearly four a game (if you discount Barrow/Telford). If I'd chosen Nuneaton versus Ebbsfleet, I'd have seen a nine goal thriller (4-5) or at Mansfield versus Newport, seven (3-4). But the value of my sequence of visits didn't rely on the number of goals scored nor even the quality of the football; it lay in the distinctiveness of the town visited, of their football teams, and of the settings in which the games were played. Barrow AFC and Holker Park (sorry, the Furness Building Society Stadium) certainly did not disappoint. In an era when new all-seater look-alike stadia are increasingly becoming the norm in the Football League, you have to move down to the Conference to get a feel for the individual, and often idiosyncratic, character that football grounds used to have. It had been a delight to stand on a dilapidated terrace, looking across at a main stand that appeared virtually unchanged since it was first erected. You feel as if football's history is being re-lived.

The post-match comments of the managers, reported in Sunday's 'Non-League' were revealing. Both claimed to be content with a point. 'I'm fairly happy that we didn't lose our first match,' said Barrow boss Dave Bayliss. I was not convinced. Many more 'well at least we didn't lose' outcomes at home, to non-favoured sides like Telford, and Barrow could be in real trouble.

# Little Hyde versus Big Luton

Hyde United vs Luton Town

Friday 17th August 2012

Hyde: a town with an unenviable public image. A town besmirched and stigmatized by not just one but three notorious serial killers: Ian Brady, Myra Hindley and Harold Shipman.

On the day of my visit, Ian Brady was back in the news (again). It was reported that he had confided to his mental health advocate, Jackie Powell, that he possessed a sealed envelope stating where Keith Bennett (the only one of his victims whose body was never found) is buried.

The letter was addressed to Keith Bennett's mother, Winnie who happened to die a week after the revelation (the letter was to have been delivered on Brady's death). Jackie Powell was herself arrested on suspicion of 'perverting the lawful burial of a body'. It was a further twist to what must be the longest-running post murder saga ever. The Moors Murders took place in1964.

But it's not just Brady and Hindley who operated from Hyde. The most prolific serial killer of them all, Harold (trust me, I'm a doctor) Shipman lived in Hyde, where his surgery was located and where large numbers of his victims lived.

It could be argued that Brady and Hindley lived in Hattersley, a bleak Manchester overspill estate east of Hyde town rather than the town itself. But Hattersley has been part of Hyde Borough Council since 1939, and the Brady/Hindley residence was only a couple of miles up the

## Chapter 2

Mottram Road from where the football ground is located. It has since been demolished, which is probably just as well, as it could have become part of a gruesome heritage trail... here's where Brady lived, there's where Shipman lived and here's his surgery...

Why should Hyde have ended up with this unenviable history? It seems a most unlikely location for such activities. It's a relatively small town, a little over 30,000 in population. Its central residential areas comprise of pleasant red-brick terraces and, further out, red brick middle-class residences in leafy avenues. The town centre used to be a place of character and vitality, with a popular market opposite the town hall. This was certainly my impression when visiting the town in 1974 when the newly-formed Tameside Planning Department wished to recruit me.

Sadly, things have changed for the worse. The market area is in the process of redevelopment, but the traditional town centre has been blighted by the proximity of a vast Asda superstore, hidden from view by the impressive red-brick Town Hall - erected in the 1930s when Hyde was a borough council, responsible for most of the public services in the town. The superstore has had a profoundly debilitating influence on the centre's viability and vitality. I know six o'clock in the evening is not the best time to judge the nature of any town centre, but I can't see what attraction there would have been in normal shopping hours. Charity shops and takeaways were there in abundance plus some oddball specialist shops (including wedding cakes) and a large pawnbroker (which are much more common than they used to be, not just in Hyde, but even in Kendal!).

Like so many of the communities surrounding Manchester, Hyde was once a cotton town. In the mid-nineteenth century there were 41 cotton mills within the borough's boundaries. It would have been a town with a veritable phalanx of mill chimneys emitting an unhealthy miasma of smoke and soot. But not any longer. There is one surviving mill (non-operational), but otherwise little trace of its once-proud industrial heritage. No alternative industry has replaced King Cotton. Hyde now gives the impression of being an unremarkable but pleasant-enough low-cost residential area within the Greater Manchester conurbation.

Manchester itself was never a mill town as such: rather it was the trading focus for the cotton-spinning activity in the large towns around it, notably Bolton, Bury, Rochdale and Oldham. The area to the east of Manchester consisted of a series of smaller towns, each with their own strong identities: Ashton-under-Lyne, Hyde, Stalybridge Mossley and Dukinfield (amongst others), all run by separate municipal boroughs or urban district councils until 1974, when they were all amalgamated into the Tameside Metropolitan Borough Council. But everyone knows that Tameside is an artificial construct. In terms of community identity, the real places remain Stalybridge, Ashton, Hyde and Droylsden (all of which have well-established non-league clubs) and the rest.

Unlike Barrow, Hyde has no local paper. There is a Tameside Advertiser (price only 36p) and a quick read led me to think that there was no news in Hyde, that particular week. Elsewhere in the borough there certainly was. 'Is family feud behind shootings?' (in Droylsden). 'Court appearance over boxers death' (likewise). 'We can't let these criminals beat us' (likewise). It sounds like Droylsden is seeking to take over Hyde's mantle of criminal notoriety! The only story of note from Hyde was headlined 'Invopak comes to rescue of charity' explaining how this local firm had generously handed over eleven plastic storage bins to West Yorkshire Dog Rescue. It didn't seem particularly newsworthy to me, but on a slow news week, maybe. There were also, mysteriously, very few houses for sale in Hyde. Plenty in Ashton, Stalybridge and (even) Droylsden, but not Hyde, which could mean it's a much-loved town that no-one wants to leave.

It would be helpful, given the notoriety of some of Hyde's best known former residents, if there were compensatory high-profile local notables with a more positive public image. Take your pick from Wayne Fontana (born there), Ricky Hatton (who has a gym there) and, allegedly L.S. Lowry, the painter, who I always thought lived in Mottram. But maybe he bought his fish and chips in Hyde?

Hyde's ground is Ewen Fields, a mile or so from the town centre. It's hard to spot from the road, because it is surrounded by leafy residential avenues. I stopped off at a pub on Mottram Road, where Hyde and Luton supporters were both drinking together quite amicably. This kind of peaceful intermingling amongst rival fans is one of the delights of the Conference. You'd be unlikely to see Newcastle fans in a West Ham-dominated pub (or vice-versa). But in the Conference there's a more relaxed attitude to such things. 'Incidents' of any kind are mercifully rare.

Approaching the stadium, I wondered how much I would remember from my previous visit, over 50 years ago, when I cycled from Stockport with my friend John Davies to watch Hyde United (as they then were) play Cheadle Rovers in the Cheshire Senior Cup. This time, having paid my £7 (Senior Citizen concession) to get in, having decided not to pay an extra £2 for the main stand, I realised that I didn't remember very much.

The ground had enjoyed a major makeover since the 1960's (of which the most recent improvements were in 2010). The old main stand was still there, but the ground now had four more covered terraced areas, one at each end of the ground, one adjacent to the main stand, and one opposite, designated for visiting supporters. I don't recall such a proliferation of constructions on my last visit. All the stands were painted blue (even though Hyde played in red) which I learned later was a response to a sponsorship deal in 2010 with Manchester City (City sponsoring Hyde, not vice versa!), which resulted in all the stands being repainted in sky blue and Hyde playing in white and blue shirts rather than the traditional red, for the 2010-11 season. The following season, however, they reverted to their familiar red and white strip. Did this reversion to their old colours signify the end of the sponsorship deal (or a move into the camp of the other Manchester giant, whose reserve side played their home matches at Hyde in the early 2000s? Clearly not, because Manchester City's academy team now play their home games at Ewen Fields, so there is still a connection, which Hyde would do well to nurture, given the apparently unlimited amount of cash available to Manchester City at the moment.

Hyde FC were founded in 1885. Two years later, they must have wondered why they'd bothered, when they experienced the most ignominious defeat ever recorded in the FA Cup - a 26-0 reverse against Preston North End (the heaviest defeat in the Football League is a mere 13-0 in comparison). But Hyde soldiered on and changed their name to Hyde United in 1919, after which they became regular members of the Cheshire County League, where they played many a thrilling local derby with nearby Stalybridge Celtic.

Hyde United joined the non-league pyramid in 1982, since when they have alternated between levels two and three, until they were promoted into the Conference at the end of the 2011-12 season. The previous three seasons had been turbulent. Hyde United were declared bankrupt in 2009 but then, with the help of a generous collection at a Manchester City home game, they contested the winding-up order in the courts and managed to get it rescinded. They then renamed the club Hyde, and after narrowly avoiding relegation in 2011, the team prospered under the managership of Garry Lowe, and won the Blue Square North League, fighting off challenges from Stalybridge Celtic, and Guiseley. So here they were, little Hyde, at the highest level of non-league football for the first time in their history.

What a contrast with the visitors, Luton Town. Of all the sleeping giants in the Conference, Luton probably feel the most aggrieved to be there in the first place, to still be there four seasons after relegation from the Football League, and the most convinced that their rightful place is not just back in that league, but in its upper reaches. As recently as 1992 they were a Division One (pre-Premiership) side, and as recently as 2007 a Championship team. There was a widespread expectation, not least in the pages of the 'Non-League Paper' that Luton would regain their league status this season. So we were faced with a (mis)match between 'little Hyde' and 'big Luton'.

One of the most endearing features of the Conference is the contrast in status amongst its membership. It operates as a transit camp. There are the 'big clubs', recently relegated from the Football League, with stadia which reflect their past glories, who are desperate to return to what they perceive as their 'rightful place'. Examples include Stockport County, Grimsby Town, Lincoln City, Wrexham, and tonight's visitors, Luton Town. But there are also the 'little clubs', typically representing small towns, who have only recently emerged from the middle reaches of the non-league pyramid, and whose aim, if they are being realistic, is simply to stay there. Supporters of Luton Town and the other 'big clubs' will probably never have heard of the likes of Hyde (who? where's that? my god, has it really come to this? only a few seasons ago we were playing Leeds United and Notts Forest!). And then there are the 'regulars' who have played in the Conference for many of the 34 years of its existence (AFC Telford United, Woking, and Forest Green Rovers). In these circumstances, there are numerous opportunities for the kind of 'giant-killing' acts more normally associated with the FA Cup. Can little Alfreton defeat the mighty Wrexham? Or Dartford overcome Grimsby? Or Braintree beat Lincoln City? And this evening, could Hyde defeat the mighty Luton Town?

The programme had the appearance of one of a club that had emerged from a lower level of the pyramid, and not yet quite adjusted to the big time. There was a series of short vacuous columns from Hyde's chairman, manager, chief executive and captain. The chairman and manager were both recent appointments. Garry Lowe had resigned before the start of the season, in protest against the meagre size of the budget allocated to strengthen his squad. The previous chairman had also resigned, perhaps in protest against the manager's protest. The new manager was Scott McNiven, who had held the post on a 'caretaker' basis in 2010-11. This degree of instability did not auger well for Hyde's prospects in the Conference. The programme contained more than the usual quota of advertisements, including one for 'Vittorio Tansella and Michael; Gents and Children's Hair Stylist', which sounded like it should be based on the Kings Road, Chelsea, rather than Mottram Road, Hyde!

What did emerge from several of the contributions was the immense pride within the club that the game was being televised. Little Hyde featured live on TV for the first time in its 127 year history! And against the mighty Luton Town, not long ago in the Premiership! Is this the side that only last season was entertaining Vauxhall Motors and Solihull Moors?

Both sides started the game unbeaten. Hyde had looked set for a win in the first game in the Conference at Braintree. But then midfielder Andy Pearson head-butted a Braintree player in the tunnel at half-time, was sent off, and 10-man Hyde just failed to hold out, conceding an equaliser in the last minute. Just Andy Pearson's luck that he was the subject of the 'Player Profile' in the programme. His explanation of what happened was somewhat incongruous… "It was just a bit of arguing in the tunnel, a little push. I got called out by the referee for head-butting, but I feel slightly hard done by, as I'm not sure how much of the incident was seen." Come on Andy, own up, did you head-butt him or didn't you? Hyde then managed a 0-0 draw at Ewen Fields with Barrow, in a game which sounds (almost) as mediocre as the Barrow/Telford game I'd watched the previous week.

Luton, meanwhile, found themselves 2-0 down at home to Gateshead by half-time, on the opening day of the season, but recovered to draw 2-2, and went on to win comfortably (2-0) at Kidderminster in mid-week.

The Hyde team featured two former Morecambe players. There was Phil Jevons, a striker Hyde had signed from Morecambe in the close-season, who had scored prolifically in 2009-10, but less so in 2010-11, and in 2011-12 his goals had dried up almost completely. At 33, he could be regarded as in the twilight of his career, but may still prove effective at Conference level. That was certainly the view of the 'Non-League Paper' who identified him as Hyde's most important pre-season signing'. The other was Matty Blinkhorn, signed on the day of the match itself and hence unacknowledged in the programme. He had joined Morecambe from Blackpool in 2007, and had contributed vital goals in their promotion season and in their first season in Division Two, before moving on to Luton Town (amongst others) and more recently York City.

Luton's line-up was formidable, by Conference standards. It included 'prolific striker' Stuart Fleetwood (signed from Hereford United in August 2011); 'prolific striker' Jon Shaw (Luton's 'trump card' signed from Gateshead pre-season); Ronnie Henry signed from Stevenage Borough (likewise) and 'commanding centre-half' Garry Richards (from Gillingham). Difficult to see how the Hydes of this world could hope to compete with a line-up like that.

As the match got underway, it became clear that there was going to be a much livelier atmosphere than the one at the previous Saturday's Barrow/Telford stalemate. For one thing, the mood was different. In the covered terrace adjacent to the main stand stood a group of, at most, fifty vociferous Hyde supporters, decked in red shirts. It is surprising how much noise fifty people can make, if they are determined enough. Opposite them stood around 250 Luton supporters, a very impressive travelling contingent on a wet Friday evening from a place 150 miles away. The support from (and banter between) the two sets of supporters created an atmosphere as lively as the Barrow game had been moribund.

Secondly the quality of the football quickly demonstrated the more positive qualities of the Conference. Both sides showed a welcome predisposition to attack. Both worked the ball forward from the back, rather than relying on the hopeful upfield punts which had characterised the Barrow/Telford game. Luton were the more dominant side, making particularly effective use of the overlapping runs of ex-Stevenage full-back Ronnie Henry, but rarely came close to scoring, despite their impressive approach work. Hyde

looked dangerous on the break, and came into the game
more as half-time approached. It was a delight to watch.

During the first half, the familiar taunt of 'Ooo are yer'
resonated across the ground from the vocal Hyde
contingent; perhaps intended sarcastically. Who are we?
Well, we're ex-League Cup winners, ex-FA Cup finalists, ex-
Division One (pre-Premiership) regulars. That's who we
are! Indeed the taunt would have made more sense if
directed at the Hyde supporters by the Luton contingent.
Who are *you*? Never heard of you! What have you ever won?

The game was scoreless and finely-balanced when half-time
arrived. Then, early in the second half, against the odds,
Hyde scored. Newcomer Matty Blinkhorn, finding space on
the edge of the penalty area, hit a beautifully judged shot
into the top corner of the net, and immediately disappeared
under a pile of his teammates. Jubilation amongst the home
supporters; silence in the stand opposite. Little Hyde 1 Big
Luton 0. Could Hyde hold out for a memorable first win
against the most formidable team in the Conference?

Sadly not. Luton composed themselves and set about
turning the game around. Ten minutes after the Hyde goal,
Luton midfielder (and 'talented youngster') J. J. O'Donnell
hit a precise shot low past the Hyde keeper. Ten minutes
later Stuart Fleetwood scored an equally precise goal,
following a swift counter attack by the visitors. Cue
euphoria from the visitors' enclosure; silence opposite.

Hyde rarely looked like saving the game in the fifteen
minutes which remained. But they had given a good
account of themselves, had contributed much to an
excellent match (4 stars in the Non League Paper) and had
demonstrated a capacity to (at least) survive at this
demanding level. Luton Town looked a powerful well-

drilled side who seemed likely to reach the play-offs by the end of the season (if not emerge as champions).

The weather forecast for the Manchester area had been for heavy rain. But by the time the match started, the rain had passed, and during the second half, pink tinges appeared on the thinning clouds, contributing to the positive experience of the visit and the game itself. What did become apparent, though, was that Hyde lay directly below the north-east approach to Manchester Airport. A succession of planes droned over Ewen Fields throughout the game, mid-way through their descents to the Airport. Perhaps that's why there were so few houses for sale in Hyde; no-one thinks there is any chance of selling them!

# Sandgrounders and Speechless Managers

Southport vs Gateshead

Tuesday 4th October 2012

Southport: a refined sophisticated upmarket seaside town. Not a seaside resort like Blackpool or Morecambe, its two main competitors in the North West. If Blackpool is unashamedly brash (though still very popular) and Morecambe is past its sell-by-date as a resort, Southport is doing very nicely, thank you, in its own quiet way.

There's only twelve miles as the crow flies between Blackpool and Southport (though three times that distance by car; the Ribble estuary gets in the way). But socially and culturally there's a vast distance between them. Southport's main attractions – Lord Street, the annual Flower Show (the biggest outside London) and the Air Show, would not fit with Blackpool's ethos, just as the gaudy trappings of the Tower and the Pleasure Beach would be out-of-place in Southport.

It would be misleading to call Southport a seaside resort, if that implies that families still take week-long holidays there. There are relatively few of the bed-and-breakfast establishments and small hotels which abound in Blackpool. And if you consider golden sands and access to the sea as essential components of a seaside holiday, Southport is not for you. But Southport remains a going concern for days-out and short breaks. It is at the end of a railway line to Liverpool, which helps in this respect. The railway is significant in another way too. You can live in Southport, catch a train and be in central Liverpool 35 minutes later. So Southport doubles as a desirable residential base for

professionals and executives who work in Liverpool.
Indeed, several of Liverpool's current squad, including
Steven Gerrard, have chosen to live there (as does ex-player
and manager Kenny Dalglish).

Driving into Southport from the north, you soon pass along
tree-lined boulevards, flanked by substantial mansions, on a
road which eventually becomes Lord Street. Lord Street, the
main shopping focus of the town, is hugely impressive.
Although there are a few larger stores, most of the shops
are small, upmarket concerns, many of them fronted by
elegant Victorian glass-topped canopies. The tourist
literature claims that the later (1870s) Paris boulevards were
modelled on Lord Street. Louis-Napoleon Bonaparte was
exiled in Southport between 1846 and 1848, and it's just
conceivable that he was so impressed by Lord Street that,
on his return to power a few years later, he did indeed use it
as the inspiration for a scheme of boulevard-construction in
Paris. Whilst not wholly convinced, I would like to believe
it; what Southport does today, Paris does tomorrow!

Southport also boasts one of the longest piers in Britain.
But it's an untypical pier. All the action (dominated by
Silcock's Amusement Hall) is at the pier's entrance which is
actually situated about half-a-mile inland from where the sea
starts. You walk past a boating lake, a Premier Inn, a
Dunelm Store and various other trappings of the modern
age, before you reach the end of the land. And even then, as
it's Southport, the likelihood is that the sea will not be
immediately in evidence, but 'out there' somewhere on the
horizon (as it was on my visit). The pier does continue out
to sea/sand for another half-mile or so, but my way was
barred by an iron gate which had been locked half-an-hour
before, at 6.00 pm. The beach itself did not inspire
admiration; couch grass beginning to spread and dark
estuarial sand rather than the golden variety.

On returning to Lord Street, I passed the impressive Victorian town hall, redolent of the days when local government was a much greater source of local pride and local choice than it is now. Southport, like Barrow is a place with a distinctive history and identity, a place which has meaning for local people. Like Barrow, it used to be a County Borough, with the full range of local powers - such as education, highways, social services, and libraries. But in 1974 the town became part of the Metropolitan Borough of Sefton, which incorporated a range of settlements from Bootle northwards, in a long, thin local authority whose only common ground was a commuter railway to Liverpool. It was, and is, a nonsensical authority as far as community identity is concerned. It soon became apparent that there was a further complication. Bootle was a Labour-dominated area, as you would expect given its rundown working-class environment. The middle belt – Crosby, Maghull and Formby – was traditional Conservative territory. You might expect Southport to have similar political leanings, but interestingly it has become a Liberal Democrat stronghold, and has retained an MP of that persuasion ever since the 1980's. (It was expected to go Conservative in 2010 but fortunately, as far as I'm concerned, resisted the temptation).

Throughout its history, Sefton borough's areal divisions – Bootle, Formby and Southport – have been reinforced by political divisions – Labour, Conservative and Liberal Democrat respectively. Since 1986 Sefton has an unbroken record of being a hung council, with no one party in overall control, which has proved a recipe for constant party-based bickering about whether Bootle – or Formby or Southport – is getting its fair share of investment and expenditure.

Various attempts have been made by Southport to extricate itself from this 'forced marriage,' so far without success. It was always a 'marriage of convenience'; Southport doesn't really see itself – or wish to be seen – as part of Merseyside. It is a place with its own identity which should be run by a council/based on the town itself, not by an amorphous fabrication like Sefton (the name is a giveaway – where in the council area is a place called Sefton to be found?).

The respectability and gentility of Southport was confirmed by a look through the local paper, the Southport Visitor. 'Monday rain fails to dampen spirits at another superb Southport Country Fair event', 'Elvis impersonator King Louis hopes to bring the sun back to Southport', 'Gloster Meteor is set for homecoming at Air Show'. What a contrast with the tales of gang warfare and unsolved murders in the Tameside Advertiser, although to be fair, there were one or two indications that Southport is not entirely problem-free, e.g. 'Brave butcher clings to his van as thief roars off in it', 'Thug attacks woman in front of daughter'. But then no town the size of Southport will be wholly thief- or thug-free, will it.

Haig Avenue – long-term home of Southport FC – is a couple of miles east of the town centre, in a leafy residential area. There are no pubs close to the ground. The nearest one I could find was the Richmond Arms, about half-a-mile away, which did have the good judgement to sell Holts Ales (Holts is an independent brewery based in north Manchester.) There was no sign that anyone else in the pub was on their way to the match.

The ground is situated adjacent to substantial houses with well-maintained gardens. They provide a suitably middle-class setting for a respectable laid-back club. I'd last been at Haig Avenue in the late 1950s to watch a third round cup tie between Southport and Stockport County (a 1-1 draw; Stockport won the replay) but had very little recollection of what it was like. It turned out to be a most attractive, trim, well-maintained ground, with an old main stand (in which I sat), a newer covered end terrace, and the rest of the terracing open, with the other end terrace reserved for visiting supporters. The terrace barriers and stands were newly painted in yellow. A greater contrast with Barrow's decaying Holker Street home could hardly be imagined.

Southport are yet another Northern club that has seen better days. So are Gateshead, the evening's opposition, for that matter; a Southport versus Gateshead match was a regular occurrence in the Third Division North of the 1950s, but whereas Gateshead never won anything (including promotion) in their time in the Football League, Southport did. In 1967 they were promoted from Division Four to Division Three, where they survived for three seasons before returning to their accustomed level. In 1973 they were promoted again as Division Four champions, but went straight back down the following season. The club's failure to achieve re-election in 1978 was controversial. They had finished $23^{rd}$ and many expected Rochdale ($24^{th}$) to be voted out. But the outcome of the first ballot resulted in survival for Rochdale and a tie between Wigan Athletic and Southport. On the second ballot, the intense canvassing of the Wigan club (including the gift to all participants of some very superior pens) led to Southport's elimination.

Since their arguably unjust demotion, Southport have soldiered on, experiencing spells in the Conference (though rarely threatening promotion) and spells in the Northern Premier League (later the Conference North). Gateshead have had a similar recent history, since their failure to gain re-election in 1960.

Last season, however, things began to look up for both teams. Both were challenging for play-off places until late in the season. Southport finished seventh (5 points short of the total achieved by fifth-placed play-off finalists Luton),

whilst Gateshead finished eighth, with two points fewer.
Southport had a formidable sequence of eight successive
away wins; ultimately it was inconsistency at home which
led to missing out on the play-offs. Both clubs did the
double over Stockport County; but then so did several
others! Both must have hoped to build on their impressive
(for them) level of success in 2011-12 over the coming
season.

In fact there had been a stark contrast to the starts made by
the two sides. Six games into the season Gateshead
remained unbeaten and were in fourth place. Southport,
however, had won only one game (at Hyde) and languished
in twentieth place. Worse, two of their three defeats had
been ignominious 3-0 reverses at home to unfancied sides
(Tamworth and AFC Telford respectively). The manager,
Liam Watson, in his column in the programme, was duly
apologetic… 'I was once again left speechless at how we
can go from a horror last week to a much improved display
at Hyde to another horror showing against Telford.' Having
recovered his powers of speech he added magnanimously…
'Please get behind the lads throughout the game… I am
happy for you to have a go at me, if you have to, but give
the lads your encouragement.' Right Liam, we'll bear in
mind your advice.

Almost all Southport's playing staff had been signed from
non-league clubs, typically at sub-Conference level. Last
season's leading scorer Tony Gray was signed from
Droylsden. Stalybridge Celtic, Hyde United, Burscough and
Skelmersdale all featured prominently in the previous
attachments of the current squad. Southport's most
significant close-season signing (according to the Non-
League Paper) was one Aaron Chalmers, signed from
Stockport Sports (who?) but with previous experience at
Oldham Athletic. Given that most other Conference clubs

had several players signed from league clubs, one suspects that the scouring of the lower reaches of the non-league pyramid is a deliberate (and on the face of it, effective) policy at Southport.

By contrast, Gateshead's squad included several players with recent league experience including Adam Bartlett (goalkeeper, Hereford United), Ben Clark (Hartlepool United), Chris Bush (AFC Wimbledon) and Yemi Odubade (Oxford United).

As kick-off time approached, it was clear that the crowd was going to be sparse. The home defeats against Tamworth and Telford had no doubt had an impact, and Tuesday evening attendances tend to be smaller than Saturdays anyway. The atmosphere was eerily quiet as the teams emerged to a subdued reception.

As the game started, the (impressive) main stand was at best a quarter full, and there were only two or three hundred scattered around the terracing, including 25 Gateshead diehards in the visiting supporters enclosure (plus a few behind me in the stand judging from their Geordie accents). But then it is 160 miles from Gateshead to Southport, it was Tuesday evening, and Gateshead aren't one of the best-supported Conference sides.

As the game got under way, Gateshead soon established a dominance which persisted throughout the first half. Southport were clearly intent on avoiding another 3-0 reverse (or worse). It wasn't apparent what formation they were playing, but it certainly involved only one player up front (Gray) and even he took on a defensive role at regular intervals.

Gateshead's approach work was immaculate, although not particularly incisive. Long sequences of passes were strung together, helped by the fact that Southport had chosen to

give their opponents the freedom of the midfield area,
which facilitated their remorseless, measured build-ups. The
majority of the chances in the first half fell to Gateshead,
although not perhaps as many as one might have expected
from their dominance. The ever-dangerous Odubade was
frequently involved in creating space in, and around, the
penalty area. Southport had a couple of half-chances
following breakaways, but that was it. It was one of the
most one-sided 45 minutes of football I'd ever seen.
Gateshead could and should have been two or three goals
up by half-time. But the home crowd seemed pleased
enough, and applauded Southport off the field, on the basis,
I assume, of 'well at least we're not 3-0 down again'.

Then, in the second half, the balance of play began to
change, Gateshead remained dominant in terms of
possession, but Southport's counter-attacks became more
frequent and more menacing. The atmosphere on the
terraces changed too. Southport were now attacking the
goal behind which the home crowd were gathered, in the
covered terrace. This was clearly the natural home of the
Southport faithful, whose encouragement was becoming
much more vocal than it had been in the first half. As at
Hyde, there was a nucleus of only around fifty or sixty
younger vociferous fans, but that was enough to create a
suitably supportive atmosphere. Southport's nickname is
'the Sandgrounders' , which is apparently also applied more
generally to the town's residents, and which refers to the
sandy terrain on which the ground (and the town) has been
built. But 'come on you Sandgrounders' is a bit too much of
a mouthful for an effective chant. So what we got was
'come on you Yellows'. Even the occupants of the main
stand became more vocal, with a distinctly middle-class
tinge to their comments; but that's Southport.

A supporter seated behind me was becoming increasingly critical of the linesman, whom he felt should have been more forthcoming in drawing the referee's attention to the use of arms by the central defender who was marking Southport's lone striker. 'Come on liner, show some guts!' was his frustrated exhortation, delivered in a plummy accent. Liner? What kind of expression is that? I've never heard a linesman called a 'liner' before. Is it a quirky expression specific to the Southport area, or was it a slip of the tongue from someone who thought he was watching rugby? It sounded bizarre.

Then, suddenly, in the $70^{th}$ minute, Southport took the lead, to the amazement and delight of their supporters. Shaun Whalley (ex-Hyde United), their increasingly influential wing-player, wrestled his way past Paddy Boyle, cut in on goal and delicately chipped the ball over the head of the advancing Adam Bartlett. A passionate embrace between scorer and manager ensued. Four minutes later, Gateshead equalised (a deflected shot from Josh Gillies), sending their 25 supporters behind the goal into paroxysms of joy. 'Aah well, it was good while it lasted,' was the resigned comment of adjacent Southport supporters in the stand. Then, three minutes from the end of normal time, with both sides apparently settling for a draw, Southport's substitute Russell Benjamin dispossessed the hapless Paddy Boyle, who was trying to waste time in the vicinity of the corner flag, and crossed for Karl Ledsham to smash home the winning goal; totally undeserved on the run of play, but deserved, perhaps as retribution for defenders seeking to waste time around the corner flag! When the final whistle came, the Southport team received a (scarcely deserved) standing ovation, whilst Gateshead's players looked devastated in the realisation they had lost a game which they clearly should have won.

## Chapter 3

As I drove out of Southport I reflected on the prospects of the six teams I had so far seen. My forecast on the basis of the evidence would be that the side finishing highest would be Luton Town, followed by Gateshead, AFC Telford, Southport, Hyde and Barrow, in that order. But early results can, of course, be deceptive.

Southport left a positive impression on me. Like Barrow and Hyde, it is a distinctive place with an interesting history. It has survived the decline of the traditional British seaside holiday resort better than most. I liked the laid-back, gentle atmosphere of the town and indeed of the crowd at Haig Avenue. No doubt there are pockets of deprivation in Southport which I didn't see, and (as in all seaside towns) a sizeable proportion of the population subsisting on the low wages associated with the tourist trade. But it does feel like a town at ease with itself. I hope that, in the next bout of local government reorganisation, Southport escapes from the unwelcome clutches of Sefton, detaches itself from Merseyside (where it doesn't belong), and regains its independence as a Southport council for Southport people.

# Dancing Bears and Famous Authors

Nuneaton Town vs Macclesfield Town

Saturday 15th September 2012

Nuneaton: a medium-sized town in middle England. If you were seeking to locate the central point of the country, it would not be far away from Nuneaton. If, as a resident of the town, you wanted to enjoy a day at the seaside, you'd have to travel across Lincolnshire to Skegness or Mablethorpe, or perhaps Cleethorpes, where you could watch Nuneaton Town play Grimsby Town.

I was already familiar with Nuneaton. I worked in Leicester for thirteen years between 1996 and 2009, and my rail journey from the north always involved a change at Nuneaton - from a Virgin train bound for London onto a cross-country train from Birmingham to Leicester. That would not be possible now. Much to the annoyance of local residents, fast London- or Liverpool- bound trains no longer stop at Nuneaton. Instead, there's a slow train from Crewe to London (via Stoke, Nuneaton, Northampton and many other stops) which has almost doubled the journey time in both directions. That's a big blow to the status of the town, as well as being highly inconvenient to local rail travellers. This sense of a loss of status mirrors a decline in the town's economic fortunes. Nuneaton first developed as the focal point of the north Warwickshire coal-mining area (a few spoil-heaps can still be seen). It diversified into textiles, brewing and brick-making in the latter part of the nineteenth century, all of which declined drastically after 1945. Currently there are no major employers in, or around the town, although Holland and Barrett have their

# Chapter 4

headquarters there. The town's main function nowadays is as a commuter town for Coventry, ten miles to the south.

It is acknowledged that there are numerous towns like Nuneaton across the country: places that once had a good reason to be there, like a steelworks, a textile industry or a car plant, but which had since lost their original raison d'etre. When towns lose their economic reason for being, they have to find a new role. Morecambe, for example, has established itself as the DHSS bed-and-breakfast capital of the north-west, having lost its position as a credible seaside resort. Nuneaton survives as a source of reasonably-priced housing (and a substantial shopping centre) in an area where there are limited alternative opportunities.

Nuneaton does have one very famous son – or rather daughter. George Eliot was born and brought up in a village close to the town. Her first work of fiction 'Scenes from Clerical Life' is based on a 'thinly-disguised' Nuneaton. Her statue adorns Newdegate Square in the town centre, and the local hospital is named after her. In the local paper, her continuing salience as a tourist attraction was illustrated by an item reporting the recent visit of a party of Japanese academics to the area, to visit the various sites associated with the author. One of them had, apparently, recently translated Middlemarch into Japanese - all 850 pages of it. The town also has a link with someone of more disputed historical significance; Mary Whitehouse was born here.

The football team - Nuneaton Town - rose out of the ashes of Nuneaton Borough, which folded in 2009, and quickly reformed under its new name. Apparently clubs that are wound up and then reform can't adopt the name of their previous incarnation; hence AFC Telford, FC Halifax and – most bizarrely – Darlington 1883! Nuneaton Borough had, for a long time, operated at relatively senior levels of non-league football: Southern Premier League, Conference

North and intermittently in the Conference itself, without ever looking likely to achieve promotion to the Football League. The reformed Nuneaton Town were demoted two levels to the Southern League Division One (Midlands) but quickly fought their way back up the pyramid, to reach the play-offs of the Conference North in 2011-12, which they won, defeating Gainsborough in the final. So they are now back where they belong.

Shortly before Nuneaton Borough went out of existence, the club switched grounds (in 2007) to a new stadium – the Triton Showers Community Arena, otherwise known as Liberty Way. I had visited their previous ground – Manor Park – a few years before the move, to watch Morecambe who, at the time, were pushing for promotion (they drew 1-1, and failed to achieve it, although they managed to do so, a season or two later). It was a wonderful ramshackle relic, reminiscent of Barrow's Holker Street ground. It was like walking back into the 1950's.

Nuneaton Town started the season with an action-packed 4-5 reverse at home to Ebbsfleet (whilst I was watching the unedifying 0-0 stalemate at Barrow). This was followed by a 4-0 defeat at Newport. Since then things had improved, although a 6-1 defeat at Woking the previous Saturday suggested that the earlier defensive problems remained. So traumatised was the manager following this result, that he made *no reference* to it in his 'From the Dugout' column. The chairman and a fellow director had no such inhibitions however. Nuneaton started the game in 20th position, a point ahead of Barrow and three ahead of Hyde.

The visitors, Macclesfield Town, had been relegated from the Football League the previous season, after a disastrous run of 25 games without a win. They had gained promotion from the Conference in 1997, and under Sammy McIlroy, won promotion to Division One the following season, but came straight back down. They were currently sitting on top of the Conference, having won six of their eight games. So, it was another David versus Goliath contest; newly-promoted Nuneaton against newly-relegated Macclesfield.

Macclesfield's line-up included Kieron Charnock, who had recently spent a couple of fairly undistinguished seasons with Morecambe (he did once play for Wigan Athletic, though). Their most significant close-season signing (according to the Non-League Paper) was Lance Cronin, the keeper, a former Crystal Palace youngster, who had recently had spells with Bristol Rovers and Gillingham (usually as a substitute). Otherwise the squad unusually boasted two players with double-barrelled surnames: Craig Braham-Barrett and Matthew Barnes-Homer; a reflection perhaps of Macclesfield's location in the affluent north Cheshire commuter belt.

Nuneaton's team relied more on players with previous careers at non-league clubs such as Kettering Town, Boston United and Worcester City. Their key signing was, (according to the Non-League Paper once more), one Kyle Perry a striker who had 'endured a miserable time at Lincoln and on loan at Telford last term, scoring just four goals'. Why a sideways move to Nuneaton was expected to revitalise his flagging career wasn't apparent.

Having dropped my son off earlier in Northampton to resume his university career (no, I didn't know Northampton had a university either, until Callum got a place there), I didn't have time to explore Nuneaton before the game started. Neither did I have time to look for a local pub, to soak up the pre-match atmosphere. However, even if I had, it's unlikely I would have found one. Nuneaton's ground is in an industrial estate, adjacent to the Leicester railway line, and the area appeared totally bereft of pubs.

The stadium was a pleasant surprise. Despite being new, it had a lot more character than most contemporary arenas. There was a small stand on one side of the ground, untypically positioned at one end, rather than in the middle. Opposite it, there was an open terrace, which was well-populated partly, no doubt, as a result of the pleasant autumn sunshine which lasted throughout the game. There were covered terraces at either end, numerous food and drink outlets (I can recommend the steak-and-ale pies) and various hoardings including one which drew our attention to 'Nuneaton Roof Truss Ltd – supporting the local community'. There was also a nice laid-back atmosphere; the contingent of Macclesfield fans was not segregated (perhaps as a result of the fact that they'd won an award for 'best away fans in the League' the previous season?). We were all entertained by the 'Crew Girls', dancing energetically in their black tops and skirts (revealing large expanses of midriff) and brandishing purple and white pom-poms. Sadly 'the girls have had a pretty quiet time recently events-wise' the programme informed us; but with Christmas not too far away, no doubt their engagements diaries would start to fill up.

The programme, which was very informative and well-produced, included news of a unilateral decision by the Community Club, which had been an integral part of the re-launch of Nuneaton Town in 2009, to sever links with the football club. It wasn't clear what had caused this schism, but it all sounded very acrimonious. The 'view from the boardroom' included the following ponderous statement: 'suffice to say we refute any suggestions or assertion that we have behaved in a way which would, either by perception or fact, give the Community Club cause to react in such extreme circumstance.' Not the kind of thing you'd expect to encounter in a football programme.

# Chapter 4

There had also been problems with Nuneaton Rugby Club. Initially the stadium was a shared venture between the two codes, with the rugby club originally paying a weekly rental of £35 for the hire of the pitch. However disputes arose over the appropriate level of the rental once this agreement terminated, and Nuneaton RFC now play most of their games elsewhere (although 'several' still at the new stadium). So it appears that all is not sweetness and light at the Triton Showers Community Arena!

It turned out to be a strange though exciting match. Macclesfield dominated possession, especially in the first half, but created very few clear-cut chances. For most of the game, all the evidence was that Nuneaton was the more committed and determined side, winning most of the 50/50 balls in midfield, and timing their defensive tackles well. They went ahead in the sixth minute, when the ball dropped kindly in the area to Andy Brown, who took his chance confidently. They went further ahead seven minutes later when Mathew Barnes-Homer handled in the box, and James Arnson dispatched the resulting penalty with conviction. It began to look like a major upset was imminent. Nuneaton then tended to play it defensively for the rest of the half, but always looked comfortable.

The Nuneaton supporters were most appreciative – in a laid-back kind of way – of their team's efforts. They still refer to Nuneaton as 'The Borough' having understandably refused to take seriously the change of name imposed on their team by the authorities in 2008. It's been 'Borough' since 1938, and no doubt always will be. In contrast, the sixty or so vociferous Macclesfield fans were far from happy about their team's display. 'It's just like last season, this rubbish,' commented one, no doubt reflecting on the 26-matches-without-a-win sequence which resulted in their demotion.

One of the delights of the Conference, in the games I've so far seen, has been the way in which visiting supporters have mingled with those of the home team, both on the way to the game and during it. At Hyde, although the large contingent of visiting fans had been directed to a separate enclosure, they could be seen before the game drinking and chatting amicably with home supporters in a pub close to the ground on Mottram Road. At Barrow, although there was a separate area earmarked for visiting supporters, most of the AFC Telford United fans were to be found on the open terrace, side-by-side with groups of Barrow fans, with whom they co-existed harmoniously. Behind me, in the main stand at Southport, was a group of Geordie-accented Gateshead supporters, whom it had not been felt necessary to segregate (or perhaps they had just infiltrated the home section unchallenged). And here, at Nuneaton, the contingent of Macclesfield fans wandered freely around the terraces. There was no tension at all between the rival groups of supporters, who exchanged pleasantries and jokey put-downs as they switched ends at half-time.

This openness of access, and the informal, inclusive atmosphere on the terraces has not been possible at Football League grounds for a long time. Even at my local club, Morecambe (average attendance 2,000), the visiting fans have to be separated. What a welcome contrast the Conference provides.

The 'Crew Girls' returned at half-time for a further session of 'strutting their stuff' (the announcer's term not mine). This time they were joined by Nuneaton's mascot, the ungainly Bloo the Bear. The girls looked not best pleased at this shambolic intrusion on their professionalism.

The second half began in similar fashion to the first, with Nuneaton's 3-5-2 formation coping with everything that

## Chapter 4

Macclesfield threw at them, which in all honesty was not a lot, initiating very little in the way of counter attacks.

Then the visitors suddenly pulled a goal back as Kieran Murtagh broke through into the area, and placed the ball under the keeper's despairing dive. Was this a signal for a Macclesfield comeback, similar to the one at Stockport ten days before when they'd recovered from 2-1 down to win 4-3? It would appear not, because four minutes later, in a rare Nuneaton attack, midfielder Daniel Sleath managed to get in behind the vulnerable Macclesfield defence and restore Nuneaton's two-goal lead. There followed one of those ridiculous contrived set-pieces where the Nuneaton players grouped themselves around the scorer, all grinning shamelessly for the benefit of the photographer of the local paper, in what was clearly a well-rehearsed routine. I really don't like that kind of play-acting; whatever happened to spontaneity? You'd expect the players to be so delighted that rehearsed routines would be the last thing on their minds. Wouldn't you?

At this stage it looked like Macclesfield were down and out. But no, a crisp drive from Mathew Barnes-Homer in the 89th minute, followed by an even crisper one from Anaud Mendy a minute later levelled the scores. There was even time for the former player to look as if he might score the winner, with a clear run in on goal, which was halted by a timely intervention from a Nuneaton defender. That would have been an injustice. Indeed Steve King, the Macclesfield manager, felt that they were fortunate to emerge with a point: 'They were hungrier than us, better than us, had more desire to get to the first ball and the sécond ball – quite honestly, we didn't deserve anything from this game,' (The Non-League Paper: Sunday September 16th). Kevin Wilkin, the Nuneaton manager, agreed. 'We've managed the game very well for 85 minutes. It was just the last five minutes…'

To an impartial observer (me), there were two counter arguments. First the statistics showed that Nuneaton had only 4 shots (3 on target) compared with Macclesfield's 9 (5 on target). As an attacking force, Nuneaton were clearly second-best. Second, for a side which indulged in such banal posturing after scoring what they, no doubt, thought was a winning goal, the late equaliser was perhaps poetic justice, and the draw a fair result!

After the match I made my way to Nuneaton's town centre which I had visited several times before and liked. The local council had shown the good judgement to pedestrianize the whole area; not even buses were permitted to enter it. As a result, you could relax in a fume-free, traffic-free environment, and sit outside Wetherspoons (if it's warm enough) enjoying a pint of cut-price real ale. At 5 o'clock, on a Saturday afternoon, however, there was a different kind of atmosphere. There had been a street market, which was in the process of being dismantled, but the town centre was still quite busy. Market traders were shouting at one another. An elderly drunk was meandering down a side street, shouting something incoherent at no-one in particular. Tired, fractious obese children dressed in tacky clothes whinged and whined at tired, fractious obese parents. But it's unfair, is it not, to judge the quality of a town centre at 5 o'clock on a Saturday afternoon? A time when it is not just Nuneaton that is not at its best. I would make sure that I retained a mental picture of the more positive impact it had made on me on previous visits.

Winding its way through central Nuneaton is the River Anker – the most static river you've ever seen. It would be impossible to know which way it was flowing if it wasn't for the directional pattern of the green weed which proliferates along its reaches.

## Chapter 4

I was struck by the contrast between the atmosphere at the match, and that of the town centre. The football stadium, in the sunshine, had felt like a good place to be. The Nuneaton supporters in the area where I was standing were relaxed, perceptive and enthusiastic. They were delighted when Nuneaton looked like they were going to win the game, and resigned when, at the very end, they had to settle for a draw. 'It's more than I'd expected at kick-off,' was one comment, as both sides were applauded when they left the field.

On such occasions, the importance of the local football club as a symbol of community identity and local pride comes over strongly. Many of the older Nuneaton fans I mingled with will no doubt have been long-term residents of the area, whose life has been lived in, and around, the town. It will matter to them that the team which represents 'their town' should give a good account of itself (one can imagine the euphoria when Nuneaton Borough held Premiership side Middlesbrough to a 1-1 draw in the third round of the FA Cup in 2006). Nuneaton as a place may not strike occasional visitors as particularly impressive, but if you've lived there all (or most of) your life, you'll no doubt see it in a much more positive light. The continuing importance of locality, even in an increasingly mobile society, is epitomised by the identity so many people feel with their local football club.

When I parked the car prior to exploring Nuneaton's town centre, I'd checked the football results on Sports Report. Stockport County had lost at home, again, for the third time in four matches. It was already beginning to look as if 2012-13 was not going to be the season when they returned to their rightful place in the Football League. But the fading prospect of promotion seemed less worrying now, nine games into the season. Of course I wanted them to survive. I was increasingly enjoying the Conference; the quality of the football and the diversity of the towns I'd visited, as well as the football clubs which represented them. I could live with Stockport's presence in this world for another season or two. My affections were now more widely scattered. I wanted unfashionable part-timers like Hyde and indeed Nuneaton to survive, amidst the ex-league giants such as Luton and Grimsby with whom they now competed.

# 21$^{st}$ September 2012 – League Table

| | Team | P | W | D | L | F | A | GD | Pt |
|---|---|---|---|---|---|---|---|---|---|
| 1 | Newport County AFC | 9 | 6 | 1 | 2 | 18 | 9 | 9 | 19 |
| 2 | Macclesfield Town | 9 | 6 | 1 | 2 | 20 | 15 | 5 | 19 |
| 3 | Forest Green Rovers | 9 | 5 | 3 | 1 | 16 | 8 | 8 | 18 |
| 4 | Wrexham | 9 | 5 | 3 | 1 | 13 | 5 | 8 | 18 |
| 5 | Grimsby Town | 10 | 4 | 5 | 1 | 15 | 7 | 8 | 17 |
| 6 | Luton Town | 10 | 5 | 2 | 3 | 17 | 15 | 2 | 17 |
| 7 | Dartford | 9 | 5 | 0 | 4 | 16 | 11 | 5 | 15 |
| 8 | Gateshead | 9 | 4 | 3 | 2 | 14 | 10 | 4 | 15 |
| 9 | Mansfield Town | 9 | 5 | 0 | 4 | 17 | 18 | -1 | 15 |
| 10 | AFC Telford United | 9 | 3 | 4 | 2 | 15 | 11 | 4 | 13 |
| 11 | Tamworth | 9 | 4 | 1 | 4 | 13 | 12 | 1 | 13 |
| 12 | Hereford United | 9 | 4 | 1 | 4 | 15 | 19 | -4 | 13 |
| 13 | Woking | 9 | 4 | 0 | 5 | 17 | 18 | -1 | 12 |
| 14 | Southport | 9 | 3 | 3 | 3 | 11 | 15 | -4 | 12 |
| 15 | Braintree Town | 9 | 3 | 2 | 4 | 12 | 14 | -2 | 11 |
| 16 | Alfreton Town | 9 | 3 | 2 | 4 | 13 | 18 | -5 | 11 |
| 17 | Cambridge United | 9 | 2 | 4 | 3 | 15 | 17 | -2 | 10 |
| 18 | Lincoln City | 9 | 2 | 3 | 4 | 12 | 14 | -2 | 9 |
| 19 | Stockport County | 9 | 2 | 3 | 4 | 11 | 13 | -2 | 9 |
| 20 | Nuneaton Town | 9 | 2 | 3 | 4 | 16 | 22 | -6 | 9 |
| 21 | Ebbsfleet United | 9 | 2 | 2 | 5 | 14 | 20 | -6 | 8 |
| 22 | Barrow | 9 | 1 | 4 | 4 | 8 | 15 | -7 | 7 |
| 23 | Hyde FC | 9 | 1 | 2 | 6 | 11 | 17 | -6 | 5 |
| 24 | Kidderminster Harriers | 9 | 0 | 4 | 5 | 6 | 12 | -6 | 4 |

# Perplexing Statues and Scissor Kicks

Gateshead vs Macclesfield Town

Tuesday October 8<sup>th</sup> 2012

Gateshead has, over the years, been seen as Newcastle's 'poor relation', or 'ugly sister'. Like Salford (overshadowed by Manchester) and Bootle (likewise by Liverpool) these towns have traditionally had undistinguished town centres, palpably unable to compete with their illustrious neighbours down the road (or in Gateshead's case, across the Tyne).

After Stockport, Gateshead is the Conference town with the strongest personal associations for me. Karen was living in Gateshead and working as a probation officer in Newcastle's west end, when I first met her in 1991. I moved there in 1993 shortly before our first son, Callum, was born at the Queen Elizabeth hospital. Incidentally, if you want to know what Callum looked like as a baby (which you probably don't) check out the DVD of the TV adaptation of Catherine Cookson's 'The Dwelling Place' (1993) in which he performs brilliantly as the illegitimate infant son of an aristocratic scoundrel played by Edward Fox.

We lived in 'The Avenues' - a compact area of terraced housing adjacent to Saltwell Park, a delightful recently-restored example of Victorian parks at their best, with a bandstand, a café, and an elaborate and challenging climbing frame. We used to wheel Callum in his pram to the park, where there were often to be seen large families of orthodox Jews, relaxing or playing games in the sun.

There is a well-established Jewish college in Gateshead, and, as a result, a large Jewish population, which co-exists happily enough with the native Tynesiders. We did our weekly shop at a large Tesco store in Gateshead town centre, which we otherwise tended to avoid (see below). Once you moved away from the centre, in a northerly direction, the residential areas always seemed attractive and friendly. I enjoyed my two years I lived there, before we moved to Kendal.

The town centre was, at the time, in poor shape. It boasted one of the ugliest multi-storey car parks in the country (and that's saying something!), which was featured in 'Get Carter' (starring Michael Caine) and as a result developed a certain iconic and ironic kudos. When the council decided it wanted to demolish it, there was even a campaign to have the car park 'listed' as 'a building of significant architectural interest' which would have meant it couldn't have been demolished. The campaign failed, and the car park has now disappeared from the face of Gateshead. That's probably just as well; lumps of concrete used to fall off it from time to time.

In 1994, before the minimum wage came into operation, we saw a board outside a small shop in Gateshead offering jobs at the princely rate of £1 per hour! Apart from Tesco, the national chains have kept well away. In a sense, the 'real' shopping centre in Gateshead was (and still is) three miles to the east in Dunstan: 'the Metro Centre'.

But if we developed an affection for Gateshead, in the past, others have described it in much less charitable terms. J B Priestley in his brilliant 'English Journey', written in 1934 at the height of another economic depression, was more critical of Gateshead than of any other place he visited.

> 'There seemed a great deal of
> Gateshead and the whole town
> appeared to have been carefully

> planned by an enemy of the
> human race in its more exuberant
> aspects. Insects can do better than
> this; their habitations are equally
> monotonous but far more
> efficiently constructed'.

Priestley went on to suggest that, as the various industries of Gateshead were then in a state of rapid decline, it was possible that it would soon end up like one of those decayed mediaeval towns, those ports that the sea has left. He concluded:

> 'No true civilisation could have
> produced such a town, which is no
> better than a huge dingy
> dormitory….. a place like this
> belongs to the pioneer age of
> industrialism, and unfortunately
> the industry appears to be
> vanishing before the pioneers
> themselves have time to make
> themselves comfortable……any
> future historian of England should
> be compelled to take a good long
> slow walk through Gateshead….'.

So much for Gateshead in 1934! But maybe Priestley was nursing a hangover or chronic indigestion as he wandered around the town! Were things any better in 2012? Well the vanishing industries referred to by Priestley – the ironworks, the wire-rope manufacturing and the locomotive works - have continued to vanish, without being replaced by anything of similar substance, although the 1930's did see a pioneering venture to attract new industry, when the 'Team Valley Industrial Estate' was laid out. It's still there today, but most of its occupants would be classified as 'light industry', and neither individually nor collectively have they ever generated employment on a scale to match what was lost.

However things have changed recently in a way which challenges the traditional poor-relation ugly-sister view of Gateshead. Where is Tyneside's new prestigious concert venue, the Sage? It is in Gateshead, proudly looking down across the river, at the Law Courts in Newcastle. Where is the new Tyneside contemporary arts venue? The Baltic, an imaginatively converted flour mill, is also in Gateshead, adjacent to The Sage. And where is the huge, famous 'Angel of the North' statue…?

How did this happen? The city fathers of Newcastle must be kicking themselves for losing out. It happened because Gateshead council got its act together in the 1980s. It has always been a Labour-dominated council, and the combination of a strong (if autocratic) council leader and an astute chief executive proved more effective than its 'big city' neighbour across the river at identifying a suitable site, putting together a regeneration package which attracted the requisite artistic and financial support, and then carrying out some effective project management which ensured (relatively) speedy implementation. So now people park across the river in Newcastle and come over to Gateshead for a cultural night out. Well done Gateshead!

I travelled to Tyneside by train. It's a lovely journey from Carlisle to Newcastle, along the Tyne Valley, through the small towns of Brampton, Haltwhistle, Haydon Bridge and Hexham, particularly on a sunny autumn day, with views north to the Roman Wall, and south to the Pennine moors. Trains don't stop at Gateshead anymore, so I went on to Newcastle, and caught the excellent metro service back across the Tyne. I'd heard that the council had embarked on a comprehensive redevelopment of the town centre, and was interested to see what progress had been made, if any.

As I emerged from the elaborate Gateshead Interchange (linking the metro to the bus station) I immediately realised that not only did the council have plans, but that they were already well under way. Across the road from the Interchange was a vast building site with tall cranes and edifices of ten or so stories already on the way to completion. I was totally disoriented. Where was the Tesco store where we did our weekly shop? Where were the little streets full of charity shops, takeaway food outlets and small cut-price carpet and bedding stores?

I crossed the road to examine an information hoarding. What faced me was apparently 'Trinity Square' which, on completion, would incorporate a hotel, a multi-screen cinema, offices, shops, bars, restaurants, a student village with nearly 1000 inhabitants, a health centre, a town square, and a Tesco 'Extra' (presumably a replacement for the one we used). The inclusion of the student village was an inspiration; a reliable source of patronage of the cafes, bars, and restaurants in the evening.

So what had happened to the Gateshead town centre which I remembered? (without much affection ). I explored further, and found what was left of it on Jackson Street and High Street.

Gateshead High Street must surely be the most down-at-heel wretched falling-to-pieces example of any High Street in the land. I carried out a quick assessment of the nature of the retail outlets involved. They included seven pubs, two of them closed, one for sale, none of them of the kind that a visitor (such as me) would dream of entering! There were four (yes four) examples of Noble's amusement arcades. There was a range of fast food outlets (most of them selling pizza), two off licences, and one tanning establishment ('better body, better colour, better you'). Two shops sold Polish food, one advertised 'full body piercing', and another sold discount furniture. There were two betting shops and five establishments which were either pawnbrokers or which advertised 'payday loans', or other forms of money lending, no doubt at an astronomical rate of interest. There were two downmarket cafes, two charity shops, the premises of an organisation which dealt with drug and alcohol-related problems, and (of course) the ubiquitous Poundland. All these outlets were concentrated within four hundred yards of one another. Several, particularly at the southern end of the High Street, had their shutters down at four o'clock on a Tuesday afternoon, which may have indicated that they were no longer open for business.

All that was really needed to complete the picture was a centre for gambling addicts, so that they could seek help, close to the doorsteps of Ladbrokes or Nobles amusements, and a slimming centre to deal with the prevalence of obesity, which was apparent in my walk round the town centre.

Appropriately enough, my copy of the Newcastle Evening Chronicle (Gateshead has no daily or weekly papers) contained the news that Wonga were likely to become the new sponsors of Newcastle United's shirts. Wonga is a company which provides loans to the needy, including the kind of 'payday' loans advertised in the Gateshead money shops. But it will cost you! How it will cost you. The annual rate of interest has been calculated at over 4000%. Understandably there was a growing body of protest in Newcastle about the association of their favourite club with such a company, but the sponsorship was confirmed the following week. One wonders how much use of the 45 retail units and the cafes and restaurants (not to mention the luxury-multiplex cinema) in the Trinity Centre, will be made by the residents of Gateshead who frequent the pubs, betting shops, and money-lenders of the High Street. My guess would be 'not a lot' (apart, no doubt from the Health Centre). It is not unlikely that this very tatty area of Gateshead town centre will, in its turn, be redeveloped; it may prove embarrassing and inconvenient to have it so close to the gleaming new Trinity Square development. In which case where will its patrons go for their pizzas, loans, drink and gambling? One also wonders whether Gateshead Council may be overreaching itself in facilitating this new development. We're in the middle of a deep recession, Newcastle city centre is fifteen minutes' walk away, and the Metro Centre is only three miles to the west. A step too far? We shall see.

On the way back to the Gateshead Interchange, I passed two pieces of contemporary sculpture. The first was in the middle of the road which separated the bus station from the metro station. 'Keep off the road' warned one notice. 'Keep off the artwork' warned another. The other piece of sculpture was perplexing. It was big and black, and featured a bloke who looked (from his headgear) like he was from ancient Egypt, apparently attempting to bend an iron bar, in the midst of an unlikely mixture of animals including a turtle, a seal and a couple of what could have been wolves or could have been dogs. There was no tablet attached explaining what the statue was all about. My guess would be some kind of mythological character, but I hadn't a clue who. Please, Gateshead Council, tell us what we're supposed to be appreciating!

It was time to catch the Metro back into Newcastle and meet my friend and fellow-Stockport County supporter John Davies. There being no atmospheric pubs near the International Stadium, (or none you would want to risk

going into) we met at the picturesque Crown Pasada, close
to Newcastle's Quayside, a wonderful example of a
Victorian pub (with stained glass windows) and a totally
unthreatening clientele.

I'd been to the International Stadium once before, in 1994
when I lived in Gateshead, to watch a tedious 0-0 draw with
Telford United in the Conference, so I knew what to
expect. On the face of it, it's one of the best grounds in the
Conference. It is an all-seater stadium, built less than 25
years ago, with a spacious main stand and a capacity of
12,000. Who else in the Conference can match that?

Harry Pearson in his excellent book about North-East
football 'The Far Corner' captured the anomalies of the
stadium well:

> 'The Gateshead International
> Stadium is immaculate. It has
> comfortable seats with adequate
> leg room, excellent sight lines, a
> roof that keeps out the rain, rather
> than funnelling it down the back
> of your neck, a snack bar that
> doesn't smell like the biggest burp
> in history, and clean toilets. In
> short it's a completely unsuitable
> place to stage a football match.'

In other ways too, the stadium is a handicap rather than an
asset to Gateshead FC. The atmosphere is sterile for a
number of reasons. First, except for big games (few and far
between in recent years) the only part of the ground which
is opened is the main stand (capacity 3,000). The other three
sides are left empty. Second there's a running track circling
the football pitch itself, reflecting the fact the ground was
built as an athletics stadium (a project inspired by Brendan

Foster, who was also closely involved in making it happen).
So the (very large) pitch seems an appreciable distance away.
The Barrow screamer would have difficulty operating at
Gateshead. Thirdly, crowds are usually sparse: 500-600 on
average. There was plenty of shouting and chanting as we
took our seats (having been ushered away from the VIP
area which we had inadvertently entered earlier) but it
echoed around the cavernous interior of the stand. I
wondered how much of it actually got through to the
players out there, across the running track. It's perhaps not
surprising that it was Gateshead's home record that led to
them missing out on the playoffs last season. Their away
record was up with the best.

The Evening Chronicle reported some disquiet amongst
local athletes that they couldn't train on several Tuesday
evenings (their scheduled training night) because of
Gateshead's midweek home fixtures. There was an
apologetic rejoinder from Gateshead's manager Ian Bogie,
explaining that the Bet Square Premier League
establishment required that they play their midweek games
on Tuesdays, although in the lower levels of the pyramid
there was more flexibility. So maybe Gateshead should do
the decent thing and get themselves relegated, so that the
local athletes don't have to miss half-a-dozen Tuesday
training sessions.

Gateshead, when I looked up their league history, turned
out to have had an even briefer time in the league than
Barrow. They were elected to Division Two in 1919, from
whence they were relegated in 1928, and back to which they
never managed to return, although they were runners-up
three times in Division Three North, in an era when only
one team was promoted. They failed to achieve re-election
at the end of the 1959-60 season, the first club to suffer this
ignominy since 'New Brighton' (where are they now?) in

## Chapter 5

1951. Allowing for the war years, this means Gateshead had a mere 35 years in the Football League compared with Barrow's 44. During this time, Gateshead never once achieved promotion. Indeed we also need to take account of the fact that between 1919 and 1930 Gateshead were known as South Shields (which is ten miles to the east); not surprisingly because that is where their ground was then located. The clubs changed names and grounds (to Redheugh Park in Gateshead) in 1930 (echoes of Wimbledon's transformation into MK Dons in 2005). From this perspective the real Gateshead played in the Football League for a mere 23 seasons.

Since their fall from grace, Gateshead have struggled. They have gone through name changes (Gateshead Town, Gateshead United) and moved up and down the Pyramid levels, with only brief periods in the Conference. In 2009, they beat Telford in the Conference North play-off final to regain their Conference status for the first time since 2003, after which they decided to operate with a full-time playing squad.

Macclesfield Town were the evening's visitors. Both teams' form had declined since I last saw them. When Gateshead kicked off at Southport, they were unbeaten, and fourth in the league. Since then their record read 'played 7, won 1, drawn 2, lost 4' and they had slumped to eleventh place. The manager, in his column in the excellent programme, expressed his frustration. In the previous two games (both 1-1 draws) 'our approach play has been very good and we have dominated the opposition, but haven't been able to put the ball in the net.' A familiar refrain, but clearly heartfelt. Bogie claimed to be devastated not to have won those last two games, and reported that Scott McNiven, Hyde's manager, told him after last week's match that they (Gateshead) should have won 10-1. (It sounded a bit unlikely to me; would any manager ever really admit that his side had been so outclassed!?)

Macclesfield Town were league leaders when I had seen them at Nuneaton. Since then their record read 'played 4, drawn 1, lost 3' and they had fallen to eighth place. Both managers were, however, upbeat about their team's prospects of making the play-offs, despite a combined recent record that would place them at the bottom of the Conference. Tonight's game was going to be crucial for both sides; a turning point or a further fall down the table?

The first half-hour of the game lacked incident and incisiveness. There was some patient, good quality approach work from both sides, but a total lack of imagination and penetration in and around the penalty area and on the flanks. The midfield was always congested, the penalty area (when either side got that far) likewise. There were very few chances. Then, a few minutes before half-time, Gateshead broke the deadlock. Yemi Odubade created space in the box for Jamie Chandler to hit a low shot to the right of the keeper, which he probably should have saved but didn't. The fifty or so vociferous Gateshead supporters, located behind us in the stand, duly celebrated. 'Heed, heed' they shouted, which was not a warning about possible complacency, but is what the club is known as, locally. For outsiders, you need to know that you don't pronounce Gateshead as it is spelt, but rather as Gates*heed*.

The second half was much better; much more attacking down the wings, more incisive play in and around the penalty box. An end-to-end cut-and-thrust pattern of play developed, as Macclesfield pushed for the equaliser. But it was Gateshead who scored again, halfway through the second half, with a stooping header from James Curtis, following a left wing corner. Cue further rejoicing from the

## Chapter 5

Gateshead fans. A home win at last? Silence from the 50 or so Macclesfield fans segregated at the far end of the stand.

Game over, you might think? But Macclesfield had already demonstrated their formidable powers of recovery late in a game, when they turned a 1-3 deficit at Nuneaton into a 3-3 draw and nearly won the game. Gateshead fans would have done well to chant 'Heed, heed' at this stage. And you always have to allow for flashes of genius, at Conference as much as at Premiership level. There was a moment of pure magic, when Barnes-Homer seeing a cross coming over behind him, executed a perfect overhead bicycle-kick to rocket the ball past a motionless Gateshead keeper. It was a replica of Wayne Rooney's winner against Manchester City two seasons before. It even had the Gateshead fans applauding.

The Macclesfield supporters woke up and began to make their presence felt. Their team continued to press, and soon equalised – a rather scruffy goal from Chris Holroyd, in a goalmouth scramble following a corner – which was nonetheless well-deserved. And 2-2 was the way it stayed.

John remembered a pub (The Wheatsheaf) he had been to some years before in Felling, a mile or so down the road from the stadium. What a delight it turned out to be. A small, street-corner hostelry, with plates of cheese, pickled onions and crisps provided free for patrons, Big Lamp bitter from the brewery of the same name in nearby Newburn, and half-a-dozen musicians playing traditional Irish music to a small but appreciative audience. It made for an enjoyable postscript to what had proved (the first 30 minutes excepted) an entertaining game.

# Touchline Banter and Banished Managers

Macclesfield Town vs Newport County

Saturday 13<sup>th</sup> October 2012

Macclesfield: a cultural desert full of happy people! Or so two recent surveys would have us believe. In 2004, an exercise carried out by The Times identified Macclesfield as the most uncultured town in Britain. Apparently it had fewer cinemas, theatres or art galleries than anywhere else (although it does have four silk museums). But to balance that shortcoming, a 2008 British Household Panel survey identified Macclesfield as the fifth happiest district in Britain. So it would appear that although apparently devoid of culture, Macclesfield residents are perfectly content with their lot. Perhaps that has something to do with the fact that so many of them are well off. Macclesfield (and its surrounding area) has a distinctly affluent feel about it, and the well above-average percentage of middle-class residents in the district's social class structure bears out that impression. Alternatively both surveys could be deeply methodologically-flawed, good for a newspaper headline or two but bearing little relation to reality.

Macclesfield Town are known as the 'Silkmen', a reflection of the town's industrial heritage, although only one silk-manufacturing concern still operates in the town. Club nicknames often have this function: Stockport County and Luton Town are both known as the 'Hatters'. Grimsby Town the 'Mariners' and Newport County were the 'Ironsides' (now the Exiles, following a spell at Moreton-in Marsh, in the 1990s).

# Chapter 6

Certainly Macclesfield's industrial past was dominated by silk; in 1832 there were 71 silk mills in the town. It was also the birthplace of 'Hovis'. Nowadays what little industry there is tends to be 'light' in character and situated in nondescript industrial estates. Increasingly the Macclesfield area is becoming a pleasant up-market residential area for those working elsewhere (typically Greater Manchester). The two biggest employers are the council and the hospital.[*]

Not surprisingly Macclesfield returns Conservative MPs; always has done, probably always will do. The council is (almost) always Conservative-controlled, a situation not changed by an amalgamation with neighbours in 2009 (of which more below). Until the 2010 general election the town's MP was Nicholas Winterton, a flamboyant and well-known backbencher, who (like many of his colleagues) found his reputation tarnished by the parliamentary 'expenses' scandal of the previous year.

Macclesfield is certainly a town with a distinctive identity. The town centre is sited on top of a hill. To the east the land falls steeply away to the valley along which the River Bollin and Macclesfield canal pass. Close by are the Pennine hills, which dominate the view to the east. To the west and north lies verdant leafy rural Cheshire, dotted with picturesque villages such as Alderley Edge and Prestbury inhabited by the affluent, including a sprinkling of millionaire players from the two Manchester Premiership clubs.

But Macclesfield's distinctive identity is no longer reflected in the existence of a local council which bears its name, and

---

[*] Astra Zeneca, the pharmaceuticals firm employs 2,500 but they are over in Alderley Edge which is 10 miles from Macclesfield itself.

which provides a meaningful reference point for its residents. In 2009, as a result of a bizarre and mismanaged Labour government-initiated reorganisation initiative, Macclesfield came to be amalgamated with Congleton and Crewe and Nantwich districts, forming a new unitary authority called East Cheshire. I participated in this process, acting as advisor to Congleton and Crewe, and Nantwich, neither of whom (understandably) wished to lose their own identity and be swallowed up in a new authority which they suspected (rightly) would be dominated by Macclesfield.

Crewe and Nantwich, in particular, had reason to feel aggrieved; more often than not the council has been controlled by Labour. No chance of that in the new East Cheshire! And anyway, isn't it a pity that a place with a strong identity and industrial tradition like Crewe should not have a local council to represent it and speak out for it? We (Crewe, Congleton, and I) won the argument – well, that's my view anyway – but the decision went against us, for 'political reasons' which need not detain us here.

Macclesfield, however, was not displeased with the outcome. The new East Cheshire headquarters are in Macclesfield, and the Macclesfield area, with the largest group of Conservatives from the three predecessor authorities, enjoys a lead role. Tough on Crewe, twenty-five miles to the south-west, which is culturally totally different from 'moneybags' Macclesfield.

I was pleased to see that my view of the recent reorganisation was shared by at least one Macclesfield resident, Alan Fraser (67), who had started a petition to abolish East Cheshire Council. According to the Macclesfield Express, Mr Fraser is calling for the new authority to be dissolved and replaced by the old county and borough council set-up. He is quoted as saying '…pre-2009 you had a council which was concentrated on Macclesfield.

## Chapter 6

Individual town needs were dealt with, which they aren't now.' I'm with you there Mr Fraser. Macclesfield is a real place. East Cheshire is a meaningless fabrication.

The upmarket nature of Macclesfield and its satellite villages is apparent when you walk down its long sinuous high street. You could hardly imagine a bigger contrast between the respective high streets of Gateshead and Macclesfield (okay, Macclesfield's is actually called Mill Street, but in everything but name it *is* the High Street!). There's not a pawnbroker or a money lender to be seen. There is a predisposition to sell you gold, not buy it from you.

The cafes and restaurants are inviting rather than forbidding. True, there are the usual charity shops (and a Poundland; is there any sizeable town which doesn't have one?) but the quality of the clothes available in them is phenomenal. If you're prepared to buy quality clothing second-hand rather than new, come to Macclesfield. Mill Street is pedestrianized throughout and cobbled for most of its length. Smartly-dressed women with their equally-smartly-dressed teenage daughters parade along it. There are new developments, but they are well-integrated into the traditional ambience of the street, neither dominating nor even intruding. There is an impressive town hall, featuring a series of Doric pillars.

The affluence of Macclesfield was neatly symbolised by the headline story in the Express. It involved a Mercedes-Benz, which was being test-driven by a garage technician, and which pulled up in front of Anthony Adkins (37) on London Road, causing him to brake sharply. Mr Adkins was so incensed he drove straight to the Mercedes-Benz showroom where he shouted and swore, until manhandled out of the showroom. A manager said 'We're a million pound showroom – we can't have people shouting and swearing.' Quite so. This is Macclesfield.

Macclesfield Town's ground is the Moss Rose Stadium, a lovely name for a very attractive ground. At one end, there's an open terrace (closed to spectators, except presumably for big matches), and at the other, a covered stand with the unusual arrangement of a seated area at the front (of five or six rows), and a standing area immediately behind it, which was where the vociferous (but polite) local fans whom I'd come across at Nuneaton and Gateshead gathered.

I positioned myself on the terracing to the side of the old 'main stand'. The 200 or so Newport fans were seated opposite, at one end of a newer stand that runs the full length of the pitch.

The Newport fans must have been up early, for today's game kicked off at the unlikely (for the Conference) time of 12.30. There was a reason for this. Blue Square, who sponsors the league, had set a ground-hopping day for those who fancied seeing three games in the space of eight hours. You could start at Macclesfield at 12.30, catch a specially-provided bus to Stockport for the 3.30 kick off between Stockport County and Kidderminster Harriers, and then move on to Hyde for a 6.30 kick-off between Hyde and Tamworth. A nice idea (and it turned out there were plenty of takers) but it wouldn't have suited me. I like to savour a match in its aftermath, not rush on to another venue. I once opted to watch three Shakespeare plays within a similar time-frame. A big mistake. I fell asleep during the first act of the third play, and decided I'd had enough by the interval.

There is a case for placing Macclesfield Town in the category of 'fallen giants' together with the likes of Luton Town, Wrexham and Grimsby Town. This would, perhaps, be over-generous. There is nothing giant-like about the club, (or the ground) and Macclesfield's 15 years in the Football League (including one season in Division One) is paltry compared with the clubs mentioned above, and

others. Their promotion from the Conference in 1997 was a
just reward mind you, they'd been Champions before in
1995 but their ground had been deemed not up-to-standard.
Since then the team had usually struggled in the lower
reaches of Division Two, and not only that, their home
crowds had always been way down the attendance league
tables (2000 on a good day). Macclesfield suffers because of
the relative smallness of the town (51,000 in the 2011
Census), its proximity to the big Manchester clubs
(Manchester is 25 minutes away by train), and the lack of a
serious football tradition in an affluent country town. It
probably has more in common with Kidderminster Harriers
who (like Macclesfield) came up from the Conference and
survived for six years in Division Two before falling back
into their traditional milieu.

Macclesfield Town have suffered more than their fair share
of tragedy over the past few years (real tragedy, that is, not
last season's run of 26 games without a win and their
subsequent relegation). A popular manger - Keith
Alexander - and stalwart defender - Richard Butcher - died
suddenly in 2010 and 2011 respectively. Squad shirt No 21
is no longer used, having been 'retired in memory of
Richard Butcher'.

Although the club reacted with dignity to their relegation
from the Football League ('we've been proud to represent
the community in the Football League, and will make every
effort to regain a place') there were signs of instability
amongst the management. That very week, club chairman
Mike Rance resigned, having held the position since 2008,
during the period of the two deaths, the relegation, and
having 'helped steer Macclesfield through the stormiest of
waters'. Although his resignation statement gave little away
as to why, he had previously threatened to walk out over the
appointment of new manager Steve King in May. His

preference was for former Town striker Steve Burr, but he was overruled by the club's Iraqi owners.

The Silkmen Supporters Trust were worried about 'the lack of local decision-making left in the hierarchy' and their concern that 'decisions are now being made from afar'.* The Alkhali brothers, the Iraqi owners, were not present at the Newport game, and the impression formed is one of absentee owners and a big hole in the management structure (there's only one other director now that Rance has left). Watch this space, as they say.

Newport came to Macclesfield as league leaders – something of a surprise, as they had been close to relegation during the previous season. They were another survivor from earlier times; elected to the Football League in 1920, never achieved very much for sixty years, then a rare promotion (to Division 3, as it was then) in the early 1980s, inspired by John Aldridge. In 1988, they were relegated to the Conference where, in early 1989, they suffered the ignominy of bankruptcy and a failure to fulfil their remaining fixtures (their record was expunged). Then came a long climb back through the lower reaches of the pyramid, until they were promoted back to the Conference in 2010.

The Macclesfield Town team were becoming familiar; I'd seen them draw 3-3 at Nuneaton and 2-2 at Gateshead, in each case playing impressive football and demonstrating a capacity to come back from what appeared to be impossible positions (1-3 and 0-2 down with barely ten minutes left). They'd suffered a slump in form since I saw them at Nuneaton, with no wins in a sequence of five games. But at this stage of the season, any club in the middle of the table knew that a good run could put them in a play-off position.

---

* Macclesfield Express 10 October 2012

## Chapter 6

The first twenty minutes or so of the game were uneventful. They were, however, hugely enlivened by the banter between Newport assistant manager, Jimmy Dack, and the Macclesfield supporters on the terrace behind the Newport dugout. This is where I'd positioned myself; after watching a game at Gateshead earlier in the week from a height and a distance, I felt the need to be close to the pitch, to witness the immediacy of the play, the well-timed tackle to dispossess an opponent, and the detail of the footwork used to evade tackles.

The problem with banter is that it sounds wittier and more spontaneous at the time than it does when you write it down on paper. So you'll have to take my word for the hilarity generated by the exchanges between Jimmy Dack and the Macclesfield supporters. For example:

> 'Are you on the coaching staff; or
> have you just climbed over the
> fence?'

> 'Who's that guy with graffiti on his
> arm? Does he think he's David
> Beckham? Cos he's not.'

> 'Newport are crap…what do you
> teach them in training sessions?'
> 'How to hoof it.'

After an ineffective Newport striker is yet again caught offside, a cry of dismay from Jimmy Dack.

> 'He's shit; we'll take him off.'
> 'Great then you'll be down to ten

men, you've already used your
three subs!'

Well, I did warn you! But what I really enjoyed was the fact
that it was possible for a visiting (assistant) manager to
engage in a jokey dialogue throughout the game with a
group of home supporters. You wouldn't get that at Old
Trafford, or indeed at the vast majority of Football League
games.

Jimmy Dack was on his feet, in front of the dugout, for the
whole game, shouting instructions to the Newport players,
and registering a wide range of emotions. Every now and
then he was joined by Newport's manager Justin Edinburgh
(once a Spurs regular) who looked rather like a very cross
Steve Coogan, in need of a good night's sleep.

Newport may have been league leaders, but there was little
about their play in the first half which distinguished them
from other reasonably capable sides I'd seen this season –
Luton Town, Gateshead and indeed Macclesfield. However
they did take the lead towards the end of the first half, when
Tony James ran in from the right to side foot home a
disputed free kick. Jimmy Dack was ecstatic in his
celebrations, Justin Edinburgh rather more restrained.

Two minutes later came a moment which, if anyone was
there to film it, will no doubt end up on a 'Gaffes of the
Season' DVD. The leading scorer in the Conference,
Newport's Aaron O'Connor found the ball dropping at his
feet, 10 yards from goal, with the Macclesfield keeper
elsewhere, and no defender anywhere near him. He side-
footed the ball over the bar, when everyone's proverbial
granny could have netted it! But at least that kept the game
alive.

## Chapter 6

The second half was dominated by Macclesfield, with some impressive approach work (as against Nuneaton and Gateshead) not matched by the quality of their finishing. Both full backs proved adept at overlapping, making it to the goal line and sending over dangerous crosses. Two or three goalbound shots hit Newport defenders, in one case resulting in a dazed Ismail Yakubu (nephew of the better-known Everton and Blackburn striker) being led from the field and substituted. Just when it looked like Newport would hold out, Matthew Barnes-Homer rose impressively to head home a left-wing cross at the far post from a difficult angle. In doing so, he joined Newport's Aaron O'Connor as the Conference's leading goal scorer.

In each of the three Macclesfield games I'd seen, Barnes-Homer had scored; a crisp ground shot, a spectacular overhead kick and now a towering header. I looked up his pedigree. Unusual to say the least. Two years in America with Rochester Raging Rhinos, Syracuse Salty Dogs and Virginia Beach Mariners (can't match those names in the Football League, can we!). Then one game for Wycombe Wanderers, followed by a good season with Kidderminster Harriers (19 goals), spells with Luton Town and Nuneaton Town and a move to Sweden, before signing for Macclesfield. There's little there to predict his ten goals in fourteen games for the Silkmen. Maybe a late-flowering talent?

Either side could have scored in the ten minutes which remained, but neither did. One-all was a fair result to another excellent game. Macclesfield's midfielder Jean Paul Kissock deservedly got the man of the match award. These awards are sometimes totally mystifying – 'can they really be giving it to him?' – but not in this case. Jean Paul really was here, there, and every-bloody-where. He rarely misplaced a pass, and was a one-man engine room behind Macclesfield's second half revival.

Justin Edinburgh sounded satisfied with a point (as well he might be, Macclesfield were the more impressive side). He claimed that 'possession doesn't win matches' which of course is true, though it does help. Steve King had been banished to the stand at half-time, which I hadn't realised until I read the match report in the Non-Leaguer the next day. 'There was no altercation with the ref,' he claimed. 'I had words with him and he wasn't happy with my words.' And what precisely were those words, Steve? Maybe he should have followed Jimmy Dack's example and retained a sense of proportion (and humour) however irrational a referee's decisions may have appeared?

# 26<sup>th</sup> October 2012 – League Table

| | Team | P | W | D | L | F | A | GD | Pt |
|---|---|---|---|---|---|---|---|---|---|
| 1 | Newport County AFC | 15 | 10 | 3 | 2 | 28 | 14 | 14 | 33 |
| 2 | Wrexham | 15 | 8 | 5 | 2 | 25 | 14 | 11 | 29 |
| 3 | Dartford | 16 | 9 | 2 | 5 | 27 | 18 | 9 | 29 |
| 4 | Luton Town | 15 | 9 | 2 | 4 | 28 | 21 | 7 | 29 |
| 5 | Grimsby Town | 15 | 7 | 6 | 2 | 22 | 10 | 12 | 27 |
| 6 | Forest Green Rovers | 15 | 8 | 3 | 4 | 25 | 15 | 10 | 27 |
| 7 | Tamworth | 15 | 7 | 1 | 7 | 22 | 21 | 1 | 22 |
| 8 | AFC Telford United | 15 | 5 | 6 | 4 | 26 | 21 | 5 | 21 |
| 9 | Macclesfield Town | 14 | 6 | 3 | 5 | 25 | 25 | 0 | 21 |
| 10 | Mansfield Town | 15 | 6 | 3 | 6 | 22 | 27 | -5 | 21 |
| 11 | Stockport County | 15 | 5 | 5 | 5 | 20 | 19 | 1 | 20 |
| 12 | Gateshead | 15 | 4 | 7 | 4 | 19 | 19 | 0 | 19 |
| 13 | Woking | 15 | 6 | 1 | 8 | 27 | 29 | -2 | 19 |
| 14 | Hereford United | 15 | 5 | 4 | 6 | 22 | 26 | -4 | 19 |
| 15 | Southport | 15 | 5 | 4 | 6 | 22 | 27 | -5 | 19 |
| 16 | Cambridge United | 15 | 4 | 5 | 6 | 27 | 28 | -1 | 17 |
| 17 | Braintree Town | 15 | 4 | 5 | 6 | 18 | 22 | -4 | 17 |
| 18 | Alfreton Town | 14 | 4 | 5 | 5 | 17 | 23 | -6 | 17 |
| 19 | Barrow | 15 | 4 | 5 | 6 | 19 | 28 | -9 | 17 |
| 20 | Lincoln City | 15 | 4 | 4 | 7 | 19 | 23 | -4 | 16 |
| 21 | Kidderminster Harriers | 15 | 3 | 6 | 6 | 17 | 16 | 1 | 15 |
| 22 | Nuneaton Town | 15 | 2 | 6 | 7 | 20 | 31 | -11 | 12 |
| 23 | Ebbsfleet United | 15 | 2 | 5 | 8 | 20 | 31 | -11 | 11 |
| 24 | Hyde FC | 14 | 2 | 4 | 8 | 17 | 26 | -9 | 10 |

# Programmes, Punctuation, and Prejudgements

Alfreton Town vs AFC Telford United

Saturday October 27th 2012

Be wary of prejudgements! I'd never been to Alfreton before, but I knew what to expect, or thought I did. I knew it used to be a mining town, with three pits close by, all long since closed. A friend, who used to live in Belper, in the same part of Derbyshire, had warned me not to expect too much of Alfreton: 'Don't spend more time there than you have to; it's a rough place!'

So, as I travelled across the Pennines by train, on a sunny autumn day, when I should really have been out walking with the dog (but there were 24 visits to do before the end of April, and I'd only done 6 so far) I prepared myself for the legendary characteristics of towns that had lost their mines: high unemployment, boarded-up houses, big problems of drug addiction, a town centre full of empty shops, and environmental dereliction.

When the train arrived at Chesterfield station, those who wanted to get off had to fight their way past two occupied buggies to reach the door. When they eventually did, the door refused to open. Fingers were still frantically jabbing the 'open' button when the train moved away.

Amongst those hoping (but failing) to leave the train were four blokes who were intending to watch Chesterfield's Division Two game against Barnet. They were remarkably relaxed about the mishap (unlike a young woman who was bewailing her fate into a mobile phone). 'What's the next stop?' said one. 'Brentford I think,' said another (so confusing these football club locations, aren't they?). Eventually they figured out that Alfreton was the next stop, and with any luck, they'd get a train back to Chesterfield in time for kick-off.

As the train approached Alfreton station, we all located ourselves next to the guard, at the front of the train, on the assumption that he would be able to deal with any doors that refused to open. As it happened there was no problem and there was a train back to Chesterfield three minutes later. All was well.

As I left the station, I noticed that there was a smell of burning fossil fuel in the air; perhaps from a coking plant. It felt appropriate; the mines had gone, but their aromatic legacy still pervaded the air.

As I made my way along the Mansfield Road, towards the town centre, I began to realise that my prejudgement of the place did not correspond with reality. There were long streets of terraced houses on the right, sloping down towards a valley, but they looked in good condition and none were boarded up. The same was true of the council houses on the left. They were well-maintained; there was no rubbish in gardens, and no signs of discarded needles in the paved or grassed communal areas. I began to suspect that my friend's warnings were out-of-date, and that he hadn't actually been to Alfreton for a long while.

The town centre strengthened my suspicions. There was no evidence of empty shops, nor any sign of the pawnbrokers or money-lenders which I'd seen elsewhere. The High Street had more of the ambience of its counterpart in Macclesfield (though less opulent, of course) than of Gateshead or Hyde. There was a lively, relatively small-scale, shopping mall which adjoined the high street, and which incorporated a paved traffic-free square. I saw no reason not to 'hang around' (despite my friend's warning); there was nothing remotely threatening about the place.

Alfreton seemed to have found a way of compensating for the loss of its industrial base. Its proximity to a motorway junction on the M1 had no doubt helped. There was also, I learned later, a chocolate factory, although the opportunity to speculate about ex-miners now making chocolates (as an alternative to crisps or toilet rolls) was not really sustainable, given that all the mines had closed in the 1960s.

Alfreton is located in Amber Valley District Council (an evocative name, but the scenery doesn't live up to it!). The council was formed in 1974 from the small towns of Ripley, Belper, Heanor and Alfreton, plus a number of villages. In an ideal world all these towns would have their own councils (as they did before 1974, and as they still would if they were in France). No doubt Amber Valley is riven with conflict as to whether each of these places is getting its fair share of resources. I don't know where the district's leisure centre is located, but you can bet your life in the three unfavoured towns there is a level of bitterness as to why Belper, or Heanor, (or wherever), has been selected, when there is just as strong a case in Ripley or Alfreton.

Alfreton Town have had a remarkably swift and impressive rise to fame. The club was founded as late as 1939, and spent most of the post-war period in the Midland Counties league with a range of other small-town Derbyshire and Nottinghamshire teams such as Belper Town, Heanor Town, Ilkeston Town and Eastwood Town (not a lot of imagination about club names being shown here is there! – where's the local equivalent of Rushden and Diamonds?). But whilst all the other 'Towns' are still operating at the third level of the pyramid or below, Alfreton Town are now punching well above their weight. They had been promoted to the Conference Division North (as it then was) in the early 2000s, then narrowly missed promotion in 2009 and 2010 (losing in the play-offs on each occasion), before going up as Champions in 2011.

Last season, after a dismal first half to the campaign (they were next to the bottom at Christmas) Alfreton enjoyed a remarkable revival, finishing the season in 15th place, well clear of the danger zone. In the process they defeated Stockport County 6-1, at a time when County were also in the midst of a revival. I remember hearing the result on the car radio and being convinced I'd misheard it. How could this be possible? But it was!

One of Alfreton's strengths has been the creation, over the years, of a settled team rather than relying on the lottery of other clubs' cast-offs at the end of every season.

Alfreton were currently in the lower-middle reaches of the table. They'd had some notable victories, including a 3-0 home victory over much-fancied Luton Town and some equally inexplicable defeats (3-0 at home to Nuneaton Town). If they were still there, or thereabouts, at the end of the season, it would be a further chapter in a remarkable 'little club makes good' story. Alfreton's population is a mere 8,000. Only Nailsworth (home of Forest Green Rovers) has a smaller population. Even if you include the villages close to Alfreton (where the pits used to be) the overall population is just 24,500. And here they were, entertaining and visiting the likes of Stockport County, Luton Town, Grimsby Town and Newport County, all towns with populations over five or six times as big.

Alfreton Town (and other 'small town' clubs like them) have benefitted from the fact that the rate of turnover of clubs in the Conference is now much greater than it used to be. From 1980 until 1986 there was no automatic promotion from the Conference to the Football League, and none of its champions in this period had managed to displace clubs that finished bottom of the league. Between 1987 and 1996, three of the ten clubs that won the Conference were denied promotion because their grounds did not meet Football League requirements (from 1997 onwards, clubs who finished as champions had made sure, in advance, that their grounds were up to standard). From 2004 onwards two clubs were promoted each season to the Football League. Thus, twice as many clubs gained promotion in the 2002-12 period as had done so between 1980 and 2001.

Turnover had also been increased by changes to the pattern of relegation from the Conference. Until 1995, just two clubs were relegated each season. From 1995, the number was increased to three, then reverted to two for a while, before increasing to four in 2009. As a result, the opportunities for small-town clubs like Alfreton to move from relative obscurity to the heady heights of the Conference has also steadily increased over time.

Several of these little clubs quickly returned to their familiar environment (Leek Town, Farsley Celtic, Lewes, and St Albans City, to name but four). Others survived for a few seasons, including Leigh Railway Mechanics Institute (now there's a distinctive name for you!) and Trowbridge Town. Alfreton had survived one season; they would be doing pretty well to make it two.

AFC Telford came up with Alfreton via the play-offs in 2011. They struggled over the previous season, winning only a single away game, but doing well enough at their well-supported home stadium to finish six points clear of the relegation places. Telford had also beaten Luton Town (1-0 away) and had generally done better than their mediocre performance on the opening day of the season at Barrow might have suggested, particularly when you take account of their long list of injured players over the past month or so.

Alfreton's ground is only a short walk from the town centre (as is most of the rest of Alfreton). It goes under the name of the Impact Arena, Impact being a local marketing and publicity outfit. Sponsored-grounds like this (and Nuneaton's Triton Showers Community Arena), with instantly forgettable names, are on the increase in the Conference. Long live Haig Avenue, Moss Rose and Ewen Fields as far as I'm concerned.

It cost me £12 to get in (and would have been £18 had I not qualified for a concession) which struck me as more than a bit steep. Once through the turnstile, though, I began to understand why. I had inadvertently entered the section of the ground reserved for visiting supporters, and I guess Alfreton felt they could jack up their prices for visitors, on the basis that if they'd travelled this far, they weren't going to go away. I certainly wasn't, and was perfectly happy to masquerade as a Telford supporter for the afternoon, joining the 77 others who (we were told at half-time) were present.

The ground looked like the ground of a club that hadn't expected to reach the lofty heights of the Conference, and didn't expect to stay there once it had. Only at one end of the ground - the end reserved for visiting fans as it happened - was it possible to gain enough height to get a sense of the shape of the game. Everywhere else there were at most six or seven rows of seats. At the opposite end were to be found a group of 70 or so vociferous home fans (the self-styled Red Army!) who stood throughout the game in an entirely seated area, encouraging their team with a singularly uninspired series of chants. It beats me why such supporters should think that 'Red Army' intoned repeatedly for minutes at a time is going to inspire their team. More likely to drive them (and me) mad!

The Impact Stadium is not a ground which seemed capable of sustaining a particularly supportive atmosphere (like Gateshead's, but for different reasons) which may help to explain why Alfreton Town's away record this season was much better than its home record.

The programme too had a 'we can't really believe we're in the Conference' feel about it. It was very thin in terms of reading matter; I read the entire contents in a little over 5 minutes. There were no pen pictures of the visiting players. Instead of the usual date-sequence listing of matches, results, teams and scorers, there was a series of boxes full of initials, posing an interpretive challenge even for an inveterate solver of cryptic crosswords like me. I struggled to identify PCX2 from the key at the bottom of the page – a player whose surname began with X? – until I realised that the reference was to one Paul Clayton (PC) who had scored twice (X2) against Southport. There were scores of adverts, lots of totally undistinguished action photographs, and a series of opportunities to sponsor a range of different things – 'clean sheets', pitch squares(!), and individual players' kit (home, away and third). If you wanted to discover some fascinating facts about Ross Killock (who had recently joined Alfreton on loan from Leeds United) then this was the programme for you! Apparently his preferred choice of pre-match meal is scrambled eggs on toast, his pre-match superstition is to put on his left sock and left boot first, his favourite holiday destination is Florida, and he prefers red sauce to brown sauce. Thanks for that Ross; I feel I know you much better now! To be fair to the player concerned, he was no doubt simply responding to the familiar set list of questions which programme editors seem to think will interest their readers.

## Chapter 7

The most interesting feature in the programme was the manager's brief column; two long paragraphs without a full stop or capital letter within either of them. I know 'stream of consciousness' prose has been used to good effect in fiction, but I'm not sure it works in football programmes. Nicky Law (the manager) was clearly not happy with the attendance – 338 – at the previous Saturday's FA Cup tie against Gateshead. Come on, Nicky, get real! This is Alfreton! There are only 8,000 people who live in the town for heaven's sake. Count your blessings. Hopefully he will have been (marginally) happier with the 572 paying customers who turned up today.

There was one ex-Morecambe player on view. Centre-back Darren Kempson (or 'Kempo' as he is apparently known in Alfreton) had a couple of Conference seasons with Morecambe, in the mid-2000s, before they were promoted. 'Vastly-experienced' now, I should think, in the parlance of football programmes.

For the first half hour, the game was like a re-run of the nondescript 0-0 draw between Barrow and Telford on the first day of the season (maybe I'd better avoid Telford's away games in future). Both sides relied on long high balls out of defence (not a good idea on a windy day). Neither attack was able to turn this kind of service into goal opportunities. The ball bounced back from Alfreton player to Telford player with metronomic predictability. Interludes of head tennis varied the monotony.

Then, Alfreton began to create chances, though rarely as a result of any sustained build-up. Twice Telford's keeper Ryan Young was forced into excellent saves. Then, in the last minute of the half, Ben Tomlinson was put through on the right, and angled a right-foot shot neatly beyond the keeper's despairing drive to give Alfreton the lead, which was probably deserved. Telford had created nothing.

During half-time, I talked to a group of Telford supporters; no choice really, I was unable to gain access to any from Alfreton, given where in the ground I was. They reminded me that their side had the worst disciplinary record in the Conference (including five red cards) and were currently being 'investigated' by the FA as a result. They were encouraged by their team's improved record this season (this time last year they were in the bottom four) but felt that mid-table was the most they could realistically aspire to. The same would no doubt be the case for Alfreton. Both sides are part-time in a league where the majority of clubs are full-time. I suspect both are delighted to be in the Conference at all, and will aim simply to stay there.

The second half was much better. It was as if both managers had said at half-time 'Okay lads, the long-ball game isn't working, let's try and keep it on the ground.' Telford certainly came out with a much more determined and creatively-disposed attitude, and increasingly dominated the proceedings with some impressive approach work. Several chances were spurned until half-way through the half when one Chris Sharp (son of the more famous ex-Evertonian Graeme), a recent substitute, turned on the edge of the penalty area and hit an unstoppable shot to the left of Alfreton's keeper. We, in the Telford end, cheered and punched the air in delight.

The equaliser was well-deserved. Indeed Telford continued to dominate, and had chances to win the game, in one case being denied by a last-ditch goal line clearance by Alfreton's impressive Josh Law (the manager's son). However, the home side could easily (if undeservedly) have won it in the last few minutes, when Ryan Young again performed heroics in the Telford goal, keeping out three close-range shots in quick succession, thereby confirming his 'man-of-the-match' award, at least as far as I was concerned (of course some Alfreton player got it – the home side always does!).

In the post-match analysis in the Non-League Paper, both managers felt their side should have won, which for Telford was a welcome advance on the 'happy with a point' response to the 0-0 draw at Barrow. Nicky Law, having rediscovered the power to express himself in sentences, thought that the game should have been over by half-time. In my opinion, Telford dominated the second half as much as Alfreton had the first. But perhaps my objectivity had been compromised by my status as a (temporary) Telford supporter!

I travelled back watching the sun sink over the Pennines, past the twisted spire of the church in Chesterfield. At Chesterfield Station, I looked out for the quartet who'd failed to get out there on the way down. I later learned that they'd witnessed a 1-0 win for Barnet with a penalty in the last minute. Maybe they should have stayed in Alfreton and watched the game there with me. Then, after Sheffield, twilight descended as we sped past Grindleford, Hope and Edale. Next week the floodlights would be on for second halves all across the Conference grounds of middle England.

# Dragons, Tasteless Pies, and Goals of the Season

Wrexham vs Gateshead

Saturday 17th November 2012

In the week preceding my visit, Wrexham had been in the news, just as Hyde had been in August when I went there. The revelations about Jimmy Savile, a month or so earlier had inspired a wide range of child abuse horror stories in places far away from BBC headquarters including Wrexham.

In 2000, the report of the Waterhouse Inquiry, which had examined evidence of abuse in almost 40 children's' care homes across North Wales, including Bryn Estyn in Wrexham, had been published. A *further* report into allegations of abuse at Bryn Estyn – the Jillings Report – was commissioned by the then Clwyd County Council in 1994 but was later pulped at the insistence of insurers.

The former leader of the County Council claimed in the Wrexham Leader that the Waterhouse Inquiry was 'weak', and that the non-publication of the Jillings Report was 'terrible'. Since the Savile revelations, former residents of Bryn Estyn had contacted the police with accusations of abuse, which the BBC Newsnight team had investigated. In the programme which followed, there was a strong implication that Lord McAlpine, the former Conservative Party Treasurer, had been involved (without actually naming him). In the turmoil that ensued, Lord McAlpine issued an angry statement denying any such involvement, stating that he had only ever been to Wrexham once in his life. He was subsequently exonerated.

## Chapter 8

It is rare for Wrexham to feature in the national news headlines. Indeed it is surprising Lord McAlpine had ever been there. Wrexham isn't on the way to anywhere, and isn't the kind of place you'd normally expect senior politicians or industrialists to visit. It is a largish town in North Wales (63,000, plus a further 67,000 in its satellites) close to the border with England (Chester is only 15 miles away). It is arguably the only sizeable industrial town in North Wales, forming the focal point of an area previously dominated by steelworks (Bersham and Brymbo) and coal mining.

Both steel and coal have long disappeared, but Wrexham has survived better than other places previously dependent on such industries. One of the reasons is the proximity of a vast 'Industrial Estate', four miles to the east of the town. A former Royal Ordnance munitions factory (closed in 1970) it is the second largest industrial estate in Britain, and one of the largest in Europe. The industry attracted has been of the light, 'high tech' variety, but it has certainly facilitated Wrexham's relative economic buoyancy. In 2007 the town was the fifth most successful place in the UK for business start-up schemes.

An interesting feature of Wrexham's economic heritage is the existence, in the late nineteenth century, of 35 breweries. That would mean one brewery for every 2,000 inhabitants, which implies a lot of very heavy drinkers, or a lot of very small breweries (or both). Nowadays there's just 'Wrexham lager' brewed locally, which is well- regarded (if you like that sort of thing!).

Wrexham's stadium, the Racecourse Ground, is conveniently situated very close to the station itself. However on leaving the station, I walked in the opposite direction, towards the town centre. I had been there before, when living and working in Chester in the late 1960s and

early 1970s, but I could remember very little of what it was
like. At first, you encounter a fairly uninspiring (though
pedestrianized) high street, full of familiar chain stores, with
the sprinkling of empty shops. It became apparent that
Poundland now had rivals! There was a 'Just a Pound' store,
and '99p' one ('making everyone happy for less'). Where will
it end, I wondered. How far below 99p can you go and still
make a profit? We shall see.

Christmas was only five or six weeks away, and decorations
had begun to appear in the shops, as well as special
Christmas menus in the pubs and restaurants. There was a
bustle and vitality about the place. Two o'clock on a
Saturday is clearly a better time to visit a town centre than
five o'clock when (as in Nuneaton) energies had begun to
flag and children had begun to whinge.

As you move away from the High Street, into the more
traditional town centre area, it becomes a much more
interesting environment. The street pattern becomes more
haphazard; narrow alleyways, full of specialist local shops
and cafes, draw you in. There are three separate market halls
(Butter, Butchers, and Peoples) all of which appear to be
going concerns. There is an impressive parish church – St
Giles – situated at the highest point of the town centre. I
later learned that it was one of the 'seven wonders of
Wales', which seemed a bit excessive, and made one
speculate about the paucity of 'wonders' in the country, if St
Giles Church, attractive though it is, is so highly-placed.

I made my way to the Racecourse ground, hoping to
incorporate a visit to the Turf Hotel ,within the ground's
curtilage, which is where the teams' dressing rooms were
once located. The players used to step down a wooden
staircase and across the paddock onto the pitch. Very
picturesque! However, the pub was so packed, and the
chances of getting served within the ten minutes so remote,

that I went straight into the ground itself, pausing to buy some lunch in the area under the stand, before finding my seat.

I opted for a meat-and-potato pie, which turned out to be a mistake. At their best meat-and-potato pies can be a culinary delight; but at their worst a tasteless mush. The 'Peter's pie' I purchased was firmly in the second category. Back to the drawing board with that one, I think, Peter!

I'd visited the Racecourse Ground on several occasions when I lived in Chester, and remembered it with great affection. The ground had indeed once been the site of a racecourse, and the dog-leg format of the main stand had been a reflection of the need to respond to its oval shape. There was also in evidence in the 1970s 'one of the oddest stands ever to grace a football ground'*. The stand, which held 1,000 spectators was dubbed 'The Pigeon Loft' and stood on top of the kop. Erected in 1962 it never looked particularly safe, and indeed, in 1978, it was deemed 'unsafe' by the Football League and sold to Wrexham Rugby Club (who were apparently prepared to take a risk on it!). So, in the early 1970s, the Racecourse ground was an idiosyncratic but colourful medley of stands and terraces, built around an oval-shaped playing area (into which, of course, a rectangle had to be fitted). What was it going to look like in 2012, I thought, as I climbed the steps into the main stand.

The answer was, firstly, that it was totally unrecognisable from the ground I remembered forty years ago, and second, that it was extremely impressive. All that remained from the early 1970s was the kop, with its patchwork of old barriers (but minus the Pigeon Loft). The kop, I later learned, had also recently been deemed 'unsafe' and was shortly to be

---

* Simon Inglis: The Football Grounds of Britain, Collins Willow 1983, p222

renovated (I do hope it remains as a standing area). As a result it was unoccupied.

On the other three sides of the ground were stands, all of them relatively new. Indeed the ground had all the earmarks of a club that was thriving, which, given the recent history of bankruptcies and winding-up orders, was a welcome surprise. All trace of the racecourse shape had disappeared. The stadium now bears the imprint of Glydwr University, who own the site and are the official club sponsors. Who are Glydwr University, you may be wondering? (I certainly was). Well, it's the former North East Wales Institute of Higher Education, which was upgraded in 2008. So Wrexham has a University now; but then so do increasing numbers of places that I didn't know had them. Why hasn't Kendal got one?

The diversity of the clubs in the Conference is reflected in the variety of their grounds. The Racecourse Ground (capacity 12,000) was the first stadium I had come across on my visits which looked as if it had once graced the Football League, and would still not look out of place there. What a contrast with Alfreton's Impact Arena (capacity 4,000) where, apart from the dilapidated visitors' end, none of the other stands contained more than five or six rows of seats (at Wrexham it's four or five times as many). Ewen Fields (Hyde), and Liberty Way (Nuneaton) were similar in scale (although more interesting in design): small-scale modern or refurbished stadia, unlikely to meet Football League requirements in the (equally unlikely) event of either team qualifying for promotion. Although Holker Street, Barrow's ground, had hosted Football League matches as recently as 1972, the fact that it had been neglected ever since, and become increasingly down-at-heel, would, if Barrow were ever to achieve promotion, be likely to generate derision from visiting supporters in Division Two. Gateshead's stadium, although modern and spacious, doesn't feel at all like a football ground, and isn't (it was designed for athletics events).

There are further contrasts to look forward to on future visits: the new sustainable 'green' stadia at Dartford and Forest Green; the spacious traditional grounds accustomed to the Football League, such as Luton's Kenilworth Road and Grimsby's Blundell Park; and even a rugby ground doubling up as a soccer venue (Rodney Parade, where Newport currently play). One of the pleasures of the Conference, which you don't get in the Premiership or Championship, is that you can watch a game at Stockport's capacious Edgeley Park one week, and Tamworth's tiny (by comparison) Lamb Stadium the next.

The more I read about Wrexham in their excellent programme, and the more I looked around their ground, the more I warmed to them. Wrexham have, since 2011, been owned by a Supporters Trust which nominates the six directors (there is no chairman). Let's hope it proves more resilient than Stockport County's similar recent short-lived initiative. Home crowds average around 3,500 which many a Division Two club (Morecambe included) would be overjoyed to attract. Wrexham had the ambience of a club which should be in the Football League but then this may be my reaction when I visit Grimsby, Luton, Lincoln and Mansfield (and of course Stockport) and they can't all make it back there, (at least by the end of this season).

Wrexham FC has a long, though not particularly impressive history. It is the oldest known club in Wales, having been founded in 1873 (or perhaps 1864, as one archive-explorer would have us believe). They were founder members of the Third Division North in 1921 and then, for forty years, followed the familiar experience of the Gatesheads, Barrows and Southports of this world in never achieving promotion, nor indeed ever winning anything (apart from the Welsh Cup, where there's not a lot of serious competition!).

They missed the cut at the end of the 1958-59 season, and found themselves in the new Division Four, which has been where they have been most of the time since, apart from a (very) brief period in the then Division Three (1960-61), another more successful spell there 1970-78, and - for four glorious years (1978-82) - a stint in Division Two (now the Championship). In 1983 they went straight back down to Division Four, where they remained until 2008, when after several near-misses, they were relegated to the Conference.

A key figure during Wrexham's glory years (1969-82) was one Arfon Griffiths, a midfielder (but also a regular goal scorer) small in stature, but of outstanding ability. When I first saw him in 1968, he'd recently had a couple of seasons with Arsenal, but hadn't quite made the grade. Back at Wrexham, he was in his element, and a delight to watch. He was an artist amongst journeymen, one of those players who (amongst other qualities) could thread long passes through a mass of opposing players to land at the feet of a teammate with a clear run on goal. He played 565 games for Wrexham and was manager during the golden years of their history; the four years in the (then) Division Two. I hope he's aware how much pleasure he brought to so many football enthusiasts in Wrexham (and elsewhere) during his time there.

In the Conference, Wrexham finished mid-table for their first two years, and then reached the play-offs, but lost to Luton Town. Last season (2011-12) they were extremely unlucky not to win automatic promotion. They finished with 98 points, which in most other seasons would have been enough to top the table. However, they were up against Fleetwood Town, with big money (by Conference standards) behind them, who managed to accumulate 103.

## Chapter 8

Wrexham failed again in the play-offs, no doubt bemoaning the fact that second place doesn't guarantee promotion from the Conference (indeed it never has! It is only since 2003 that more than one club has been promoted, and play-offs have always been used to decide who goes up with the champions).

This season Wrexham had, since early September, occupied one of the top five positions in the table. They started the game against Gateshead, in fourth place, four points behind the leaders (Newport County) with a game in hand. Only four points separated the first and sixth clubs in the table. No-one had broken away from the pack, as Fleetwood and Wrexham had in 2011-12 - opening up the promotion race nicely. Gateshead had gone on doing what Gateshead do, playing good football, drawing a lot of games and hovering in the upper-middle reaches of the table, just below the play-off positions (in eighth place at the start of the game).

Wrexham's line-up included Brett Ormerod, one of the most high-profile ex-Football League players in the Conference. After an illustrious career with Blackpool (two spells), Southampton and Preston North End, he signed a two year contract with Wrexham at the start of the season. His impact so far had been limited; eight first team appearances (plus five as substitute) and two goals. But he was playing today, and I wanted to see if a former top-level 36 year-old striker would still stand out in the Conference. The Wrexham manager, Andy Morrell, had himself been a prolific goal scorer for Wrexham in the early 2000s, but hadn't selected himself on this occasion.

The match developed into an intriguing tussle between two sides who both played football of a quality that would not look out of place in Division Two. Both teams built up moves from defence, with the occasional long ball used when it seemed appropriate (rather than as a standard ploy).

## Dragons, Tasteless Pies, and Goals of the Season

Wrexham had more of the play and created more scoring opportunities. Gateshead looked dangerous on the break and at corners. The atmosphere was great, too. The crowd (we learned at the interval) was 3,011, including 33 from Gateshead, who had a whole section of one of the main stands to themselves. The home supporters made a lot of noise. Strangled cries of 'Heed, Heed' were heard from time-to-time, from the back of the stand where the Gateshead contingent was situated.

Ten minutes before half-time Wrexham scored, as they had been threatening to for a while. Nick Rushton ran onto a well-judged through pass and beat Adam Bartlett neatly. The Gateshead keeper had previously made several crucial saves, justifying the Non-Leaguer Paper's confidence in him (he was identified pre-season as Gateshead's trump card). But Gateshead were still very much in the game. There was a 'how did they not score?' incident during a goalmouth scrimmage, when any of three close-range shots could have found the net.

At half-time a strange red animal came lumbering out onto the pitch; or rather a man dressed as a strange red animal did. It was clearly Wrexham's mascot, but what was it? My best guess would have been a hippopotamus, on the basis of the large wide-jowled head, the capacious mouth and the small ears. And the creature did bear a passing resemblance to the hippo that features in the Slumberland adverts (minus the pyjamas, of course). A red hippopotamus for a mascot? Well it made a welcome change from the ubiquitous bears, monkeys and lions. But I was wrong. The creature was, I learned later, Wrex the Dragon, although a more benign (and misshapen) dragon could hardly be imagined.

The quality of the football was maintained in the second half. Brett Ormerod displayed some neat touches, but rarely looked likely to add to his formidable career goal tally. It

was the kind of game you couldn't keep your eyes off.
Wrexham continued to have more possession. Gateshead
continued to threaten in breakaways. Ryan Donaldson, a 21-
year-old former trainee with Newcastle United (where he
made a handful of first-team appearances) began to look
increasingly dangerous on the left, embarking on a mazy run
which could have resulted in a 'goal of the season'
contender had his progress not been blocked as he prepared
to shoot. However, a 'goal of the season' contender was not
long in coming. Donaldson cut in again from the left,
switched the ball to his right foot and hit a magnificent shot
from well outside the penalty area into the far corner,
leaving Wrexham's keeper with no chance.

The quality of the Conference has been epitomised, for me,
by the quality of some of the goals. I've already seen:
Barnes-Homer's overhead kick for Macclesfield (against
Gateshead), Chris Sharp's blockbuster for Telford (against
Alfreton), Matty Blinkhorn's screamer for Hyde (against
Luton) and now Donaldson's memorable effort. There have
been very few prods-over-the-line from five yards out.

Either side could have won it in the final quarter. Gateshead
brought on Yemi Odubade, who had impressed me in
earlier games, and whose formidable pace at once caused
problems for the Wrexham defence. Wrexham had a couple
of penalty shouts (reasonable, but by no means conclusive)
and Adam Bartlett came to Gateshead's rescue again on a
couple of occasions. But it ended 1-1, which I thought was
a fair result, although the Wrexham faithful were clearly
disappointed. Six of the eight Conference games I'd seen
had ended in draws, but I can live with that, given the
quality of the football (Barrow/Telford excepted).

The 'Non-League Paper' shared my enthusiasm for the
Wrexham/Gateshead game, awarding it four stars (they
rarely give five). We could have done without the headlines

– 'A Goal Don Wonder' – but the Non-League Paper is prone to that kind of thing ('Bullishly Imp-Ressive' (Lincoln's win over Hereford); 'McNiven has his Edin the clouds' (Hyde's win over Justin Edinburgh – manager at Newport). Looks like some sub-editor has ambitions to get a job with the Sun!

The five-minute walk to Wrexham General Station resulted in a ten-minute wait for the Chester train. As I waited, I watched a stream of Wrexham fans crossing the road bridge under which the railway passed on its way to Shrewsbury. The last vestiges of daylight were apparent as a backcloth to the succession of silhouetted figures returning to the town centre. It was reminiscent of an Ingmar Bergman film (or an L.S. Lowry painting) and was mesmerising.

# 26<sup>th</sup> December 2012 – League Table

| | Team | P | W | D | L | F | A | GD | Pt |
|---|---|---|---|---|---|---|---|---|---|
| 1 | Grimsby Town | 24 | 13 | 7 | 4 | 41 | 17 | 24 | 46 |
| 2 | Newport County AFC | 23 | 14 | 3 | 6 | 52 | 33 | 19 | 45 |
| 3 | Wrexham | 23 | 12 | 6 | 5 | 46 | 24 | 22 | 42 |
| 4 | Luton Town | 22 | 12 | 3 | 7 | 40 | 33 | 7 | 39 |
| 5 | Kidderminster Harriers | 24 | 10 | 8 | 6 | 35 | 22 | 13 | 38 |
| 6 | Forest Green Rovers | 23 | 11 | 5 | 7 | 37 | 26 | 11 | 38 |
| 7 | Dartford | 24 | 11 | 3 | 10 | 39 | 35 | 4 | 36 |
| 8 | Mansfield Town | 21 | 9 | 5 | 7 | 34 | 33 | 1 | 32 |
| 9 | Macclesfield Town | 23 | 9 | 5 | 9 | 35 | 38 | -3 | 32 |
| 10 | Cambridge United | 23 | 8 | 7 | 8 | 43 | 39 | 4 | 31 |
| 11 | Gateshead | 23 | 7 | 9 | 7 | 29 | 30 | -1 | 30 |
| 12 | Hyde FC | 23 | 8 | 5 | 10 | 40 | 37 | 3 | 29 |
| 13 | Lincoln City | 22 | 8 | 5 | 9 | 35 | 37 | -2 | 29 |
| 14 | Hereford United | 21 | 8 | 5 | 8 | 31 | 33 | -2 | 29 |
| 15 | Alfreton Town | 22 | 7 | 8 | 7 | 28 | 36 | -8 | 29 |
| 16 | Woking | 24 | 9 | 2 | 13 | 39 | 52 | -13 | 29 |
| 17 | Tamworth | 24 | 8 | 3 | 13 | 27 | 33 | -6 | 27 |
| 18 | Southport | 22 | 7 | 6 | 9 | 34 | 43 | -9 | 27 |
| 19 | Braintree Town | 22 | 7 | 5 | 10 | 26 | 38 | -12 | 26 |
| 20 | AFC Telford United | 22 | 5 | 10 | 7 | 32 | 33 | -1 | 25 |
| 21 | Stockport County | 22 | 6 | 6 | 10 | 30 | 36 | -6 | 24 |
| 22 | Nuneaton Town | 24 | 5 | 9 | 10 | 28 | 42 | -14 | 24 |
| 23 | Ebbsfleet United | 23 | 5 | 7 | 11 | 33 | 48 | -15 | 22 |
| 24 | Barrow | 22 | 4 | 8 | 10 | 25 | 41 | -16 | 20 |

# Sporting Cities and Dodgy Lodgings

Newport County vs Wrexham

Friday 4th January 2013

Early January, and I was back on the road – or rather the railway – again, after a barren December, as far as Conference visits were concerned; mainly due to numerous postponements because of flooded pitches.

My journey took me from Kendal to Crewe, where I changed to a train which wound its way through a lovely stretch of rural England, with stops at Shrewsbury, Church Stretton, Leominster and Hereford. The daylight held out until Hereford, where there were dramatic tinges of purple in the fading western sky.

I was on my way to Newport, to watch a top-of-the-table tussle (as Manchester's 'Football Pink' used to put it) between second-placed Newport and third-placed Wrexham. This was a kind of Welsh local derby – there are no other Conference sides in Wales – but 'local' is misleading in this context: Newport and Wrexham are over 100 miles apart. However as I left the train at Newport station and walked down the hill into the city centre, it was clear that a sizeable contingent of Wrexham fans was expected. It was only 5.30 pm, but already there was a formidable police presence on the streets, with the sound of howling dogs emanating from adjacent police vans. 'Trouble' was clearly expected!

I made my way across a bridge over the broad, tidal, River Usk onto the Chepstow Road, where my overnight accommodation was situated. From the bridge, you could

# Chapter 9

see, half a mile downriver, the tall floodlight pylons of Rodney Parade, where tonight's game was to take place.

Newport was the first of my visits to require an overnight stop. As someone whose computer skills are comparatively limited (accessing and replying to e-mails, and trawling the internet for fascinating facts about Conference towns and teams is about the sum of it) it was with some trepidation that I had decided to book my accommodation on the internet. But everyone else seems to do it that way nowadays, so I thought I'd give it a try. The place had to be within walking distance of the station and relatively cheap (I had, as yet, no publisher's advance to cover such expenses!).

The hotel I'd selected was called the Gateway Express, which the website implied, was a smaller-scale version of a Premier Inn, Travelodge or Ibis. The photos of the rooms certainly gave that impression. I was somewhat disconcerted, therefore, to discover that the stretch of Chepstow Road where the hotel was located consisted of a row of seedy-looking run-down semi-detached Victorian villas. The ambience was not dispelled by a series of passers-by who looked like they were on their way to the nearest soup kitchen. It looked like an archetypal rooming-house area for transients.

The Gateway Express Hotel sign was dimly-lit and its front door was locked. What had I let myself in for? I pressed the intercom. A voice informed me (once I'd managed to figure out what it said) that I should go to the Gateway Hotel (non-Express) a few houses down the road, to obtain a key. The Gateway Hotel was another semi-detached Victorian villa, extended at the rear. I was given a key and returned to the Gateway Express. The key didn't work. I went back to the Gateway, from whence someone returned with me to the Gateway Express, and finally managed to get me into the place. To be fair, my room turned out to be clean, well-appointed and comfortable, even if the setting of the Gateway Express displayed none of these qualities. I realised that I had not yet begun to master the art of booking accommodation on the net. Hadn't Karen said something about using 'Trip Advisor'?

I made my way to nearby Rodney Parade an hour before kick-off time. None of the pubs on Chepstow Road looked remotely inviting, but there turned out to be a bar in Rodney Parade itself (within its curtilage, but before you reached the stadium) which looked innocuous and was, at the time I visited it, reasonably quiet. Showing on the TV screen was a re-run of an earlier Sky-transmitted Conference game, which turned out to be the Barrow versus Hereford United match, played on December 7$^{th}$. It was good to see some old friends again: David Bayliss, the Barrow manager, looking extremely worried (as well he might, Barrow were losing 0-2 and bottom of the Conference); Gary Hunter (ex-Morecambe) who was looking increasingly like Ryan Giggs (but was not playing like him); and of course good old Holker Street (sorry, I mean the Furness Building Society Stadium), more thinly-populated for this evening game than when I'd been there on the opening day of the season.

The Barrow faithful looked and sounded dispirited, understandably so. I did wonder about the wisdom of Sky's decision to screen a re-run of an earlier mundane Conference game prior to the live transmission of tonight's match. 'I know, let's show Barrow versus Hereford, that should whet the viewers' appetite for what's coming up'.

Both Newport and Wrexham, despite their lofty positions had experienced mixed fortunes in the run up to tonight's game. Newport, having defeated fellow promotion candidates Forest Green Rovers 2-1 in Nailsworth on Boxing Day, contrived to lose the return match 5-0 on New Year's Day. They clearly owed their fans some recompense tonight. Wrexham had done better, winning home and away to AFC Telford, but only managing a 2-2 draw at home to lowly Tamworth on the intervening Saturday.

The holiday results were bizarre. Not only did Newport win away and then lose at home to the same opponents, but so did Hyde (to Stockport), Alfreton (to Mansfield), Kidderminster (to Hereford), and Gateshead (to Barrow). So much for the decisive influence of home support! But then that's the Conference for you. Certainly in its middle and lower reaches away records are often better than those at home. Understandable, perhaps, at Alfreton and Braintree, but less so at relatively well-supported Stockport and Hereford.

Newport County, before their ignominious demise half-way through their first season in the Conference in 1988, had been consistent underachievers ever since 1920, when they were elected to the Football League. They started out in Division Three South (where they failed to be re-elected in 1931, but were re-admitted in 1932). In the last pre-war season (1938-39) they were promoted to what was then Division Two, but came straight back down again in the first post-war season (1946-47). In 1959, they were founder members of the new Division Four, where they remained until the John Aldridge era, when they made it to Division Three for a while (1981-87), before a speedy descent into obscurity. In 1987, they were relegated to the Conference, and halfway through the following season were declared bankrupt - then failing to fulfil their fixtures (the only time this has ever happened in the Conference's 33-year history).

The mixture of pain and delight experienced by the remaining clubs on hearing the news of Newport's demise can well be imagined; delight from those who had dropped points to Newport, but anguish from those who'd defeated them and now had to forfeit the points they'd gained.

However Newport County refused to die, and have become one of a growing list of 'great survivors': clubs which have been beset by financial crises, gone out of existence, reformed, and subsequently re-emerged in the Conference (or Football League), after a long period in the nether regions of the non-league pyramid.

The most famous example of a club refusing to die is Accrington Stanley, one of the founder members of the Football League in 1888 who, in the wake of a financial crisis, were summarily ejected from Division Four in 1962 (probably unfairly so, with the benefit of hindsight). Slowly and painfully the club was nursed back into existence. By 1980 they were to be found in the Cheshire County League, Division Two. In 2001, they were promoted to the Conference, and in 2006 finally made it back to the Football League, 44 years after being kicked out of it. What a wonderful example of persistence!

Aldershot experienced a similar fall from grace after their collapse in 1989, but finally made it back in 2008. Of the clubs currently in the Conference, several have recovered from the same fate, often re-emerging with new identities (AFC Telford United, Nuneaton Town, Gateshead). And there are several more candidates for resurrection waiting in the wings, including Bradford Park Avenue, Chester, Halifax Town and Darlington 1883). Indeed, the only ex-League club that I can find which has not survived in one form or another is New Brighton, who were kicked out of the League in 1951, pottered around in the Cheshire County League (Division Two) and finally expired after finishing at its bottom in 1981. But for all I know there may yet be a campaign to coax it back into existence!

Now, both sleeping Welsh giants seemed to be on the way up. In Newport's case, their progress has been greatly aided by the decision of local lottery-winner Les Scadding to make

## Chapter 9

a chunk of his £46.5 million Euromillions win available to the club. Scadding, now apparently known locally as 'Sir Les', became Newport's chairman in September 2012 (well I guess it was the least they could do, in the circumstances). There was a photograph in the Non-League Paper of Justin Edinburgh, Newport's manager, with his arm round Sir Les and a (rare) big smile on his face, as well there might be. There are now three clubs in the Conference with multi-millionaire chairmen: Forest Green Rovers, Mansfield Town and Newport County. And it certainly helps, as Crawley Town and Fleetwood Town can testify.

If Justin Edinburgh was smiling from the pages of the Non-League paper on Sunday August 26th, he certainly wasn't on Tuesday January 1st. He admitted in the programme that he was 'absolutely gutted' by the 5-0 home defeat to Forest Green Rovers. It was 'the worst performance he had ever been involved with' (might be worth checking Spurs' record during his time there?). He cancelled the players' day-off on the following Wednesday (I bet that went down well) and forced them to watch a DVD of the game. Let's see if they could bounce back today.

In their Football League days, Newport played at Somerton Park, which you could see, decked out in the team's amber and black colours, from the railway as you approached Newport station. It has not survived. For the past few years Newport have played at Spytty Park, on the edge of the city, and before that, in their days in the wilderness, at Moreton-in-Marsh in the Cotswolds. . However at the start of the 2012-13 season they reached an agreement with Newport RUFC to share their stadium at Rodney Parade. The ground is impressive. There is a shiny new grey stand on one side, a section of which was given over to the Wrexham fans. There is an older stand opposite, with no-one in it apart from the press, but which had terracing in front that was well-populated. One end was open terracing. The other end consisted of an administrative block (with executive boxes at the top) and a smaller triangular-shaped building on the corner from which the teams in due course emerged. The fact that Rodney Parade doubled as a rugby ground was illustrated by the pitch markings, (for both codes) the space behind each goal and the unevenness of the playing surface.

Peters Pies were on sale at the refreshment bar (are they seeking a pie monopoly at Welsh football grounds?) but fortunately so were someone else's. My cheese and onion pie wasn't great (the onion was disconcertingly crunchy) but it was an improvement on Peter's meat and potato abominations.

The game developed, at a frenetic pace. 'Hotly-contested' and 'fiercely-fought' are amongst the clichés that spring to mind. The atmosphere at the ground was infectiously enthusiastic. There was a noisy contingent of around 400 Wrexham fans, who traded insults with their Newport counterparts. Both sides were adept at denying space to their opponents, but one player who seemed able to create space out of nothing was Newport's leading scorer Aaron O'Connor, who was proving to be the game's outstanding individual. In the 27th minute he was unfairly impeded in the Wrexham penalty area, when bearing down on the goal, and won Newport a penalty. But Wrexham's impressive keeper, Cameroonian international Joslain Mayebi saved Andy Sandell's spot kick.

Newport had more of the possession but Wrexham always looked dangerous in breakaways, and it was as a result of one of these, in the 34th minute, that Danny Wright latched onto an astute through ball from Adrian Cieslewicz and neatly chipped it over Newport's advancing keeper to give Wrexham the lead. Cue delirium from the far corner of the ground where the Wrexham fans were situated, and stunned silence elsewhere.

At half-time, the Newport mascot made an appearance (it may have been around before the game, but I hadn't noticed it). It was a dog, but a dog not calculated to inspire a team (or its supporters), who were 1-0 down. It had a doleful expression, two big floppy ears and it trudged forlornly around the pitch as though resigned to defeat. I thought of starting a chant of 'sack the mascot' (Spytty the Dog, I learned later) but decided against.

I had hoped to renew my acquaintance with the wise-cracking Newport assistant manager Jimmy Dack, whose exchanges with the home fans had proved so entertaining when Newport played at Macclesfield. But the Newport dug-out was situated in front of a particularly packed section of terracing, so I couldn't get near him. However, I suspect that his humorous exchanges with the crowd may well be reserved for more sparsely-attended away fixtures.

The second half was even more absorbing than the first. There was more intense pressure from Newport which finally paid off when Max Porter's lob from the edge of the area was deflected past the unlucky Joslain Mayebi. An ecstatic response (mingled with relief) emanated from the Newport fans around me. Then both sides continued to create and miss chances. Another mazy run by Newport's Aaron O'Conner ended with a disappointingly tame shot. Cieslewicz's header rebounded from the post at one end, whilst Matt Flynn's did the same at the other. Joslain Mayebi was carrying the ball to the edge of his penalty area, when a nudge from a Newport player caused him to take it further than he'd intended, outside the area. The referee awarded Newport a free kick (wrongly in my view), which incensed not just Mayebi, but most of the Wrexham team.

But the free-kick was blocked and Wrexham deservedly held out until the final whistle.

So, another 1-1 draw, the fourth I'd seen in a row (seven of my nine games so far had been drawn). But I'm not complaining. It was good to see both Newport and Wrexham get something from tonight's game, and I'd had a similar reaction at Gateshead, Macclesfield, Nuneaton, Alfreton and Wrexham. This season, the Conference proved very even, a fact reflected in the prevalence of drawn games (just under 30% at the last count).

Justin Edinburgh felt that Newport deserved to win, but he would, wouldn't he (and remember what you said after the Macclesfield game, Justin… 'possession doesn't win matches'). Both managers felt the game was a great advert for the Conference (it had been shown on Sky) and indeed it was. I've seen worse games in Division One.

As I left the ground, I noticed two giant eyes, perched on metal structures, peering down over Rodney Parade. Was this Newport County's guardian angel perhaps? In fact they were part of the Millennium bridge structure, which linked the city centre of Newport with Rodney Parade and its surroundings. I walked back to the Gateway Express, surrounded by departing Newport supporters, through streets of terraced houses, which evoked memories of similar experiences at Edgeley Park and Maine Road in the 1950s and 60s.

Next morning, after an excellent breakfast at the Gateway (non-Express), I walked back into Newport past a credible rival to Gateshead in the 'ugliest multi-storey car park in Britain' contest, past the remains of a castle by the River Usk, and went on to explore the city centre in daylight. Newport was designated a city in 1992, and certainly has the feel of one. The shops on the High Street are substantial stone-faced four-storey Victorian terraces, similar to those you see in Cardiff. Civic buildings abound, including a magnificent glass-roofed Market Hall, and the Council Offices, which stand on a small hill overlooking the town centre. I noticed, with some amusement, a poster displayed in several locations, with the wording 'Newport: Sporting City' and a depiction of a footballer and a rugby player. Now what could be the basis for this claim? A football club playing outside the Football League in the Conference and a rugby club (Newport Gwent Dragons) languishing next to the bottom of the Rabo Direct Pro 12 league, with only Zebre (who? where?) below them. It hardly justifies the claim, does it? Liverpool or Manchester as 'Sporting Cities' perhaps. But surely not Newport!

Despite the imposing facades of the main shopping area, the impressive Millennium Bridge, the unusual 'Newport Wave' steel sculpture adjacent to the river, and the light and airy Market Hall, I found it difficult to warm to Newport; there was something off-putting about the ambience of the place: not just the seedy area in which my hotel was located, but the city centre too. Newport is reasonably prosperous, mainly thanks to the new business parks clustered around the motorway junctions to the east and west, the range of public sector jobs in the centre, and the presence of large firms such as Panasonic, the Quinn Group (radiator manufacturers) and Sim Metal Management (the world's largest industrial shredder for scrap metal and the world's largest car crusher!). But the sense of well-being, which prosperity tends to generate in towns such as Macclesfield and Southport, did not seem apparent in Newport.

The headlines in the South Wales Argus tended to confirm these (admittedly superficial) impressions. 'Woman punched her husband after love affair taunts', 'Homeless man hid screwdriver down trousers', 'Deputy Head banned from teaching for life' (for incompetence!) and my favourite 'Man blamed voices in head'. This was the defence put forward by a local 21-year-old who had pleaded guilty to 'assault, occasioning actual bodily harm' on his girlfriend (now ex-girlfriend) and to two counts of criminal damage. When arrested in May, the defendant had told police that he had heard voices in his head, telling him to take them (he and his girlfriend) to a better place. Cardiff perhaps? Or heaven? You have to give him credit for ingenuity. I must remember his defence if ever I have to appear in court. 'I'm sorry I assaulted the Jehovah's Witness who wouldn't go away, your honour, but I heard these voices in my head....'

As the train moved out of Newport station, en route for Tamworth my next Conference destination, I was rewarded with another view of the concrete monstrosity of a car park, and the villas of Chepstow Road. Further to the south, I caught a glimpse of Newport's 'transporter bridge' (the answer to the question 'what do Middlesbrough and Newport have in common') in the now largely derelict docks area, which used to ship out huge quantities of coal from the valleys which descend into Newport. The coal has gone, the docks have gone, and the steelworks at Llanwern no longer manufacture steel (it houses only rolling mills). It is as if Newport has lost all the distinctive activities which had given the city its identity, and is now 'just another town along the road'.

# Brummie Accents and 'Massive Games'

Tamworth vs Braintree Town

Saturday 5<sup>th</sup> January 2013

I travelled on to Tamworth from Newport, the morning after the absorbing Newport/Wrexham match.

Tamworth lies about ten miles north-west of Nuneaton, and is similar to Nuneaton in population size. There is a fierce local rivalry between their football teams, both currently in the Conference. However, there are important differences. Nuneaton is a well-established manufacturing centre, which has expanded in size only slowly since the end of the war. By contrast Tamworth was a small market town, rich in history, which has grown spectacularly since the 1960s, when it was designated as an 'expanded town', and earmarked to receive large amounts of (what was then termed) 'overspill' population from the West Midlands conurbation, and Birmingham in particular. Over a 50 year period, it has been transformed, with its population rising from 25,000 to 74,000. The attractive old town centre is now encircled by a plethora of housing estates, displaying the various changes in housing design over the period, including an unpopular estate of tower blocks.

The town centre is a short walk from the station. It has an irregular street pattern, much of it pedestrianized, with a sprinkling of old buildings which reflect its historical development: a small domestic-scale castle (reminiscent of Lindisfarne), an ancient and impressive parish church, an early nineteenth century town hall (commissioned by Sir Robert Peel, of whom more later), and the Victorian Assembly Rooms, where the Beatles played, early in their career. As you wander around, the flat soothing tones of the Brummie accents remind you of the origins of most of the local population.

Pleasant though the town centre is, some of the encircling housing and industrial estates are, by reputation, pretty soulless. Indeed, in William Trevor's novel 'Felicia's Journey' the heroine travels to Tamworth to locate the man who has (unknowingly) made her pregnant, and who had moved from Dublin to Tamworth to find work. She traipses around the town's various light industrial estates, trying, without success, to find him. Trevor obviously felt Tamworth was an ideal location for a young girl's dispiriting and inconclusive search for an absentee father-to-be.

Tamworth's most famous ex-resident (by far) is Sir Robert Peel, MP for Tamworth from 1830 to 1850, and Prime Minister briefly (1834-35) and then again between 1841 and 1846. When Home Secretary in 1829, Sir Robert established the Metropolitan Police Force, whose employees became known as 'Peelers' or (later) 'Bobbies'. He also played a leading role in the formation of the Conservative Party as we know it today. What became known as the 'Tamworth Manifesto' (1834) set out the basis on which the new party (built out of the disintegration of the old 'Tories') would operate. So without the Tamworth Manifesto, I guess we might not have to deal with the likes of George Osborne, Iain Duncan Smith and Michael Gove. Thanks a lot, Tamworth!

The Peel dynasty was a dominant force in the Tamworth area for over a hundred years, residing at Drayton Manor (now a theme park). It's just as well there's a Peel association; Tamworth's next most famous former resident is probably Julian Cope of the band 'Teardrop Explodes'!

There is a big new shopping centre in Tamworth:
Ankerside. The name seemed strangely familiar. And then I
remembered. The sluggish, at times almost static river
which graces Nuneaton with its presence is the River Anker.
By the time it reaches Tamworth, it has become much more
like a real river, as I saw when I wandered to the rear of
Ankerside, and looked down on a broader and more mobile
watercourse. It flows through an attractive area of parkland
known as Castle Gardens, which I proceeded to explore.
The level of activity was phenomenal for the first Saturday
in January. Admittedly it was warm for the time of the year,
but even so, I was amazed by the sheer volume of park
users. There was a challenging skate park full of
skateboarders, an equally imaginative playground full of
young children, the park café was packed, and the volume
of kids' scooter traffic made progress along the main paths -
hazardous for me and the host of other promenaders. What
must the park be like on a sunny summer bank holiday?

It was time to find a suitable hostelry for a pre-match pint. I
hadn't noticed anywhere particularly inviting in the town
itself, so I followed a sign in the park to the 'Jolly Sailor'
which had to be a pub, didn't it? I found the Jolly Sailor car
park (ominously deserted) but no sign, whatsoever, of an
adjacent public house. Perhaps it had been demolished to
make way for the new Co-operative store situated nearby? I
wandered off in another direction, towards the SnowDome
(Britain's first indoor ski slope) which dominated a group of
other retail establishments including a Wimpy outlet. I
thought Wimpy establishments had been phased out in the
1980's, but apparently not in Tamworth! There was also a
place called the Q-Lounge, which didn't look particularly
inviting, but I thought I'd give it a try. But no, when I
approached the entrance, it was clear that the Q-Lounge
was closed for business. There was nothing for it but to go

back into the town centre, where I selected the 'Terrace Bar' mainly because you could sit out in the open on a balcony and look out over Castle Gardens. A big mistake! It turned out to be a dark, dingy, unkempt establishment full of pool tables, utilised by menacing-looking youths. There seemed to be no bitter of any description (and certainly no hand pumps). Scanning the rows of lager taps, I was relieved to see a Guinness dispenser. I asked for a pint, and was totally taken aback when the girl behind the bar cracked open a 500m can, and then topped it up from the dispenser. A novel way indeed to serve a pint of Guinness! I decided not to protest, given the presence of a thick-set bloke with a shaved head, sitting next to the bar, who might just have been the proprietor. I took my drink outside, where I was regaled with a series of heavy metal numbers, played far too loud for comfort. If you're a lager-drinking, pool-playing heavy metal enthusiast, then the Terrace Bar, Tamworth is the place for you. Otherwise not; definitely not. I descended to the peace of the Castle Gardens and headed in the direction of the football ground.

Tamworth FC gained promotion to the Conference in 2009, having previously spent four seasons there (2003-07). Last year (2011-12) they started well, but suffered a serious decline in the second half of the season, winning only two more games and finishing eighteenth, escaping relegation thanks to the points accumulated in the first half of the campaign. They did, however, enjoy a brief moment of glory, reaching the 3rd round of the FA Cup and restricting Everton to a 2-0 win at Goodison Park, before a crowd of 27,564, with a 'terrific performance' (well that's what the programme said anyway). Maybe the two events are not unconnected. It must be difficult motivating yourself to perform before 600 stalwarts at Alfreton Town (away) when you've recently excelled yourself against Premiership opposition in front of 27,000 people.

It is the FA Cup, which draws the attention of the wider public to clubs in the Conference (and indeed, those below). Giant-killing achievements in which non-league clubs defeat, or hold to a draw, those in the higher echelons of the Football League invariably hit the headlines (of the sports pages, at least). High profile wins by Hereford United and Peterborough United undoubtedly aided their progress to league status, before the Conference was formed in 1979. Tamworth's impressive result at Everton the previous season was matched by Wrexham's pair of one-all draws against Brighton (then a Championship side). In 2010-11, Forest Green Rovers and Barrow both made it to the third round, where they lost to Notts County and Sunderland respectively. 2009-10 proved a particularly successful season for non-league clubs, with Kidderminster Harriers, Kettering Town, Histon, and Forest Green Rovers (again) of the Conference all making it to the third round, before losing to much more highly-placed opposition (Forest Green Rovers lost 4-3 at Derby, in what must have been a real thriller; 'this is what the FA Cup's all about, Brian'). Kettering actually reached round four, before losing 4-2 at home to Fulham. Barrow, Blyth Spartans, Eastwood Town and Salisbury City, from further down the pyramid, also reached the third round before losing (gallantly, no doubt!).

The quality of football in the Conference (and indeed below) is demonstrated by the fact that so many clubs get this far and that, when they do, they invariably give a good account of themselves, as Tamworth had at Everton. Embarrassing defeats are rare. Giant-killing achievements (or even performing well against giants) are good news financially for the clubs involved, but also provide good publicity for the Conference itself. Today, there was a

## Chapter 10

chance for Luton and Mansfield to see what they could do against Wolves and Liverpool respectively.

Braintree Town, today's opponents at Tamworth, were promoted to the Conference at the end of the 2010-11 season, for the first time in their history, thus becoming susceptible to chants of 'Ooo are yer?' on their travels. Contrary to expectations, they did well, disappointing those who had predicted a quick return to where they had come from: they finished a respectable twelfth, having never looked remotely vulnerable to relegation.

Tamworth are known as 'the Lambs' (which isn't exactly going to strike dread into the hearts of opponents is it?) and play at - 'The Lamb Ground'. It is situated adjacent to the biggest roundabout in the town (and there are lots of roundabouts in Tamworth), a 20 minute walk away from the centre.

Having purchased a seat in the main stand (well, the only stand actually) for £9 (please take note of the price, Alfreton!) half-an-hour before kick-off, I had plenty of time to explore the ground. On the pitch, in front of the open end terrace, the squads of both teams were doing warm-up exercises, exuding the evocative smell of liniment (familiar from my days as midfield dynamo in the Manchester Amateur Sunday League Division Six, and the Chester and District Amateur League Division Four). The ground was reminiscent of Alfreton Town's stadium, compact and short on elevation. The main stand had only six rows of seats, whilst the covered end and side terraces looked like they had, at most, five steps. The open end terrace provided slightly more height, but not as much as the visitors' end at Alfreton. The total capacity comes in at just over 4,000, but it looks a lot less.

I'd assumed that the 'lamb' motif would result in an appropriate, if unusual, choice of mascot. But no lamb appeared as kick-off approached. I guess the problem would be that, unlike bears and monkeys, lambs aren't known for their capacity to operate on two legs, but I'm sure that, with a bit of imagination, a workable solution could have been found.

As I approached the refreshment bar, I noticed to my horror an advert for Peter's Pies. Is Peter seeking a pie monopoly throughout the Conference, I wonder? ('We'll start with Wrexham and Newport and work our way eastward....!). However, I am happy to report that Peter's Steak and Kidney pies are much tastier than the Meat and Potato variety. Okay Peter, I take it all back – well, most of it anyway – but I'd still recommend the deletion of 'meat and potato' from your pie portfolio.

The programme was a bargain; two for the price of one! Depending on which side you picked up, it was either the programme for Tamworth versus Nuneaton (Wednesday 2 January) or Tamworth versus Braintree (Saturday 5 January), meeting in the middle with the two respective team sheets, one top to bottom, the other bottom to top. Not that I'm complaining; the programme was full of interesting information about both visiting clubs, as well as a month-by month review of Tamworth's fortunes on the pitch throughout 2012.

Tamworth had started this season well, taking 10 points from their first four games including a 3-0 win at Southport which rendered their opponent's manager 'speechless', at least for a time. Since then their form had been patchy, with a lot of home defeats against unfavoured clubs (including Barrow and Ebbsfleet United) balanced by some impressive away victories (including Woking and Forest Green Rovers). Currently they were in 16th position, with 31 points, five more than the visitors, who were in 21st position with 26 points, having suffered a decline in form after a reasonable start to the season. Braintree had lost both holiday fixtures (Boxing Day and New Year's Day) to Cambridge United. Tamworth had lost 2-1 at Nuneaton, but won the return (also 2-1), an outcome aided by the half-time dismissal of the visitors' Gavin Cowan, apparently for raking his boots down an opponent's heel as the teams left the pitch ('Cowan cowers after Red Disgrace' as the Non-League Paper put it).

In the Tamworth Herald, manager Marcus Law saw today's game as a crucial one. 'They are below us in the table, so nothing other than a win will do, to be honest. It's a massive game, no doubt about it...' Probably his Braintree counterpart, Alan Devonshire, had expressed similar views in the Braintree Gazette (or whatever). So Tamworth versus Braintree: a massive game. I couldn't wait! Marcus Law was encouraged by the likelihood that there would be no more than a handful of visiting supporters present, and that home support would therefore dominate. As it happened he was right; the Braintree contingent numbered 30 at most, although this was an improvement on the number of visiting supporters from Ebbsfleet (11) and Gateshead (11) who had made it to Newport earlier in the season.(Statistics noted from Newport County's programme, the previous evening).

I scanned the team sheets for familiar names. There was one: Lee Hendrie, who played for Aston Villa from 1995 to 2006. He appeared once for England (coming on as a substitute) and played in the 2000 FA Cup Final. After moving to other League clubs (Sheffield United, Leicester City, Brighton), his football career and personal life appeared to have nose-dived, to the extent that he was declared bankrupt in January 2012, at a time when he was

playing for Redditch United (and later Chasetown).
However Tamworth were impressed enough with his
physical fitness and attitude to sign him in the summer of
2012, at the age of 35. I can recollect an article in the Non-
League Paper in the autumn where Hendrie claimed to have
overcome his various problems (drink, gambling, lack of
discipline) and still felt he could deliver at this level. Well I
guess Tamworth is very much 'last chance saloon' for Lee.
Good luck to him. It would be interesting to see how he
performed today.

Tamworth started with an urgency which suggested they
wanted to get the game over in the first fifteen minutes,
which they totally dominated, without making the
breakthrough their pressure might have justified. Then, over
a three minute period, the whole complexion of the game
changed. In Braintree's first attack, Don Holman
unexpectedly found himself in space in the Tamworth
penalty area, and slotted the ball past the home keeper Tony
Breedon. Soon afterwards, in their second attack, Matt
Paine hit an innocuous-looking half-volley which Breedon
inexplicably fumbled into his own net. 'Oww dear!'
exclaimed a matronly Tamworth supporter in the seats
behind me. At least it wasn't to be yet another 1-1 draw.
Shortly afterwards Braintree should have added a third,
when Breedon found himself stranded well away from the
goal area. After these unexpected reverses, Tamworth
struggled to make any impression on a well-organised and
muscular Braintree defence, and departed at half-time 2-0
down to the disgruntlement of their supporters behind me
in the stand (all of them VIPs, according to the lettering on
their seats).

The second half did little to dispel their disaffection. On 60
minutes the visitors' Luke Daley tapped in a third goal. It all
looked so easy for Braintree. It wasn't that they were playing

particularly well, but they appeared to be doing more than enough to return to Essex with three points. Lee Hendrie was anonymous; but then so were most of his teammates.

I'd repositioned myself on the open terrace at the end of the ground Tamworth were attacking in the hope of witnessing a late revival. Certainly the home team began to look more dangerous (they could hardly have looked less so!) particularly after the introduction of leading scorer Adam Cunnington, who was back on the bench after a spell out injured.

Standing near me was Tamworth's answer to the Barrow screamer, a pasty-faced middle-aged man (they usually are) who howled abuse at the referee, the linesman, and various Tamworth players for not following up in support of attackers who found their options closed down. He developed a refrain about the need for his side to show some pride, in the face of an impending defeat. 'Do you want to play for Tamworth?' he screamed 'Then show a bit of pride!' He turned to me, 'They need to show a bit of pride,' he shouted. 'Indeed they do,' I replied, playing it safe. A few minutes later, they did, insofar as they pulled a goal back. Adam Cunnington was pushed in the penalty area and took the penalty himself. He saw it saved by Braintree's impressive Nathan McDonald, but was on hand to net the rebound. Game on? Well no, not really. There was a period of sustained Tamworth pressure, but the Braintree defence coped with it, and two minutes from the end, they gained a penalty themselves, which the captain Kenny Davis duly converted. Game over.

Although Braintree were no doubt delighted with the outcome (and I'd seen five goals for a change), the game was an anti-climax after the Newport/Wrexham contest the previous evening. It looked like a game between two strugglers for survival (as indeed it was), as opposed to one between two promotion candidates. Yet only a week previously Tamworth had earned an impressive 2-2 draw at Wrexham, whilst Braintree, before the two Cambridge defeats, had beaten much-fancied Forest Green Rovers (who went on to thrash Newport County 5-0 at Rodney Parade). The Conference continued to be full of surprises. With just over half the games played, a mere 11 points separated bottom club Barrow (23) from tenth-placed Hereford United (33), which suggested that 15 of the 24 clubs should still be seriously concerned about relegation. A healthy situation, at this stage of the season!

# Benign Bulls and Helpful Stewards

Hereford United vs Alfreton Town

Saturday 12<sup>th</sup> January 2013

A week after visiting Newport, I was back on the Shrewsbury to Cardiff train for a visit to Hereford, where I'd seen the spectacular purple sunset. There was a light dusting of snow on the Long Mynd, the line of rolling hills above Church Stretton, and bursts of winter sunshine brightened the attractive undulating countryside of Shropshire and Herefordshire. Snow was forecast for later in the day and a chilly easterly wind was blowing as I walked out of Hereford Station.

Like Newport, Hereford is classed as a city, but that's because it possesses a cathedral, not because it has a particularly sizeable population. Its most famous ex-resident (if you discount Beryl Reid and Gilbert Harding) is Edward Elgar who lived there between 1904 and 1911, and whose music was frequently played at the Three Choirs Festival, which alternates between Worcester, Gloucester and Hereford. Of the three cathedral cities, Hereford is the most remote. It's close to the Welsh border, but unlike its two counterparts, no motorway passes anywhere near it. I remember it from some research I did there in the early 2000's. It had, and still has, a vibrant and attractive city centre.

The city of Hereford itself has a population of only 56,000, but it is a focal point for the whole of rural Herefordshire, which surrounds it. As I walked through the city centre, which was all the better for being traffic-free, I pondered on

# Chapter 11

the credibility of the various articles on the 'Death of the High Street' which I'd read recently. The High Street in Hereford was very much alive and well, on a cold Saturday in January. That had also been the case in Macclesfield, Tamworth and Wrexham. There was a lively street market and the big central square known as High Town was teeming with shoppers.

There had been a series of recent High Street casualties: Woolworths, Blockbuster, Currys, and only a few days earlier: Jessops. The impending doom of HMV was also widely anticipated (in fact it went bust the very next week). At first the main cause of the decline of the High Street was seen to be the out-of-town shopping centre. Now it's Amazon and the Internet.

Yet the High Street survives in Hereford and elsewhere, because it can offer a range of experiences which the out-of-town centre and the Internet cannot. There is the opportunity to visit a range of small specialist shops, which rarely make it to the edge of town. There is the social experience of shopping and meeting friends in a familiar traditional traffic-free area, full of coffee-shops (now there is a growth industry), and old-fashioned pubs (you can't do any of this on the Internet). Karen assures me that shopping for women's clothes remains a valued feature of the High Street, because of the opportunity to inspect, try on, compare and (eventually) choose. So, long live the High Street and the traditional town and city centre.

The quality of Hereford's city centre is enhanced by the historic buildings dotted around it. Hereford is steeped in history. I seem to recall various Earls of Hereford making frequent appearances in Shakespeare's historical plays. There's not just the lovely Cathedral (modest in size) which houses the Mappa Mundi (a medieval map of the world, dating from the thirteenth century), but also the timber-framed 'Old House' built in 1621, the Bishops Palace, and many other gems.

Although most people would probably regard Gloucestershire and Somerset as the quintessential 'West Country' counties, Hereford and Herefordshire also have a distinctive 'West Country' feel about them. The speech of the locals is slow-paced and relaxed. On the edge of the city is based Bulmers, the firm which produces and distributes vast amounts of cider (having taken over Woodpecker, previously its main rival), and which draws on the vast number of orchards in the surrounding area for its raw materials. The rurality of the West Country is also apparent in other Hereford industries: Cargill meat products which no doubt utilises the famous breed of Herefordshire cattle: a leather goods manufactory, and two real ale breweries. It seems incongruous that the SAS should have its headquarters in such a serene place.

Walking towards the football ground from the city centre, I passed two gun shops (one of them established in 1845), presumably there to supply the local hunting and shooting fraternity. There was more than the usual quota of traditional family enterprises of this nature in Hereford – hardware stores, gents clothing emporiums, and tobacconists. Hereford has the feel of a place which is resisting the temptation to 'change with the times', and looks all the better for it.

In 1974, Herefordshire and Worcestershire were merged into a combined county council, much to the dismay of Herefordshire's local inhabitants (or at least those who were concerned about such things). Everyone knows that Herefordshire and Worcestershire have their own distinctive identities and cultures, don't they? Apparently not. After twenty years of tension between representatives of the two former counties, the case for a divorce of the

## Chapter 11

recently-married partners was recognised (it had after all been an 'arranged marriage') and Herefordshire was reinstated as a distinctive entity.

Hereford United's history is an interesting mixture of highlights and lowlights, certainly from 1972 onwards. The club motto is 'Our greatest glory lies not in never having fallen, but in rising when we fall', which sounds more like a strapline for a public school or a regiment. But it does fit well with Hereford United's recent history; they've done a fair bit of rising and falling over the past forty years.

The club was founded in 1924 but achieved little in the period up to the outbreak of war. After the war they joined the Southern League, in which they performed consistently well, with occasional feats of FA Cup giant-killing heightening the sense of a club that was going places. This sense of momentum was highlighted in 1966 when John Charles, the legendary Welsh international who'd had a spell with Italian giants Juventus, signed for Hereford, admittedly in the twilight of his playing career. He became manager a year later, and spearheaded a series of attempts by the club to get themselves elected to the Football League. They finally made it in 1972, on the back of an historic FA Cup victory at Edgar Street against Newcastle United on a mud bath of a pitch. Their equalising goal, a 40 yard drive from Ronnie Radford must be one of the most replayed film clips in the history of FA Cup. Hereford had also finished second in the Southern League, and at the AGM of the Football League displaced our old friends Barrow (who have since caught up with them again, as co-members of the Conference). By 1976-77 Hereford had reached the lofty heights of Division Two, but only survived there for one season. A second relegation followed to Division Four the following year. In the course of a mere six years Hereford had experienced two promotions and two relegations. Let's hope the club's motto was comforting to the Edgar Street regulars. There followed a less frenetic 20 years in the middle to lower reaches of Division Four, until a fateful day – the last of the season – in 1997 when Carlisle United's goalkeeper Philip Glass scored in the 92nd minute of the game against Plymouth Argyle, which clinched the victory which sent Hereford down to the Conference.

Hereford made it back to Division Two (as it had by then become) in 2006 after a play-off victory against Halifax (Hereford had beaten my local team Morecambe in the first stage of the play offs) and went on to gain promotion to Division One the next season, only to come straight back down again (again). Last season, after a couple of narrow escapes in 2011 and 2012, Hereford were once more relegated. Which is why I am here today... at Edgar Street.

Since returning to the Conference (which is where you feel Hereford really belongs) their form has been erratic, like that of the vast majority of their fellow members. After four games they sat in second place but that was as good as it got. Currently they were in 11th with an outside chance of making the play-offs. Their away record was better than their home record (another attribute they have in common with most of the clubs in the middle reaches of the table). The Edgar Street faithful had seen only one victory in the last six home games (but it was against high-flying Luton Town) whereas those travelling to away games had witnessed only one defeat in the previous nine. There was a welcome run in the FA Cup, including a victory over Shrewsbury Town, a Division One side, which helped alleviate Hereford's growing financial problems (will the nearest multi-million pound lottery winner please step forward!).

There was an impressive 1-1 away draw with league leaders Grimsby the previous Saturday, followed by a disappointing

## Chapter 11

1-1 home draw against strugglers AFC Telford in mid-week, preceded by a 1-0 win at Kidderminster and 0-1 defeat at home to Kidderminster over the holiday period. That sequence just about summed up Hereford's season. Alfreton too had proven to be a model of inconsistency, winning at Mansfield on Boxing Day, then losing the return on New Year's Day and succumbing to Wrexham last Saturday, despite the visitors having a player sent off early in the second half. It was unlikely, I felt, that many Alfreton supporters would be making the long journey to Hereford.

I'd been looking forward to seeing Edgar Street again. I had been there once before, to watch an evening match against Notts Forest, during Hereford's one and only season in Division Two (1976-77). Notts Forest, who had recently appointed Brian Clough as their manager, won 1-0 and went on to (much) greater things a few years later.

Edgar Street is a strange mixture of the old and the (relatively) new. At both ends of the ground are slightly-curved covered terraces (there used to be a running track surrounding the pitch, which accounts for their shape). One of them was clearly the main gathering point for home supporters, whilst the other was empty, either designated as unsafe or earmarked for improvement (or both).

The Main Stand, which was where I chose to go (it was a bitterly cold day, and I wanted protection from the east wind) had been erected in 1968 to strengthen Hereford's case for league status, which was then gathering momentum. It looked and felt older. It was a cantilevered stand, as was the Cargill Community Stand, situated opposite, which had been built in 1974 (but looked newer). There can't be many Conference grounds with two cantilever stands, although admittedly they are both small and narrow examples of the genre. The handful of Alfreton supporters had been directed to an area of terracing at the foot of the Cargill Community Stand, the seated area of which was very sparsely populated – a hundred at most. By contrast the Main Stand was about three-quarters full. At the foot of this stand, where you might have expected five or six steps of terracing, as for the stand opposite, there is nothing. In 'Football Grounds of Great Britain' Simon Inglis explains that this area used to be fronted by large windows, fronting the Vice-Presidents Club, which had to be boarded up when legislation in 1985 prohibited the consumption of alcohol within sight of the pitch (even when consumed behind a plate glass window?). 'This at least saved players from what must have been a tempting view of the bar,' noted Inglis wryly (p 87).

Hereford's nickname is 'the Bulls' which reflects the fame of the local Herefordshire breed of cattle. Whenever Hereford play Tamworth, it's the Bulls versus the Lambs. Now there's a one-sided contest for you! In fact the Lambs managed a 2-2 draw with the Bulls earlier in the season, which just goes to show. Hereford's mascot was a benign-looking bull, with a silly grin on its face, which lumbered around trying to generate some vocal support from the crowd. This proved an uphill struggle; the Hereford supporters were one of the more passive groups I've encountered in the Conference. He was the fourth of a strange miscellany of club mascots I've so far seen this season. There's been Nuneaton's Bloo the Bear (ungainly), Wrexham's Wrex the Dragon (ludicrous), Newport's Spytty the Dog (pathetic) and now an ineffectual bull. My next visit is to Kidderminster Harriers, where I guess I can expect to see Harry the Harrier.

Mascots cavorting around the pitch before kick-off have typically been all that has been on offer for pre-match entertainment, apart from a series of middle-of-the-road pop songs relayed over a loudspeaker (usually too loud, too crackly, or both). At Nuneaton there were the Crew Girls, of course, which was a welcome exception to the norm. But usually there has been little to divert one from reading the programme and munching a pie. It was so different at Maine Road and Old Trafford in the 1950s, and early 60s, when we enjoyed an hour's pre-match entertainment from the Beswick Prize Band (vocalist Sylvia Farmer). Sometimes the band would parade round the pitch, and the band-leader would throw the mace he held in front of him high into the air. I was always afraid he'd drop it... but he never did.

After an early spell of scrappy indecisive play, Hereford scored with their first incisive attacking move. They broke on the right to send Chris Sharp clear. He sent a low cross into the box which Ryan Bowman confidently side-footed into the net. It was Chris Sharp who had scored a stunning equaliser when playing for AFC Telford at Alfreton earlier in the season. They must be sick of the sight of him! But the lead did not last long. Alfreton were counter-attacking with increasing conviction, and after a right-wing cross had not been cleared properly by the Hereford defence, Paul Clayton pounced to hammer a loose ball home. Clayton had been ineffective in the game against Telford but looked much more dangerous today. The game ebbed and flowed, with Alfreton playing the neater football, whilst Hereford relied more on long balls into their opponent's penalty area. Just before half-time Alfreton conceded a needless free-kick on the edge of their area and Stefan Stam rose majestically to head emphatically home. So Hereford went into the break with a lead they scarcely deserved.

I had been unable to buy a programme before the game. I had been assured that a lady in an orange jacket would be circulating throughout the main stand before kick-off, but she never appeared. At half-time, I approached a steward and asked him where I could buy a programme (programmes are an essential source of background information for me about the clubs and the match). 'I'll get one for you,' was his obliging response. 'Just tell me where you're sitting, and I'll bring it over.' As indeed he did, a few minutes later. Now that's what I call customer service!

The electronic scoreboard kept us all informed of the progress of other Conference games (plus the Premiership and Championship). However, its small size meant that other important messages it was trying to convey to us had to be transmitted in stages. Thus we were informed that 'Racial Abuse will not be…' Not be what? Taken seriously? Held against you? As we discovered a minute later, it was (of course)… 'tolerated'. 'Any offenders will be… (long pause) Ignored? Ostracised? Spoken to severely? No, they will be 'prosecuted'. Quite right too.

Three minutes into the second half another high cross into the Alfreton box was headed home by Ryan Bowman. Alfreton just didn't seem able to deal with such crosses, despite the presence of the towering Kempo (aka Darren Kempson) in their defence. The Hereford faithful sat back contentedly in anticipation of an unproblematic home win.

Their confidence turned out to be premature. Within ten minutes Alfreton had pulled a goal back. Nathan Arnold picked up a long throw from the right and had time and space to turn and hit a crisp cross shot into the far corner of the net. Five minutes later an innocuous-looking header from Connor Franklin squirmed through the grasp of Hereford keeper James Bittner and trickled into the net. The vociferous contingent of visiting Alfreton supporters (all 56 of them) celebrated joyfully.

The natives began to get restless. How could a 3-1 lead have been squandered so quickly, one of them wondered, by a side which had conceded a mere three goals in its previous

## Chapter 11

four games? At this stage in the game, every Alfreton attack was looking dangerous. I began to warm to this team of part-timers, representing a small Derbyshire town, who were up against a set of full-timers who only last year were playing in the Football League. The quality of Alfreton's approach work was far superior to that of Hereford's, reflecting the fact that many of the team had played together for a long period. Paul Clayton, Josh Law (the manager's son, as you will recall) Anton Brown and Theo Streete have all been with Alfreton for four or more seasons. This kind of collective experience is an asset which rightly often pays dividends.

The Hereford fans who had witnessed only one win at home in their last seven league games became increasingly critical. There was a nice example of local speech idiosyncrasies when Hereford's left back, who had been struggling since coming on as a substitute, made himself available for a lay-off. 'Don't pass it to 'e' ' cried someone in a nearby seat. You wouldn't hear that at Old Trafford.

Neither side really threatened to win the game in the last ten minutes. Nicky Law of Alfreton was the more satisfied of the two managers. He felt, with some justification, that his team should have won. Martin Foyle, Hereford's boss, was reportedly furious; 'There seems to be a sort of stage fright here, and we showed it again today.' Hereford will, I'm sure, survive… though I can't see them making the play-offs. So no rising or falling is likely this season for Hereford. Maybe they should temporarily adopt a new motto: 'We will overcome our fear of playing at Edgar Street, or perish in the attempt.' Alfreton too will survive, I think; which would be a major achievement for a small, unfashionable club.

# Carpets, Stranded Seals, and Succulent Pies

Kidderminster Harriers vs AFC Telford United

Tuesday 29th January 2013

After a further plethora of postponements in mid-January, due to snowfall and frozen pitches rather than flooding, I made my way to Kidderminster for a Tuesday evening fixture against AFC Telford United.

To reach Kidderminster by train from the north, you have to change in Birmingham. I walked from the profoundly depressing subterranean New Street Station across the city centre to Snow Hill. It's probably nearly fifty years since I last caught a train from Snow Hill. In the early 1960's it was a lovely spacious smoky cavern of a place with steam trains in abundance. It took some finding in 2013. What used to be Snow Hill now appeared to be a collection of tall glass-sided office blocks. Then I noticed a station sign which directed me down an escalator into (another) subterranean station concourse that was very similar (though smaller in scale) to New Street. Snow Hill as I remember it had, sadly, totally disappeared.

Arriving in Kidderminster, I walked down the hill from the railway station towards the town centre, passing the imposing town hall, which is fronted by a statue of Sir Rowland Hill, who was responsible for the introduction of the postage stamp, and is undoubtedly the town's most famous son. But it was dark cold and rainy, so I decided to revisit the town centre the next day, and then make a more balanced appraisal of its qualities.

# Chapter 12

En route to the Travelodge into which I had (unimaginatively) booked myself, I passed one of Kidderminster's two remaining carpet factories. If Macclesfield's development was fuelled by silk, Stockport's by hats (with a bit of help from cotton), and Barrow's by iron and steel and then shipbuilding - in Kidderminster carpets proved the economic driver.

In 1785, Brintons opened their first carpet factory, which still exists today, currently employing several hundred workers. Throughout the nineteenth century and the first half of the twentieth, Kidderminster was the carpet capital of Britain. Carpet-making is still the town's largest employer, although it has greatly declined over the past 50 years. Kidderminster's other large manufacturing firm is the Roxel Group which manufactures solid fuel rocket motors. With its retention of a reasonable range of manufacturing industry and the usual range of public service and retail opportunities, Kidderminster has (so far) proved reasonably resilient to the recession.

You might expect to find carpets featuring somewhere in Kidderminster's nickname. They don't, perhaps because it's difficult to contain it to the requisite two syllables. 'Carpetbaggers' would have a nice resonance, or 'Carpetbaggies' perhaps (West Bromwich is a mere 12 miles down the road). But just as 'come on you Sandgrounders' was too much of a mouthful for Southport fans, so I suppose, 'come on you Carpetbaggers' would be for Kidderminster supporters. 'Kiddy' tends to be the term of affection used instead.

Kidderminster is close to the Black Country – there are only five miles of countryside between it and Stourbridge – but it is not part of it. Its links have always been with Worcestershire and when, in 1972, a Local Government Royal Commission proposed making Kidderminster part of a new conurbation-based 'West Midlands County Council' this change was fiercely – and successfully – resisted.

Although echoes of the Birmingham accent can be heard in the pubs and streets of Kidderminster, so can something closer to the West Country drawl I encountered in Hereford.

The local council is not called Kidderminster, but rather Wyre Forest, after a large sparsely-populated woodland area on the west side of the borough. The choice was confusing, not least because there is a Wyre Borough Council (based in Fleetwood) in Lancashire, and who (local residents apart) knows where Wyre Forest is?

If you are interested in politics, you will know that Wyre Forest hit the headlines in the 2001 General Election when it returned to parliament a candidate unaffiliated to any national party, who stood solely on the basis of his opposition to the downgrading of the local hospital. So strong was the local feeling about this issue, that not only was Dr Richard Taylor of the Kidderminster Health Action Group elected with a large majority, he was re-elected in 2005, a very rare achievement for an independent parliamentary candidate in recent decades. Although Dr Taylor was defeated in 2010, when Wyre Forest reverted to the normality of electing a mainstream party MP, there are still eight Kidderminster Health Action Group members on the borough council.

The council hit the headlines for very different reasons a couple of decades ago when it emerged that its chief executive was involved in concurrent affairs with the female leaders of both the Conservatives and Liberal Democrat party groups. Who says local government is boring!

Flicking through the pages of the local paper - the 'Kidderminster Shuttle', I noted that thousands of Wyre

## Chapter 12

Forest residents had signed a petition to 'save Keith the seal' who had somehow found himself in the River Severn at Bewdley, where he had been delighting wildlife lovers. But he was liable to be shot, if the local Angling Trust had its way, and the challenge was to get Keith back down the river to the sea with all due haste.

Having deposited my rucksack at the Travelodge, I walked towards Aggborough, (Kidderminster Harriers' ground) via a route that took me under a roundabout that matched the biggest Tamworth could offer. Aggborough turned out to be a delight. It's a compact well-maintained ground with a nice symmetry. On one side, there's a newish construction (the Reynolds Stand), which houses the changing rooms, administration facilities and hospitality. Facing it is the even newer East Stand, opened in 2003, where I chose to sit. To the north and south are identical terraces, in one of which the home supporters congregate. The other is sub-divided; one-half reserved for away supporters, the other for home supporters who want to distance themselves from the incessant chanting of 'Red Army'.

After a brief visit to the friendly Supporters Club Bar (temporary membership £1), I moved on to the refreshment bar under the East Stand, where I purchased a cheese and onion pie which I can unreservedly say was the best pie I have ever consumed at a football ground. It was £4 (which is more than usual) but it was worth every penny. It took me the best part of 15 minutes to finish the succulent blend of cheese, onion and potato. It was a meal in itself, otherwise I would have returned to see if the cottage pie was of the same quality.

Why is there this obsession with pies, I wonder, amongst authors whose books on football involve a series of visits to different clubs? If you're doing the rounds of many different stadia, as I was, you don't have time for a 3-course lunch in the town centre, because logistics mean that you only have time for a quick pint before making your way to the ground. Once there, the options are invariably burgers, hot dogs or pies. Burgers and hot dogs vary little wherever you go, but pies differ hugely from venue to venue. They are also a traditional English delicacy, unlike their two American competitors. So the one variable is the pie! There was an advert in the Kidderminster programme in which Brian and Joan Murdoch (who run the catering) thank all their home and away fans for their support over the last 50 years at Aggborough – 'serving you all the best food in British Football'! An ambitious claim, but one I'm happy to support.

Kidderminster Harriers – now there's an imaginative name (take note all you boring South Derbyshire settlements who have settled for 'Town'). This seven-syllable club name is suitable for the ubiquitous 'we hate...' chant beloved by football supporters everywhere. We hate Kidderminster Harriers, we hate Tamworth too, we hate Cambridge United, but Braintree (or whoever) we love you. Five syllables are ideal (Forest Green Rovers, Ebbsfleet United) for the first and third objects of hatred, but six or seven are usable. Anything less wouldn't sound right. There's not a lot of choice in the Conference at present. Maybe next season there'll be some additional targets of hatred – Stalybridge, Celtic? Gainsborough Trinity? Rushden and Diamonds fitted well, and they have a nice stadium. Let's hope they make it back to the Conference soon.

Kidderminster's opponents this evening were AFC Telford United. I know I said, after the Alfreton versus Telford game, that I'd try to avoid them in future, but when you've 13 games to cover and the end of the season is only 3 months away you take what you can get! The two clubs had enjoyed contrasting seasons (or in Telford's case, maybe not). Kidderminster started the season abysmally, losing the first five games, and drawing the next five. Their manager, Steve Burr, must have been a worried man, although he could take some comfort from the fact that a lot of people at Macclesfield Town would like to see him there. Then they hit a hugely impressive streak, including seven straight wins in November and December, and had taken 39 points from the last 18 games (won 12, drawn 3, lost 3), a record which would have put them well clear at the top of the league, if the season had started on September 25th. As it was, they'd moved from bottom of the league to fifth, with every chance of making the play-offs, or even, given the stuttering form of the other contenders, ending up as champions.

AFC Telford United, in contrast, had experienced a very different pattern of results. They started well (for an unfancied part-time club) and lost only 3 of their first 14 games, climbing to seventh in the table. Since then they had not recorded a single victory, and had amassed a mere 8 further points from 15 games. Currently they languished in 21st place, and manager Andy Sinton had felt it necessary to issue a statement to the effect that changing the manager at this stage would be counterproductive. So it was a crucial game for both clubs. A Telford win would get them out of the bottom four; a Kidderminster victory would take them to within 5 points of Grimsby Town, the current league leaders.

Kidderminster have had experience of playing in the Football League, but not very much. They were promoted as Conference champions in 2001, under the managerial guidance of former Liverpool favourite Jan Molby. After four uneventful mid-table seasons, they were relegated back to the Conference in 2006, and have stayed there ever since. Three times they have just missed the play-offs (2009, 2011,

2012). Their earlier history was played out mainly in the
Midlands Combination, before they eventually reached the
Conference in the 1980s. All things considered, you feel that
the Conference is where they really belong. But the two-up,
two-down system between Division Two and the
Conference since 2003 has shaken things up. Division Two
now has a large quota of clubs that have recently played in
the Conference, and the Conference has an equally large
quota of clubs who have played recently in the League. This
is, arguably, a much healthier situation than the 'old pals act'
which, until 1987, resulted in the regular re-election of the
same old Division Four (as it was then) failures, with only
the occasional casualties, such as Barrow, Gateshead, and
Southport.

Kidderminster are one of seven clubs to have won the
Conference title twice. They, Macclesfield Town, Maidstone
United and Stevenage Borough were all denied entry to the
Football League first time round, because of the perceived
inadequacy of their grounds (in 1994, a couple of years after
the horrendous Bradford City fire, Kidderminster were
rejected because Aggborough had too many wooden seats).
Barnet were promoted as champions in1991, came back
down again in 2001, but were re-promoted in 2005 (they
currently look likely candidates for a further demotion!). Of
the other two-time champions, Altrincham (1980 and 1981)
have since oscillated between the Conference and the
second tier, whilst Enfield (1983 and 1986) have only
recently re-emerged as a force in non-league football (as
Enfield Town) after a long spell in the doldrums. Maidstone
United (1984 and 1989), whose spell in the Football League
lasted only two seasons, subsequently went bust (a
successor club now plays in the Rymans League). These
varying fortunes illustrate a dilemma facing several
Conference clubs. Do you invest heavily in pushing hard for

promotion to the Football League (a high-risk strategy, as we have seen) knowing it could all end in tears? Or do you settle for the safer environment of the Conference? Not a difficult choice for Hyde, Braintree, or Alfreton, all with average gates of well under a thousand. But much more problematic for Kidderminster, Macclesfield, and Hereford.

As kick-off approached, I wondered whether I should continue my support of Telford (having found myself in the visitors' enclosure when they played at Alfreton). I decided not. Things were not looking good for Stockport County at the moment, and it would be helpful if Telford, a fellow relegation candidate, continued to lose.

As the teams came out, my eye was caught by an advertisement hoarding at the home supporters' end. It read 'Doolittle and Dalley; Letting and Selling Properties'. But not very quickly it would seem!

There was a swirling wind, which typically adversely affects the quality of football, but both sides coped with it well. Kidderminster did most of the attacking, but Telford were well-organised in defence (their defensive record is better than those of their fellow relegation candidates) and counter-attacked, without ever looking particularly dangerous. Ryan Young, their keeper, who was so excellent at Alfreton, was equally impressive here, beating away a couple of fierce Kidderminster shots. But he could do little about a Kidderminster goal, towards the end of the first half, when an astute lofted pass from Lee Vaughan (perhaps aided by the wind) sent Marvin Johnson clear on the left. He advanced into the penalty area and beat the advancing Young with a well-placed shot. It was no more than Kidderminster deserved. Their approach play had been excellent.

No Kidderminster mascot appeared before the game, or at half-time, and when I read through the programme, I realised why not. There is a mascot – predictably Harry the Harrier (a variety of hawk) – or rather, there is a mascot costume, but no-one is prepared to put it on! 'Help: Harry the Harrier' bewailed the Aggborough News section of the programme – 'the club is in urgent need of someone to help with the operation of the official team mascot.' You'd have thought some extrovert poser would have given it a go, wouldn't you?

The second half followed a similar pattern to the first. Kidderminster had more of the play and looked the more likely to score. But Telford were still in the game, and mounted periodic counter-attacks, spurred on by a vociferous contingent of two hundred or so travelling supporters (Kidderminster is their nearest thing to a local derby). Ryan Young pulled off another couple of impressive saves (where would they be without him?) but the player who really caught the eye was Kidderminster defender Lee Vaughan who was involved in most of his team's creative moves. I noticed the way in which, having made a pass, he was always running into space, seeking a return. He covered a prodigious amount of ground and was as likely to be seen in his opponents' penalty area (where he managed a couple of decent goal attempts) as he was defending resolutely in his own. I noted that he had already scored three goals this season; not bad for a back four defender. He will go far, I think. Remember when you see him playing in the Premiership in a couple of season's time that you first saw this outcome predicted here.

In the end Kidderminster ran out worthy 1-0 winners (and Lee Vaughan was deservedly named man-of-the-match). It could have been more, but the vagaries of the wind impeded the accuracy of their shooting. Telford acquitted themselves well, but as in the other games I'd seen them play, lacked that bit of inspiration amongst their strikers to create clear-cut goal opportunities. Their relegation worries have increased.

I walked back into Kidderminster's town centre the next morning, en route for the station. My course followed a street that incorporated an off-centre range of retail establishments similar to those I had seen on Gateshead's High Street, although Kidderminster could not match the latter's sense of desolation, nor its profusion of unhealthy outlets.

The first building I passed was a large store called 'Bed City'. Now that's an interesting concept; a city of beds. There must be other possibilities: Bathroom City? Furniture City? Or, of course, Carpet City. There followed Shipley's Luxury Bingo (what distinguishes luxury bingo from common-or-garden bingo, one wonders), Fireplace World, and a shop which called itself 'First Choice Nutrition', but the window of which was stocked with large tins of paint.

I then passed a succession of hairdressers, takeaways, pubs, nail manicure establishments, and the 'Select Café' (which I didn't, despite having not yet breakfasted). There was a closed-down butchers, a Coral betting shop, and a wedding dress establishment, full of lovely specimens of the genre, which was called '2 Have and 2 Hold'.

I then reached the town centre itself, which was largely pedestrianized, with an irregular street pattern and an undulating terrain, all of which are positive townscape qualities. But it also contained some depressing examples of brutalistic 1960s and 1970s town centre architecture, and there was a proliferation of 'To Let' signs, including five in a row on one street. A short walk away was the inevitable new shopping complex - Weavers Wharf - which had no doubt contributed to its decline.

I began to see a pattern in the distribution of shopping and service outlets in the medium-sized towns I'd visited. There is the traditional core centre, most of it pedestrianized, with a range of familiar retail outlets, specialist shops, civic buildings and markets (indoor and/or outdoor). They usually proved pleasant enough environments to wander around, and you feel you are somewhere with a distinctive individual character.

On the edge of the 'traditional' centre (or sometimes integrated within it) is the new (or newish) retail complex, with a predictable set of retail outlets. Then, on the main arteries heading out of town you'll find a mix of takeaway outlets, downmarket cafes, specialist shops that can't afford the town centre rents, and other establishments that wouldn't quite fit (nails, tattoos, downmarket hairdressers, wedding cakes, wedding dresses). Reviewing the range of services offered in the Kidderminster street I'd earlier walked down, it was clear that they all offered goods or services you wouldn't find in the huge Tesco store, located a hundred yards away (which was probably why the butcher's shop hadn't survived). You can't get a wedding dress, a wedding cake, a fireplace, or your nails manicured at Tesco, can you? Well not yet anyway!

My return journey to Birmingham took me back through the succession of Black Country towns I'd passed in darkness the previous evening. The train stopped at Stourbridge Junction, where the shortest branch line in Britain (one mile) provides a connection to Stourbridge Town itself. The link train was the smallest train I'd ever come across on the British Rail network, a single unit bus-like vehicle which can't have accommodated more than 40 people. Just as well Stourbridge Town aren't in the Conference!

From Stourbridge Junction, the train passed through undulating territory with lots of small hills and small towns which all looked similar (although they have reputations for fierce independence). Each little community used to have its own metal manufacturing speciality. There were derelict factories, scrapyards, patches of scrubby wasteland, and a mixture of housing developments ranging from run-down 1930s council estates to areas of more pretentious detached residences. All these ingredients were jumbled together in a continuous splurge of development from Stourbridge onwards. You can't tell where Rowley Regis ends and Cradley Heath begins. It is not a pretty sight. But it was a nostalgic journey for me. When I was at Birmingham University in the 1960s, I guested occasionally for a Sunday football team of staggering ineptitude, run by one of my fellow students, which played in a Black Country league. I remember losing 13-0 on a pitch atop a hill at Old Hill, which is one of the stations on the line.

Later that week, AFC Telford United sacked manager Andy Sinton, despite his earlier warnings. As someone who had presided over the club's ascent from the middle reaches of the pyramid, after Telford United went bust in 2004, he can count himself unlucky. He joined a growing number of victims of 'relegation panic', including Jim Gannon (Stockport County), Ian Bogie (Gateshead), and Marcus Law (Tamworth).

# Nostalgia, New Managers, and Mary Portas

Stockport County vs Nuneaton Town

Saturday February 2<sup>nd</sup> 2013

Travelling to Stockport was like going home. I spent my adolescent years in Heaton Moor, a suburb of Stockport, and Stockport County was my local team. My parents lived there until 1975, when they moved to Alderley Edge, in opulent north Cheshire. I have so many positive memories of the place and the team. Since 1975, I have, every now and then, visited Edgeley Park to watch Stockport County but Stockport town centre hardly at all. So it was a nostalgia-seeped return trip.

But, more importantly, Stockport County were in trouble. They were lying 20<sup>th</sup> in the Conference, a mere two points above relegation-zoned AFC Telford United. Ten days before the game, they had sacked their manager Jim Gannon, an iconic figure in County's recent history, both as a player and as a manager. In his place they had appointed a Bosnian, Darije Kalezic, whose most recent managerial experience was with Zulte Waregem (Belgium) from which he was dismissed in February 2012, and, as his assistant, Stuart Watkiss, who has management experience in the Conference. Today's game against fellow-strugglers Nuneaton Town was crucial. The previous twelve Conference games I'd witnessed, I hadn't really cared who'd won (probably just as well, as eight ended in draws). In this case, I cared desperately. If County won they would reach the mid-table comfort zone, at least for a week. If they lost, they would probably be back in the relegation quartet.

## Chapter 13

Stockport is one of the large towns circling Manchester which developed and flourished as centres of the cotton-spinning industry in the nineteenth century. We moved there in 1958 when I was fifteen. I remember going to sleep to the sound of goods wagons being shunted down in the yards in the Mersey Valley, a mile or so away, and watching steam trains crossing the imposing viaduct in the dark, 'setting the night on fire', as Ewan MacColl so eloquently put it in 'Dirty Old Town'.

I remember getting work on the Christmas post for three successive years, including a stint in the sorting office at the Armoury, near Edgeley Park, surrounded by voluptuous female students (or maybe that's a distortion of memory!). I joined Stockport Youth Campaign for Nuclear Disarmament, with whom I walked on two Aldermaston Marches. There were cheap lunches (3/6d for 3 courses, I seem to recall) at the Rajah Indian Restaurant, under the arches of the railway viaduct, and mouth-watering fudge and toffee could be purchased at Duerden's home-made sweets stall in Stockport Market. Opposite the market were lively traditional pubs selling Robinson's excellent ales, where you could get delicious pea and ham soup at lunchtime. I always enjoyed returning to Stockport, after I went away to university in Birmingham in 1962, and when I got my first job (as a very junior planning officer) with Manchester City Council in 1965. Stockport continued to be a focal point for me, both socially and in terms of football.

My friend John Davies had moved to Heaton Moor a couple of years before my family did (in 1957), and soon began to watch Stockport County. The first game for which I joined him was a Division Three (North) match against Workington, towards the end of the 1956-57 season. Both clubs had an outside chance of promotion, which all but disappeared for Stockport after a 1-0 defeat (and in the end

Workington didn't go up either; only one club got promoted in those days).

I attended numerous games the following season, including the memorable 3-0 win in the FA Cup Third Round against Luton Town who, at the time, were fourth in Division One. That match was the start of a 56-year (and counting) attachment to Stockport County.

Stockport, like so many towns, has had a chequered industrial/economic history. The first mechanised silk manufacturer premises in the UK were built in Stockport in the eighteenth century. The silk industry waxed and waned over the next hundred years, with Stockport losing its dominance to nearby Macclesfield (you will recall that Macclesfield Town are known as the 'Silkmen'). Then the geography (river valleys) and micro-climate (damp) of Stockport made it an ideal venue for the emergent cotton industry in the nineteenth century, although cotton was less dominant in Stockport than it was in towns such as Oldham, 'Ashton-under-Lyne, Bury and Rochdale to the north. There was never the same 'forest of tall chimneys' phenomenon in Stockport that there was in Chadderton (near Oldham) and Bolton, for example.

The third industry which developed at around the same time as cotton was more unusual: hat-making. Hat-making became a big deal around the turn of the century, and 3,000 people were employed in Stockport by 1930 (only textiles and engineering employed more). But hat-making then declined, with Stockport being overtaken by Luton as the centre of this industry in the UK. The last hat-making factory closed in 1997. Since both Stockport County, and Luton Town are known as 'the Hatters', the famous 1958 cup-tie which Stockport won 3-0 could perhaps be seen as revenge for Luton's role in eroding Stockport's economic base!

# Chapter 13

Cotton also declined before, and after, the Second World War, creating the need for a more varied range of industries, which the town has been reasonably successful in attracting. To the south of Stockport (but within its boundaries) there is the Woodford-based Avro-De-Havilland aircraft factory, home of the famous Avro Delta which was a familiar sight in the skies above Stockport in the 1960's.

There are two distinct 'town centres' in Stockport. There's Merseyway and its various offshoots, which is boringly predictable, with all the usual high street stores (albeit a diminishing species, currently). It's not even enlivened by the sight of the River Mersey, which has long been built over, in this part of Stockport. Adjacent to Merseyway and up a steep hill is the old centre of Stockport: the Market Hall, the Market Place, Great and Little Underbank, St Petersgate, and Robinson's Unicorn Brewery. This was the Stockport I came to know and love during my teens and twenties. It was thus with some trepidation that I parked the car in St Petersgate, and walked over the bridge which straddles Little Underbank, towards the Market. I'd not been here for the best part of forty years. Would pea and ham soup still be on the menu at the 'Boars Head'? Would Duerdens fudge and toffee stall still be in operation? Would there be honey still for tea?

Well, the Boars Head was closed and boarded up. The Duerdens had, I was told, retired many years ago, having clearly been unable to persuade any offspring to keep the stall going (it can't have been a particularly attractive prospect for an 18- year old in the 1980s or 1990s). There was another Robinsons pub on the edge of the Market Place which had closed, as had a baronial Josiah Holt's establishment on Little Underbank. The whole area, although it had retained its distinctiveness, was clearly in decline, as most old market areas are nowadays.

In Little Underbank there had been some attempt to introduce more trendy establishments (the kind of thing you see in Camden Market). But the few examples co-existed uneasily with more traditional outlets (and a fair bit of dereliction) and there were few young people in evidence at lunchtime on a sunny Saturday. Some of the outdoor market stalls contained the most uninspiring collections of miscellaneous tat you can imagine. One stall promised free delivery (within a 3-mile radius) of any item purchased which cost £3 or more. I couldn't even find a Robinson's pub in the area, and had to settle for a pint of Samuel Smiths, which seemed sacrilegious given the looming presence of the Robinson's brewery! But what did I expect, for heaven's sake? Time to stand still for forty years? The market area to have somehow survived the ravages of time and changes in shopping habits and preferences? I had intended to get my lunch there, but changed my mind, and made my way past the railway viaduct, past the Armoury, and on to Castle Street, which is the local shopping centre that serves Edgeley, and which is close to Edgeley Park itself.

Edgeley is a compact, intact, well-defined area of red-brick terraced housing, dating from the 1880s or '90s. At one time it was surrounded on all sides by railways, thus emphasising its distinctiveness. One of the railways has since been uprooted – the old Manchester Central to London St Pancras line (via Buxton) but that, in turn, has been replaced by the M60, so Edgeley residents still have a well-defined territory. This archetypal working-class suburb is only ten minutes' walk from the town centre (via the railway station) but feels totally detached from it. It is a world of its own with a shopping centre of its own. Whilst it remains a working-class area (no gentrification in Edgeley), it has a relaxed unthreatening feel to it (although an off-duty policeman had been murdered close to Castle Street the previous Saturday). The terraced houses appeared well-maintained, as did the small front gardens some of them possess. The area reminded me of Hindpool in Barrow (see Chapter 1).

Castle Street itself has survived better than the Market area. There is nothing remotely sophisticated about it, but there is an interesting variety of small shops, none of which were vacant. A small Co-op does not appear to have damaged the livelihoods of the other shopkeepers. At 2.00, the street was full of shoppers, plus groups of County supporters on their way to the match. There were two pubs, both well-patronised (partly, but not wholly, by the latter). If the Underbanks had proved disappointing, Edgeley and Castle Street had not.

I arrived at Edgeley Park an hour before kick-off and bought my ticket (£11; concession) for the old main stand, which has been there since 1902, and looks as if it has. Emerging from the club shop under the Cheadle End Stand, clutching my DVD of highlights of the 2006-07 season (when County were promoted to Division One after a memorable Wembley play-off final against Rochdale) I noticed that a small crowd had gathered nearby. Something was about to be unveiled, and who was there to unveil it but Darije Kalezic himself. (No, I can't pronounce his name either). I liked the look of him. He was small, and neat, but un-flamboyant in appearance and coiffure (Roberto Mancini would do well to take note: his overblown overgrown locks would benefit from a visit to 'Vittorio Tansella and Michael' of Mottram Road, Hyde (see Chapter 2)). Darije gave a short, well-judged speech saying how pleased he was to have been appointed as County's manager, and made the familiar reference to 'sleeping giants'. Then, to warm applause, he unveiled what turned out to be the 'County

Wall', consisting of a group of plaques which I assumed contained details of Stockport County greats of the past (or possibly recent benefactors).

The main stand had been renamed the Danny Bergera stand since I was last there, appropriately so, because it was Bergera who had transformed County in the late 1980's from a perennial failing re-election-seeking club to one which, eight years later in 1996, attained the lofty heights of the Championship (by which time Bergera had been dismissed, after thumping the Chairman in a nearby hotel).

In one sense Stockport County can be seen as yet another lower-division northern club which, after an undistinguished history, has ended up in the Conference. But that would be an unfair characterisation. Whilst Barrow, Gateshead and Southport achieved very little in their relatively brief histories in the Football League, Stockport have had their moments of glory. They also have a much longer track record in the League. They were elected to Division Two of the League in 1900, whilst Barrow, Gateshead and Southport were elected to the league much later (and departed much earlier!). By 2011 County had participated in 100 years of league football (compared with Barrow's meagre 44 and Gateshead's even more paltry 25). Most of these years have been spent in the League's lowest division, but there have been brief spells in the League's second level. Since 1956, in particular, they've had a roller-coaster ride. They spent five seasons in the Championship (1997-2002); appeared in three Wembley play-off finals (losing two - 1992, 1994 - and winning one (2008)); reached the semi-final of League Cup in 1997 (when it was a much bigger deal than it is now) beating the first division sides Blackburn Rovers, Southampton, and West Ham United on the way. They've achieved three promotions, and suffered four relegations, including two in quick succession in 2010 and 2011, which saw them fall into the Conference. They have, over the years, given their supporters a potent mixture of joy, depression, heartache and pride. None of the other ex-league clubs now in the Conference could boast a similarly impressive history, apart from Luton Town (though I acknowledge possible accusations of bias here).

The collective consciousness of football clubs and their supporters is littered with ghosts from the past. As far as the leading Premiership clubs are concerned, everyone with an interest in football knows their ghosts: Duncan Edwards, Georgie Best and Dennis Law in the case of Manchester United; Tommy Smith, Ian Rush and Steve Heighway at Liverpool. But the ghosts of the likes of Stockport County are just as evocative for their supporters, who still talk of goal-scoring legend Jack Connor, who played his last game for County a season or so before I started watching them, and whose grandson, James, is currently on County's books. There was the diminutive winger Gene Wilson, hair always parted meticulously down the middle who, so legend has it, once pushed the ball through the legs of the opposing full-back, and then crawled through them himself! There was Mike Davock, who sped energetically up and down the left touchline, in the days when there were outside-lefts, and that was what was expected of them. There was the giant goal-scoring legend Kevin Francis who went on to play for Birmingham City, midfield genius Chris Marsden who went on to Southampton, and Bill Holden who scored twice in the epic cup defeat of Luton Town. None of these names are well-known or celebrated outside Stockport but they remain key reference points for County supporters, just as Best, Law and Edwards do for United fans.

Today's opponents - Nuneaton Town - have never graced the Football League with their presence, nor are they likely to. They are Conference regulars, having been there or thereabouts since its inception in 1979. They had languished in the bottom four of the Conference throughout this season, but have recently shown signs of a revival, with a 3-1 win at in-form Cambridge United.

Stockport are presently unique in the Conference (and probably the entire British professional football spectrum) in having a lord as chairman of the club. But Lord Peter Snape isn't a real lord in the aristocratic sense. He's a former railway signalman and Labour M.P. for West Bromwich East, who has returned to his Stockport roots to try to turn round County's fortunes.

My seat was at the back of the main stand. Surveying the pitch I noticed that it was in good condition, with plenty of grass. For several years in the 2000s, Edgeley Park was shared with Sale Sharks RUFC, an arrangement which was not conducive to quality football. In January 2003, I came to see Stockport County play Swindon Town, on a mud bath with hardly a blade of grass remaining. It's good to see the back of Sale Sharks (and rugby union is, in my view, a singularly boring game anyway).

I glanced through the pages of the Stockport Express, whilst munching my way through a piping hot steak and kidney pie. There were some nice examples of quintessential local paper headlines. 'Police probe into mystery substance after three dogs die in park horror', 'It's no yolk….chicken lays 'the worlds' smallest egg'', 'calls for action after stone yob attacks'. Where would we be without the Stockport Expresses of this world?! There was a report of the visit of 'retail queen and TV star Mary Portas' to Stockport, to see how the £100,000 Portas Pilot money was being spent. She enthused fulsomely about the potential of the Market area and the Underbanks, but regretted the controversy that has broken out over the composition of the 'town team committee' which runs the project. Just take it over and run

## Chapter 13

it yourself, Mary! There were four pages covering the new appointments at Stockport County, which included a reference to the fact that both the new manager and his assistant were initially on three-month contracts. Hardly a vote of confidence!

Sitting next to me in the stand was a friendly elderly couple who reminded me of my mum and dad. He was sporting one of those tweedy flat caps (as my dad used to) whilst she had her hair done in what used to be called a 'perm' (short for 'permanent wave' – except it wasn't), which was what my mum did. I asked her about the circumstances surrounding Jim Gannon's departure. She was very unhappy about the abrupt and ungrateful way he had been dismissed. However, she felt that the team had not been playing for him. The contrast between the ignominious 1-3 home defeat to Mansfield Town a fortnight or so ago, and the 2-1 win against highly-placed Forest Green Rovers a few days later, (after Gannon had gone) was, she said, remarkable. 'You wouldn't have thought they were the same players.' We then swapped some 'personal history' details. They had lived in Reddish, but then moved to Heaton Chapel, which is just down the road from Heaton Moor, where we used to live. They'd had a caravan which they took regularly for holidays to Kendal, which is where I now live. It was like stepping back into the cosy familiar Stockport world of the 1960s and '70s.

The game began with County attacking the open end (a seated terrace earmarked for visitors, where there were about 150 Nuneaton supporters). After five minutes, County were ahead. A free kick on the left, taken by Jon Nolan, was steered home by an unmarked Connor Jennings. Five minutes later, County were two up, when Danny Whitehead raced clear on the right, and his low cross was side-footed home from close range by Danny Hattersley.

The Edgeley faithful couldn't believe it (when had County last been 2-0 up after 10 minutes?) and roared their delight, which I shared. I'll settle for this, I thought, a nice straightforward 3-0 or 4-0 win, with no nail-biting tension in the last ten minutes.

If only! Four minutes later Nuneaton's Adam Walker made it to the by-line and put over a low cross which Andy Brown glanced into the far corner. A further four minutes elapsed before a free-kick from the very same Adam Walker was headed home by the very same Andy Brown. Back to square one, with a mere eighteen minutes on the clock. The prospect of a nail-biting finish re-emerged. On the opening day of the season, when I witnessed a dreary 0-0 draw at Barrow, Nuneaton Town were losing 4-5 at home to Ebbsfleet. It looked like a similar scoreline was on the cards, with hopefully Nuneaton (again) on the wrong end of it.

County's young team (average age 23) were understandably shaken by these reverses, and Nuneaton for a time looked dangerous every time they attacked, although Danny Whitehead did hit the bar with a powerful shot a few minutes before the break. I'd noticed the contrasting style of the two managers. Nuneaton's Kevin Wilkin was on his feet outside the visitors' dugout the whole time (as was his assistant) gesticulating, shouting instructions, and expressing a wide range of emotions. In contrast, Darije Kalezic and Stuart Watkiss stayed put in their dugout, making only the occasional gesture, and only rarely emerging. Jim Gannon would have been out there with Kevin Wilkin.

Nuneaton started the stronger in the second half, but County began to come back into the game. Both sides had, for long periods in the first half, sought to progress patiently using a short passing game, both reasonably effectively. After the interval there were more long, hopeful up-field punts which, given the limited height of both sets of strikers, never looked likely to create scoring opportunities. It was a relief when both sides reverted to their earlier strategy.

Just when it looked like the early 2-2 scoreline might prove to be the end result, County forced a corner, and when Connor Jennings' shot was half-cleared, it fell to Jon Nolan, who slammed it first time into the roof of the net, and promptly disappeared under a mass of ecstatic team-mates.

It was appropriate that Nolan should score what turned out to be the winning goal, because he had made a major contribution to the match, with his enthusiasm, his tireless running, his tenacious tackling and his constant probing for attacking options. Towards the end, he was rightly singled out as man of the match by the sponsors (Robinson's Brewery).

Stockport held out without too much trouble, and were applauded from the field by manager and their supporters (including me). I breathed a huge sigh of relief. The illusory security of mid-table beckoned. A delighted Darije Kalezic said afterwards that it had been his dream to win this game for everyone inside the club, and for the fans. Well he had, and it felt like it just might be the start of a new era (another Danny Bergera?).

Other results meant that Stockport finished the day sixteenth in the table on 34 points, five more than Telford in 21st place, who had played three games more. The spectre of visits next season from (and to) the likes of Vauxhall Motors and Solihull Moors began mercifully to recede. But away next Saturday to second-placed Wrexham could be a tough follow-up!

Wandering through Stockport and Edgeley, and witnessing a crucial County victory made me realise how much the town and the team still meant to me. Stockport was where I spent my formative years. Adolescence is a time when experience has a particular intensity; first girl-friends, first shared drinking sessions with groups of mates, and a heightened concern about the fortunes of whichever football club you had attached yourself to. Why else would I have travelled to Accrington on a cold February afternoon in 1959, with my friend John, to watch County scrape a 2-2 draw with Accrington Stanley, in an ultimately futile attempt to avoid relegation? These allegiances come to be engrained into your persona and stay with you for the rest of your life. Stockport County was the reason I was writing this book, and today, they had done me proud.

# The Wooden Man and Peppa Pig

Dartford vs Luton Town

Tuesday 12<sup>th</sup> February 2013

What associations does Dartford stimulate in the popular mind? My guess would be the Tunnel and the Crossing. One pictures Dartford as a place of transit; a town you pass by on the way to somewhere else (the Channel Tunnel, the commuter belt of north-east Kent).There may be a growing awareness that Dartford is the nearest town to the vast Bluewater shopping complex, which lies three miles away to the east, and which no doubt explains why Dartford town centre has been selected as one of Mary Portas's 'high-street revitalisation projects (in common with Stockport). Rolling Stones fans, however, will know it as the place where Mick Jagger and Keith Richards were born and brought up (they first met at Dartford Station).

Dartford was new territory for me. I'd glanced down on it from the Crossing, and descended into its Tunnel, but I'd never stopped there before. Of the Conference towns there were only five (Dartford, Woking, Braintree, Alfreton, and Nailsworth) that I had not previously visited. I caught the train from Charing Cross, and at 5.45 on a cold February evening descended from Dartford station into unknown territory.

The short walk into Dartford's town centre quickly led me to the conclusion that the task of reviving it needed much more than the attentions of Mary Portas, and the paltry grant involved. It was totally knackered, as bad as Gateshead, and without the new investment which may (or may not) transform the future of the latter. Quite apart from the Bluewater Centre (which had a special bus lane to transport you there from the town centre) there was a large Sainsbury's to the south of the High Street, a large Waitrose to the north. What was left for a traditional town centre in these circumstances? Well, very little really. It can best be described as 'residual'. Not a single butcher, baker and confectioner, fishmonger or (new) clothes shop was to be seen. Instead there were cash converters (and the like), a 'shoppers amusements' establishment, 'Lucky Nails' (now there's a growth industry) and the increasingly familiar range of takeaways, and cut-price stores. Banks and estate agents added a spurious sense of gravitas.

There were two more modern shopping precincts adjoining the High Street – the Priory Centre and the Orchard Centre – which were no doubt seen as Dartford's salvation when they were erected thirty years or so ago, but which were now well past their sell-by date; they seemed forlorn, uncared-for, and full of empty or downmarket shops. The one unexpected element was the 'What If Gallery' selling paintings and other quality artefacts. Will it still be there in twelve months' time, I wondered?

I bought my copy of the Dartford Messenger, and entered one of the High Street pubs, a cavernous bar attached to the only hotel in the town centre, which had the feeling of a place which no longer expected people to stay there (with some justification). The paper contained an item about the Mary Portas revitalisation initiative. Apparently the only use so far made of the £100,000 grant had been to invite 'Peppa Pig' to wander around the town centre the previous Saturday, an initiative which generated an understandable level of ridicule amongst the Messenger's readers. 'Peppa Pig saves Dartford'? I don't think so!

I didn't have time to visit the Bluewater Centre, but I didn't need to. I'd been to its north-western and north-eastern equivalents, the Trafford Centre and the Metro Centre (in Gateshead) and I know what these places are like. The Trafford Centre I remember best for its dimly-lit subterranean Hades-like concourse full of overpriced eating-places. Whilst my family went through the motions of shopping there, I returned to the car-park for some forgotten item. As I left the centre itself, I was accosted by a smart young woman with a clipboard. 'Can I ask you a few questions,' she requested, with an over-bright smile. 'Certainly,' I replied. 'How would you describe your impressions of the Trafford Centre?' she asked. 'Horrendous,' I said, 'I couldn't get out of it quickly enough, and there's no way I'm ever going to return.' 'Oh dear,' she responded, glancing down her printed questionnaire, 'I don't think I've got a category for that.'

Dartford's most famous son is probably Wat Tyler, although this claim is disputed by Deptford, Colchester and Maidstone, all of which claim ownership of the famed leader of the Peasants' Revolt. I noticed that there was a pub in the town centre named after him, but this is hardly conclusive evidence. If you're not convinced of the authenticity of the Wat Tyler connection then there are links with Anne of Cleeves (after her divorce from Henry VIII), Peter Blake (the pop artist), Malcolm Allison (football manager), and two of the Rolling Stones (see above). And Dartford also played an important part in Margaret Thatcher's political career. Her first election contests were in Dartford, in 1950 and 1951, and although she didn't manage to unseat the sitting Labour MP, she performed well enough to get herself noticed, and to earn a winnable seat (Finchley) at the 1955 General Election. The rest - as they say - is history!

## Chapter 14

In 1840 Dartford boasted the largest mustard factory in the kingdom. Later, there developed a varied industrial mix including a large chemical works, a gunpowder factory, a paper mill, a heavy engineering plant and a vast cement-manufacturing concern (now the Bluewater Centre site). In its inter-war heyday Dartford must have been a veritable hotbed of heavy industry, albeit at the cost of a noxious melange of air pollutants. However, like so many traditional industrial towns, Dartford's industrial base has been spectacularly eroded since the Second World War, and there is little of it now remaining. It now operates as a commuter area for central London. Another town that's lost its identity, like Newport, 'just another town along the road'.

I made my way to Princes Park, Dartford F.C.'s ground, a 20 minute walk from the town centre. Princes Park is a new stadium, built in 2006, but very different from the familiar identikit new stadia you find elsewhere. It certainly looked distinctive from the photographs on the club's website. It had apparently been built on 'sustainable' principles, producing electricity from solar panels, collecting rainwater for use within the stadium, and having timber beams to support the roof (which is itself covered with green vegetation). Opposite the Main Stand the 'Wooden Man' sculpture stands on top of the terrace, gazing benignly down at the pitch. I approached it full of anticipation.

I was not disappointed. Princes Park proved a delight. It cost me a mere £8 to get in (only Hyde have beaten that). I visited the bar (open to all, apart from away supporters) which was friendly and comfortable, filled with the anticipatory hubbub you'd expect half-an-hour before a game. The bar is located in the main stand, above the seated area. The other three sides of the ground are standing areas, which feels the right balance for a club of this status. All the stands are covered with roofs with gentle convex curves, which avoids the regimentation of the more familiar square-shaped layouts. The abundance of wood in the structures is unusual, but welcome. I also noticed two raised areas specially designed for wheelchair users in different parts of the ground. Princes Park is at the other end of the spectrum from Hereford's Edgar Street ground, an imaginatively-designed modern stadium as opposed to a decaying relic of the past.

Dartford had been promoted from Blue Square Bet South the previous season, via the play offs, where they beat nearby Welling. Like many non-league clubs, their history has been a topsy-turvy one. Founded as early as 1888, they were consistent performers in the Southern League, both before and after World War Two. They were the first non-league club ever to reach the third round of the FA Cup in successive seasons (1937 and 1938), and were FA Trophy finalists in 1974 (beaten 3-0 by Morecambe!).

Dartford were promoted to the Conference in 1981, but went straight back down again in 1982. Undaunted, they regained their Conference place in 1984, under the astute management of John Still (currently manager of Dagenham and Redbridge) and finished third in 1985, only five points behind champions Wealdstone. The following season, however, they were relegated again (with Barrow), and spent the next five seasons back in the Southern League, several times coming close to promotion, but never quite making it.

Then, at the start of the 1990s, Dartford hit hard times. After the Bradford City fire in 1987, Dartford were required to upgrade their ground at Watling Street. The costs of doing so placed a considerable financial burden on the club, but fortunately (or so it seemed at the time) Maidstone United had recently sold their local ground to raise money to fund their ambition to become a Football League club, and were looking for a ground-share opportunity. They

negotiated a deal with Dartford to share Watling Street, and
paid for some of the ground improvements, plus a
substantial rental, which together provided a welcome
solution to Dartford's financial problems. So far so good;
even better when Maidstone won promotion to the League
in 1989.

What Dartford hadn't anticipated was that Maidstone
United would go bust in 1991, when they were forced to
resign from the League. Dartford's bankruptcy followed in
September 1992, when they had to withdraw from the
Southern League four games into the season. They were
kept alive by the club's Supporters Association, but for the
next fourteen years struggled in the lower reaches of the
pyramid, without a ground of their own. As recently as
2007-08 they were languishing in the Ryman League
Division One (the fourth tier). But from 2008 onwards,
Dartford have developed a momentum, and enjoyed a
succession of promotions.

Their performance in the Conference this season had, so
far, exceeded expectations (including, I suspect, their own).
They remain a part-time outfit, but looking at the
appearances record of the current squad in the excellent
programme, I noticed that six of the players had over a
hundred appearances under their belt, in one case (Ryan
Hayes) over 350. That indicated a settled side with long-
term knowledge of one another, rather than a random
collection of short-term imports. Alfreton Town were
similar, in this respect; I'm sure it helps smaller clubs
survive in the Conference.

Dartford had lost their first three games but then embarked
on an impressive run which took them into a play-off
position by November, with notable victories over Newport
County, Grimsby Town and Luton Town in the process.
Since then, their form had been less consistent and they

currently lay tenth in the table, in what I would call the 'safe' zone. They were well clear of threats of relegation, although unlikely to make the play-offs. Indeed I suspected that Dartford would not necessarily welcome the prospect of promotion to the Football League. With an average crowd of 1,471 in a stadium which holds only 4,000 I suspect that the Conference is, for the present, the limit of their ambitions.

The day's opponents, Luton Town, were currently seventh-placed, just outside the play-off positions, but with a couple of games in hand over some of the other contenders. Pre-season predictions would have placed them in a stronger position at this stage of the season. Luton's problem was that they had become distracted by the magic of the FA Cup. After beating Wolves and Norwich City, they had a tie against Millwall four days hence. The FA Cup had proved great for headlines, not just the 'Non-League Paper' but the national press had also featured and acclaimed the achievements of this plucky non-league side. But cup success had played havoc with Luton's league form: a 0-0 draw at Telford, and most worryingly a 1-0 defeat at Barrow the previous week. So Luton travel to Premiership Norwich City one week and beat them 1-0, then move on to relegation-threatened Barrow the next, and lose. And the next week Barrow lost 8-1 at Mansfield. Funny game, football!

I was interested to see to what extent the prospect of the 'big game' next Saturday would affect the commitment of the Luton players. They really needed to get something out of this match if they were to keep up with other play-off contenders.

There were two or three hundred Luton fans at the end of the ground reserved for visiting supporters, which was not bad for a very cold evening in February, and which helped

# Chapter 14

create a lively atmosphere. But then Luton are the best-supported club in the Conference (average home gate 6,126; 2,400 ahead of the next best – Grimsby Town). There was certainly no lack of commitment from Luton in the early stages. They looked the more dangerous side and the Dartford goal had a couple of narrow escapes.

Dartford looked well-organised, without being particular inventive, and played with only one striker upfront, which resulted in a crowded midfield and a resultant lack of space. Everyone seemed to be under immediate pressure when they received the ball, leading to a fair number of hasty misplaced passes. It wasn't a particularly inspiring game, by any standards. After Luton's early pressure, Dartford had a spell of domination, without creating very much, following which spells of territorial domination tended to alternate.

Luton had recently signed a central defender called Steve McNulty, who had previously been with Fleetwood Town. I don't know what activities he'd been pursuing over the past couple of months, but training and/or playing football didn't seem to be amongst them. He was noticeably overweight. 'Who ate all the pies'? chanted a group of youngsters standing in front of me. The mother of one of them, who was standing next to me, asked to see my programme to identify him. 'Chunky I'd call him,' she said. So Chunky McNulty he became. We tried to remember previous overweight footballers and came up with Mickey Quinn, the talented but portly striker who played for Coventry City, amongst others. Not that Chunky McNulty's bulk seemed to adversely affect his performance. He was more than a match for Dartford's lone striker.

The game was still goalless at half-time with neither side (after Luton's early flurry) looking likely to break the deadlock. The second half developed a similar rhythm to the first, although Dartford gradually began to dominate in terms of possession. Luton occasionally looked threatening on the break but Dartford's keeper, Marcus Bettinelli, exuded composure and competence in dealing with anything that came his way. I noticed that although (in general) Luton's players were taking the game seriously (after all, they needed to get something out of it, to maintain their challenge for a play-off place) there was one notable exception. I'd seen Arnaud Mendy play for Macclesfield at Nuneaton in September where he'd looked good and scored an impressive goal. He'd signed for Luton in October, and was described in the programme as a combative and creative central midfielder. Well tonight he was neither combative nor creative. He strolled through the game nonchalantly, doing, it seemed to me, as little as possible. Whenever he received the ball, his aim seemed to be to get rid of it as quickly as possible. Nor did he show any inclination to find space for a return pass. He alone played like someone who had next Saturday's cup tie on his mind, and it was no surprise when he was substituted half way through the second half.

With less than 20 minutes left, the game had 0-0 written all over it. But Ryan Hayes, Dartford's lively right-sided attacker had other ideas. Finding himself with the ball near the right side corner flag, he switched the ball from right to left foot, cut in diagonally for a few yards and then unleashed a viscously swerving left foot drive into the top corner of the net. Another top quality goal to add to those by Blinkhorn, Sharp, Donaldson and Barnes-Homer.

With time running out, Luton came out of their collective shell and pushed forward. But none of their renowned strikers was proving effective. Jon Shaw, who hit 28 goals in the Conference for Gateshead in 2011-12, had made little impression, and was replaced by Scott Rendell, who hustled and scurried around a lot to no particular purpose. Andre

Gray looked the sharpest of the three but rarely managed to find space for a telling shot. An equaliser never looked on the cards, and 1-0 was the way it finished, just about what Dartford deserved, but bad news for Luton. Cup glory is all very well (and certainly helpful in financial terms) but their priority must be a return to the Football League, which was beginning to look increasingly unlikely.

On the way back to Dartford station, I had a narrow escape on the A207 when I stupidly misjudged the direction of traffic flow. I narrowly avoided ending up as a mangled heap on the road. Proceeding shakily towards the station, and muttering prayers of thanks to any higher being that might be up there, I noticed a police cordon across the end of a road close to the station, and a phalanx of police cars. Next day I learned that there had been a murder the previous evening close to that very spot, and that a 32 year old man had been arrested. It must have happened whilst I'd been at Princes Park. I would remember my visit to Dartford, not for the unremarkable match I'd witnessed, but for the near-death experience and the proximity to the scene of a recent murder.

Four days later Luton's cup dream was over. They lost 3-0 at home to Millwall, and could concentrate on the Conference, although they had a fair bit of catching up to do. Dartford also lost 3-0, at Grimsby in the first leg of the FA Trophy semi-final, and now looked unlikely to match their appearance in the final of that competition in 1974, which heads the 'Darts Roll of Honour' in the programme. But if, as seems likely, Dartford were to finish in the Conference top ten, that will have been a major achievement for a friendly, unpretentious club with a great little stadium.

# Cathedrals, Imps, and Free Tickets

Lincoln City vs Barrow

Saturday 23rd February 2013

'Conference Season' is by no means the first football book to involve numerous journeys to diverse places over the course of a season. Harry Pearson's 'mazy dribble through North-East football' (The Far Corner, 1994) took him to twenty-five different venues, ranging from St James's Park to Blackworth Miners Welfare Ground, home of West Allotment Celtic.(I gave him a lift to an FA Trophy tie at Blyth Spartans). In 'Playing at Home' (1998), John Aislewood somehow managed to fit in visits to matches at all ninety-two football league clubs.

I'm sure both authors (and many others) must have wondered, at some stage in their perambulations, what on earth induced them to embark on such projects. My moment of truth came as I drove to Lincoln, to watch them play Barrow. It was a bitterly cold February day. You can do almost all the journey by motorway, but to do so adds around 80 miles to the most direct route, which was the option I chose. As I, and a stream of other drivers, crawled up the Woodhead Road, between Manchester and Sheffield, behind a big lorry, at 25 miles per hour, I wondered why I was doing this! My mood deteriorated as the temperature fell to -2 degrees, and one of the forecast snow showers began to hit my windscreen.

But as I came within striking distance of Lincoln, and saw the majestic cathedral perched on a hilltop above the town centre, my mood lifted. Lincoln is one of the two 'showpiece' cities in the Conference, the other being Cambridge. Only Hereford comes close to these two architecturally-renowned heritage sites.

The city of Lincoln first developed in a gap in a long limestone ridge, which runs north to south. Its castle was sensibly built on the ridge itself, overlooking the town from the north. The cathedral later came to be built close to the castle, and the bishop's palace likewise. So one has the unusual phenomenon of a cathedral not in the midst of the town (as in York, Canterbury and Norwich) but spectacularly perched above it, visible from afar long before you see the town itself.

There is an upper town, and a lower town, where the main shopping centre is located. The two are linked by a couple of steep, winding lanes. Although upper Lincoln is the main focus of tourist attention, the town centre below it is also full of interest: narrow alleyways; a scattering of historic buildings; and a nice spread of specialist shops amongst the more familiar high street names and the more modern precincts.

The high street in Lincoln and its environs was as vibrant and bustling as its counterpart in Hereford had been on an equally cold Saturday in January. No need for Mary Portas here!

Nowadays Lincoln is relatively untroubled by the noise and smell of heavy industry. Its current economic base is IT-dominated, with many e-commerce mail-order companies having established themselves around the city, particularly to the south and east. Like most county towns, its biggest employers are concerned with public services: Lincolnshire County Council, Lincoln City Council and the local hospital. Such organisations act as a buffer to the growth of unemployment in times of recession. Towns of similar size which lack such employers tend to be much more vulnerable.

In the nineteenth century, Lincoln was a very different kind of city. With the arrival of the railway, it developed a strong manufacturing base, including heavy engineering, diesel engine locomotives, steam shovels and other types of heavy machinery. It must have been much less attractive in those days with the smoke and noise pollution then associated with such activities. But, fortunately for the tourist trade, all that has now gone. The largest remaining industrial site is Siemens, which manufactures gas turbine engines and employs 1,300 people at a large plant in the suburb of Pelham.

I parked the car in a densely-populated terraced area to the south of the city centre, within walking distance of the ground. It reminded me of Edgeley (in Stockport) and Hindpool (in Barrow), an intact traditional working-class area with corner shops and back alleys. It's good that many of these areas have survived, although some towns and cities have been more ruthless than others in demolishing them and replacing them with new building forms which rarely have the warmth and vitality of the Edgeleys of this world.

Sincil Bank was admired in its mid-1980s format by Simon Inglis in his book 'The Football Grounds of Great Britain'. It was in a process of transition at the time, in the aftermath of the Bradford City fire (1985) when anything deemed as a fire risk (including all wooden structures) was required to be replaced or (less commonly) fireproofed. Inglis notes that even with the recent changes, the ground retained much of its picturesque quality. Would it still be 'picturesque', I wondered, as I approached it 25 years later?

## Chapter 15

I wandered around the ground before deciding where to locate myself. However my problem was solved as I walked past the rear of the Main Stand, where the ticket office is situated. A middle-aged man approached me and asked me if I was intending to buy a ticket. 'Yes,' I replied, guardedly 'Well would you like this one?' he asked, producing a £15 ticket for the main stand (Row P). 'How much do you want for it?' I asked. 'Nothing,' he replied. 'I've a friend who's a season ticket holder and he can't come today. He asked me to pass it on to someone.' Well this was too good a chance to miss. I thanked him and accepted it. 'It looks like it's my lucky day,' I said. 'You wait till you've seen the game,' he responded ominously.

I entered the ground, bought a pie and found my way to my seat. I looked around the ground. Picturesque is not a phrase which came to mind. The Lincolnshire Echo Stand, where I was situated, was big (26 rows of seats) and had been in the process of construction when Simon Inglis last visited Sincil Bank. However, it runs only half the length of the pitch, straddling the half-way line. To the left of it is a tiny covered Family Stand. Opposite is an even larger all-seater affair - the 'Co-op Community Stand' - which was completed in 1995. At both ends are smaller all-seater stands (there are no standing areas anywhere in the stadium, which is a shortcoming as far as I'm concerned). One is called the Stacey West Stand, after the two Lincoln City supporters who died in the Bradford City fire (Lincoln were Bradford's opponents that day). The other – the Bridge McFarlane Stand – has a row of executive boxes running across the back, which seems over-the-top for a struggling Conference side, but no doubt Lincoln City hope to return to their place in the Football League as soon as possible, and don't really see themselves as Conference regulars any more than Luton Town do. In overall terms, Sincil Bank reminded me much more of Wrexham's Racecourse Ground and Kidderminster's Aggborough Stadium than the more picturesque small-scale stadia of Tamworth or Alfreton. These were the premises of a club that had aspirations to greater things; aspirations that were, however, unlikely to be realised this season!

Lincoln City have one of the more impressive previous records of the Football League clubs now in the Conference. They've been around for a long time. Founded in 1884, they played in the League's Division Two between 1892 (the first year it existed) and 1908, then failed to be re-elected, but returned the next year. The same sequence of events was experienced in 1911 and 1912. The League clearly couldn't make up its mind about Lincoln's worthiness to be included.

After the war, Lincoln City became founder members of Division Three (North) where they performed unremarkably between 1921 and 1952, with only two (very) brief spells in Division Two (1932-34; 1948-49). In 1952, however, they were again promoted and this time stayed in Division Two for nine glorious (by their standards) years peaking at eighth in 1956. Since then they have spent most of their time in the basement of the Football League although in 1976, the subsequently much-ridiculed England boss Graham Taylor led them to the Fourth Division title. The club won 32 of its 46 fixtures and lost only four, scoring over 100 goals in the process. At home they won 21, and drew the other two. Taylor later remarked: "Teams were petrified of coming to Sincil Bank."

Lincoln stayed in Division Three for ten years until relegation in 1986, a fate which was repeated the following year, when they became the first club to suffer automatic relegation to the Conference. They came straight back the next season, under the guidance of the eccentric long-ball enthusiast Colin Murphy. During his time at Lincoln, Murphy gained cult status for his notes in the match-day programme. His column demonstrated a level of inventiveness with the English language that marked it out from any other offering in this medium. Lincoln programmes from this era are now collectors' items. Here is one example;

'Of the keys on the ring at the moment, we should be selecting more correctly to unlock opposing mechanisms. However there is not a lock that cannot be unlocked, so we shall continue to endeavour to unlock the lock, but in doing so, we must not get locked out.'

It makes Nicky Low's stream of consciousness contribution to the Alfreton programme sound relatively coherent!

But the most successful manager of recent years was probably Keith Alexander who, in 2002, took over a club that had just gone into administration, and which had lost the cream of its playing staff. Against all the odds he took them to a play-off place in 2002, and then managed to do likewise in each of the next four seasons, twice reaching the final, but never managing to get any further. He then left for Macclesfield Town, where he suffered an untimely death in 2010. Five successive play-off failures is, I discovered, a record, albeit an unenviable one.

In 2011, however, Lincoln were back in the Conference, and have not (yet) looked like getting out of it.

Overall, Lincoln City have spent 102 seasons in the Football League; no team has played so long without ever reaching the top tier. On the basis of this long and chequered history, they are justifiably viewed as one of the biggest of the Conference's sleeping giants, on a par with Wrexham, Stockport County, Grimsby Town and Luton Town. But since descending to the Conference (for a second time) at the end of the 2010-11 season, they have hardly lived up to that status. They finished last season in seventeenth place (one behind Stockport) with safety not assured until relatively late in the campaign. This season, although they looked relatively comfortable for a while, peaking at ninth in November, they had since slumped to eighteenth, only two points clear of the relegation zone. Their last ten league games had yielded a paltry six points. In the circumstances it was perhaps not surprising that their manager David Holdsworth (brother of the more famous Dean) was relieved of his duties during the previous week. The official announcement said that it was by 'mutual agreement', but it didn't look like that to me. There was a column in the programme by one of the directors which included the statement: 'However the recent run of two wins from the last 16 league and cup matches…meant that the Board had no alternative but to part company with him.' One wonders what the basis of the mutual agreement was! 'Look Dave, we're going to sack you anyway, so can you do us a favour and tell the media we're parting by mutual agreement. That way, it'll look better for all of us.'

A growing sense of panic was apparent elsewhere in the director's column: 'We find ourselves as a Club in a perilous position; relegation from this League would have dire consequences, even down to the players becoming part-time.' Well, Dartford and Southport have shown this season that being part-time need not be a fate worse than death. But I suppose that, for a big club like Lincoln (or Stockport), it's bound to be seen that way.

The programme was unimpressive by Conference standards. There were no pen pictures of opposition players, no reviews of previous meetings between the teams, and too high a proportion of space devoted to adverts. Part-time Dartford's programme was much superior.

## Chapter 15

Barrow were the visitors. It would be the first time I'd seen them since the opening day of the season, when they played abysmally against the (almost as bad) AFC Telford United. They were currently in the relegation zone, having performed erratically (to say the least) since Christmas (and indeed before). Recent results included an 8-1 reverse at Mansfield, a 6-1 beating at Luton, and a 5-2 defeat at Southport, which had all contributed to the worst goal difference (by far) in the Conference: -28. But interspersed between these dispiriting defeats were a 1-0 win at home to Luton, a similar success at Gateshead, and only four days previously, a 2-0 victory over mid-table Woking. So all was not yet lost. Indeed nearly half the Conference was still vulnerable to relegation. Only eleven points separated bottom-placed Telford from mid-table Tamworth.

Barrow's leading scorer, Adam Boyes, was unfit, which was not helpful to their chances of a good result, given the paucity of goals from anyone else in the team. But they may have derived some comfort from the recent 'on loan' signing of forty-year old Efe Sodje, who had played for Nigeria in two World Cups, and was currently in Division One Bury's squad. When the teams emerged (to the tune of the Dambusters march – the Dambusters squadron had been based at an airfield near Lincoln), Sodje was instantly recognisable on account of his height and his wide headband. Also in the side were Danny L. Rowe (previously with Stockport County), not to be confused with his colleague Danny M. Rowe (also previously with Stockport County). Danny L. had played in the opening match, to no great effect, but had stood out when he played for Kendal Town (which in all honesty isn't difficult). Danny M. was a more recent acquisition from Stockport.

There were around 50 Barrow fans in one corner of the stand opposite. I was in Row P of the Main Stand, with a great view both of Lincoln Cathedral to the north, and the pattern of play on the field some distance below. It soon became apparent that Barrow had changed their tactics – for the better – since I saw them in August. The lofted upfield punt had been eschewed in favour of a more measured passing game (which will have no doubt come as a relief to ex-Morecambe midfielder Gary Hunter for one). They began to dominate the game, but were frustrated by Lincoln's keeper, Paul Farman, who made an excellent save early on, and followed it with an even better one later in the half.

Lincoln were devoid of inspiration and (in several cases) short on basic skills. It was they who were relying on long speculative upfield punts, which proved as ineffective as they had for Barrow in August. But Barrow were a revelation. They created numerous chances, as a result of imaginative inter-passing movements, particularly down the right side.

Danny L. Rowe was the fulcrum of many of the attacks. Although at times he looked ponderous, he was able to find space and time to create openings for others, or in some cases himself – a rare skill at this level. Efe Sodje coped confidently with anything in the air, using his formidable height to his advantage. Gavin Skelton was a hugely effective attacking full-back on the left, regularly finding space on the overlap. Barrow could, and should, have been two or three goals up by half-time. But they lacked composure in front of goal, and came in at the interval with nothing to show for their superiority.

It was the same story in the second half. Lincoln City were turning out to be the worst Conference side I'd seen all season (run close by Tamworth and by Barrow before their rebirth). The home crowd had a reputation for the intensity of their vocal support, but it was not apparent today. They sounded dispirited (with good reason). Three substitutions were made by Lincoln's caretaker manager, Grant Brown, but none made any difference to his side's performance.

Barrow's build-up continued to be imaginative and penetrative, with numerous chances being created and missed. Paul Furman continued to pull off important saves, and deservedly won the man-of-the-match award at the end of the game (opposition players are routinely excluded from consideration by the match sponsors, otherwise there would have been several Barrow contenders).

I noticed that each of the three substituted Lincoln players went through the motions of applauding the home supporters, as they trotted off the pitch. In no case was the applause returned. It seems that however well or badly you've played, this is what you are now expected to do (unless you are a temperamental Premiership prima donna, in which case you may exclude yourself from the ritual if you don't think the substitution is justified). I remember a few seasons ago how, at the end of a 6-0 thrashing at Carlisle United, the Stockport County players bravely walked to the away fans enclosure to show their appreciation in the usual manner, and were rudely (and appropriately) booed and ridiculed for their incompetence.

As the game neared the end, it looked increasingly unlikely that the excellence of Barrow's performance would be rewarded with the goal (and win) it deserved. My fear (as a neutral) was that Lincoln, in a rare breakaway, might snatch a totally underserved victory. That outcome looked a real possibility when Colin Larkin found himself one-against-one with Barrow keeper Danny Hurst. Fortunately Hurst managed to block the shot.

So 0-0 it finished. But it was a better no-score draw than the early season game between Barrow and Telford. I came away greatly impressed with the transformation in the quality of Barrow's football, and with the hope that they would survive in the Conference (although not at the expense of Stockport). On this performance, they certainly deserved to.

# Braintree, Bocking, and the Future of the World

Braintree Town vs Luton Town

Tuesday 26th February 2013

Braintree was another new location for me. I'd never been there before, and all I knew of it was the slogan which the local council adopted in the early 1990s: 'Braintree Means Business' (presumably the double meaning was intentional).

The early 1990's was a time when many local authorities thought it was a good idea to try to encapsulate the main purpose of their existence in a few well-chosen words. Sadly, they were usually wrong! There was 'Wolverhampton: The Pace Setter' (it certainly wasn't), 'Harrow: A Sensible London Borough' (so don't expect any fireworks there), 'Wandsworth: the Brighter Borough' (in contrast to Lambeth or Southwark, presumably), 'Lancashire: The Place where everyone matters' and 'Hampshire: The County that believes in Partnership'. The last two well demonstrate the dangers of this kind of word-spinning. Is it conceivable that any council would claim the opposite? If not, we're dealing with vacuous 'of course' statements. Would we ever be likely to come across 'Surrey: where only the better-off matter' or 'Derbyshire: the County that couldn't give a shit about partnership'? In my time as a local government consultant, I was sometimes tempted to make suggestions about slogans. 'New Forest: determined to keep out Southampton's overspill' (which would, at least, have been honest). 'Walsall: no-worse than anywhere else', 'Tendring: the place that no-one's ever heard of', and (my favourite) 'Hull City Council: Serves You Right'.

## Chapter 16

It was February, and most of England was shrouded in grey. For the past few days, the weather had been static; cold, cloudy with an easterly wind and occasional snow flurries. As it had been when I travelled to Lincoln, so it was as I made my way to Braintree.

Braintree was one of several clubs in the Conference with a formidable backlog of fixtures to fulfil. Their ground was prone to waterlogging (like Gateshead's but not quite as bad). At least the current spell of settled weather should have given it the chance to dry out. Braintree, Gateshead, Ebbsfleet and Luton all had sixteen games remaining; that's two a week until the end of the season, assuming no further weather problems.

The train journey from London Liverpool Street to Braintree passed through the East End. There was a veritable pick-and-mix of post-World War One public housing designs to be seen: walk-up tenement blocks, deck access maisonettes, high rise blocks of various shapes and colours (including some crescent-shaped examples) and streets of newish terraced housing (a 1970s response to the disrepute into which high rise had fallen; the Ronan Point explosion had happened not far away in Newham). There were a few remaining pockets of traditional yellow-brick East End terraces, familiar from the evocative 'Call the Midwife' books and TV series.

It all looked dreary and inhospitable, the kind of environment from which people would want to escape if they could. And indeed much of southern Essex, including Braintree, did provide an escape route from the densely-populated East End in the post-war period. Witham, which is within Braintree District Council's boundaries, includes a sizeable overspill estate, which catered for less affluent East Enders. Braintree town itself tended to attract those who could afford to buy their own homes.

After calling at Stratford, the train passed the Olympic Games site which looked eerily deserted. Much of it seemed to be in the process of demolition. Despite the government's claims, I find it hard to believe that the Olympics proved a viable economic proposition, and actually generated a profit, rather than costing a hell of a lot, in overall terms.

The approach to Braintree was uninspiring – flat, arable Essex countryside. Shortly before arriving at the town itself, the train stops at Braintree Freeport. Freeport? Braintree is about 50 miles away from the sea, and no river of any significance flows through it or near it. It looked from the train like another Trafford Centre (or Bluewater). Would I encounter another disintegrating town centre in Braintree, as I had in Dartford?

On the contrary, even on a dismal grey day Braintree's centre proved to be attractive. The street pattern was haphazard rather than gridiron, and the central zone traffic-free, apart from the occasional bus. There was a nice traditional town hall ('available for functions') and an imaginatively-designed circular library building. But the most impressive feature was the relatively new shopping precinct. It had been blended in so sensitively to the existing environment that you would hardly recognise it as a separate entity. It was open air, rather than covered, and was built in brick which matched that of the older buildings around it. The buildings were grouped around a new dog-leg street which looked like it could have been part of the previous street pattern (but probably wasn't). It just shows what can be achieved by sensitive architects and planners who don't want to build monuments to their own egos. The town centre certainly didn't look as if it had been badly-harmed by the Freeport development, although later, at the match, I was told that it had been adversely affected.

# Chapter 16

The benign and relaxed feel of the town was not reinforced by the lead stories in the Braintree and Witham Times. On the contrary, Braintree sounded like a place to avoid, with echoes of Nuneaton and Newport. 'Family fury after murderer's wish to be buried next to the daughter he killed', 'I lost my mum, my job and now my home too', 'Benefit cuts could kill me says dad' (a homeless man who can't afford medication), 'Police find young mother dead at flat'. So, all is not sweetness and light in Braintree. But then why would it be? Even Macclesfield, in the heart of opulent North Cheshire, had its share of problem areas, problem families and personal tragedies. At a time of economic depression nowhere is likely to escape such phenomena.

In the nineteenth century Braintree had developed as a thriving agricultural and textile centre. George Courtauld opened a silk mill there in the 1820s and a local textile industry quickly developed. The Courtauld family were greatly influential in Braintree, both as providers of local employment and benefactors; the town hall, the public gardens and the Julian Courtauld hospital were all funded by the family. At one time Braintree must, like Barrow, have felt like a company town. There is now no textile industry left; it declined steadily after the Second World War, and finally disappeared altogether when ICI took over Courtaulds in the 1970s. Now Braintree's main function is as a commuter town for those working in London, although there is some light industry on its outskirts.

Contiguous with Braintree to the north is a separate settlement called Bocking. In his book 'What is Coming: A European Forecast' (1916) the once popular writer (and Fabian socialist) H.G. Wells bizarrely entitled the fourth chapter 'Braintree, Bocking and the Future of the World'. Fame at last for these two unremarkable Essex towns? Well not really. H.G Wells was using differences between

Braintree and Bocking, divided (as he pointed out) by a single road, to explain the difficulties he expected in establishing world peace through a world state.

> 'The curious enquirer….will find a Bocking water main supplying the houses on the north side, and a Braintree water main supplying the houses on the south. I rather suspect that the drains are also in duplicate. The total population is probably little more than 13,000… but for that there are two water suppliers, two sets of schools, two administrations. To the passing observer the rurality of the Bocking side is indistinguishable from the urbanity of the Braintree side; it is just a little muddier.'

Not sure that I'm happy with where the author's argument is leading here. It sounds like the advocacy of a move to big local authorities, where all services are provided across a large area, but where the distinctiveness of the Braintrees and Bockings of this world are disregarded. Sefton and Tameside here we come! Well, at least Wells would be pleased to see that Braintree and Bocking are now united as a single entity on the road signs as you enter the town, and indeed that both places are now administered by a council which covers a wider area, including the town of Witham, eight miles to the east. But it's still called Braintree District Council, and as far as I'm concerned, that's as far as it should go, whatever the detrimental impact on world peace and world government! Local identity matters, and local councils need to correspond to real places.

I walked to the Braintree ground along streets of dreary inter-war semis. The ground is now known as the Amlin

# Chapter 16

Stadium, (Amlin are a local insurance company who have sponsored some renovation of it), but most people still know it by its traditional name – Cressing Road. It's a modest little ground with a capacity of just over 4,000 (so they'd better not win promotion just yet). There's a seated area on one side of the pitch, and a covered terrace facing it. The open end reserved for visiting supporters is known as the 'Quag End', reflecting the tendency of the whole ground to turn into a quagmire in wet weather. I stood at the opposite end (also open to the elements) close to, but not amongst, a group of around eighty noisy home supporters.

The programme which cost a mere £2 – the cheapest I've encountered so far – was very informative. There were columns from the manager ('The Gaffer gives it to you straight'), the captain ('Proud to wear the skipper's armband'), and a lot of interesting comment on the visitors (Arsenal to Alfreton: The Highs and Lows of Luton Town). The quality of programmes on my travels has varied. It has not always been the bigger clubs who have had the better programmes. Tamworth's and Dartford's, as well as Braintree's have been up with the best, although those of Hyde and Alfreton remained redolent of the Blue Square Bet North, from which both clubs had only recently emerged. Of the bigger clubs, Lincoln's was the most disappointing; no mention at all of their opponent (Barrow). Programmes have been a crucial resource in this project. They may seem overpriced (typically £3 for 40 or so A3 pages, many of them featuring adverts for worthy local enterprises) but they have been full of invaluable background information, which is why I went to such lengths to secure one at half-time at Hereford. Especially revealing have been the manager's columns, particularly when the team has been struggling. There's a good deal of humour too, not all of it intentional! In the Barrow programme (vs AFC Telford United, 11 August 2013) Dave Bayliss, Barrow's manager, discussed the pre-season 'bonding session' in the Lake District, enthusing about its benefits. 'But 'what happens in boot camp stays in boot camp' as they say,' he comments '…however we could well have done without Matt Flynn picking up a jaw fracture.' Some bonding session!

I'd previously seen Braintree in January at Tamworth, where they'd comfortably beaten a lacklustre home side 4-1, without themselves looking particularly impressive. They are one of the 'little clubs' in the Conference with a small ground and attendances to match. They have only recently emerged as a force in non-league football.

Seven seasons ago they were playing in the Isthmian League, the third level of the pyramid, before grafting their way up to the Conference South. Indeed they had worked their way up from the sixth level (Isthmian League Division Three) where they found themselves in 1996, having tried and failed to gain a sideways move from a higher league, where their travelling costs had proved prohibitive. After a couple of near misses in the play-offs, they won the Conference South and promotion to the Conference itself in 2011.

Last season they performed much better than expected, finishing a respectable twelfth. This season, their form had been all over the place. Impressive wins (for example 3-2 at Luton) alternated with unexpected defeats (for example 2-3 at home to Barrow). They currently stood sixteenth in the Conference, not yet out of the danger zone, but better-placed than several of their fellow-strugglers, if only because they had played fewer games.

# Chapter 16

Luton Town – many people's early season tip for automatic promotion – looked like they'd blown it. Their slump in form since January had seen them drop from fifth on January 13th to eighth on February 23rd, when they lost a crucial home game to fellow play-off contenders Mansfield Town 3-2. They'd amassed a mere three points from the previous six games. Their decline in the Conference coincided with their exploits in the FA Cup, where they reached the Fifth Round before succumbing to Millwall the previous weekend.

Added to their current struggles on the field, their manager, Paul Buckle, had resigned the previous week for 'personal' reasons. This may have had something to do with the move of his partner, TV presenter Rebecca Lowe, to the USA in the summer ('Buckle in turmoil' as the Non-League Paper put it). In reality he would have been unlikely to survive as manager if Luton did not make the play-offs.

His replacement, announced earlier in the week, was John Still, manager of Dagenham and Redbridge. He had presided over their promotion from the Conference to Division Two in 2007, and (briefly) to Division One in 2010. His annual salary at Luton was reported to be £200,000, which must be three or four times as much as some of his Conference counterparts, and which was presumably a major factor in his decision to move out of League football to the Conference. He had not yet formally taken charge, but would be watching from the stand tonight.

I'd seen Luton play at Dartford the previous week. Tonight's game against a well-organised, muscular, but not particularly inventive Braintree side (on the evidence of their game at Tamworth) was very much the 'last chance saloon' for the visitors. Anything other than a win, and even the play-offs would become an increasingly forlorn hope.

## Braintree, Bocking, and the Future of the World

As so often with Conference games I've seen, the first twenty minutes or so were taken up with some rather cautious sparring, as though each team were sounding out their opponents, before finalising their game plan. Braintree had the majority of the possession without creating any clear-cut opportunities, whilst Luton relied on long high speculative balls out of defence for their three strikers to chase, with a similar lack of positive outcome. The first incident of note took place on 22 minutes when Braintree's Matt Paine received a straight red card for what turned out to be a high challenge/violent conduct (I was unsighted). The Braintree fans around me felt it was a harsh decision ('most refs would have given a yellow'). The reaction of Braintree's manager was to withdraw Luke Daley, who had scored twice in the previous game against Grimsby and replace him with a defender, Nicky Simons. The response turned out to be a tad premature. After a further 13 minutes, in which Luton had shown little sign of capitalising on their numerical superiority, their midfielder Wayne Thomas was sent off, for what appeared to be a head-butt on Braintree's Sean Marks (who certainly made the most of it). This decision too seemed harsh, even to the partisan Braintree fans (it could have been more of a clash of heads than a head butt). Maybe the referee thought he had over reacted with the first sending-off and wanted to show he was even-handed? Whatever his reasoning (or lack of it) it certainly enhanced the prospects of a more even game. 0-0 in terms of goals; 1-1 in terms of dismissals.

The midfield battle continued, with little in the way of goal opportunities, until three minutes before half-time, when Braintree's Dan Holman created space near the right corner to put over a low cross, which Sean Marks neatly back-heeled into the net from close range.

## Chapter 16

At half-time I chatted with the Braintree supporters next to me. 'Why are Braintree known as 'The Iron?' I asked. 'Haven't a clue,' was the first response. But someone alongside did know. Apparently there used to be a galvanised-iron manufactory in Braintree, long since closed down, but in operation at the time Braintree Town was formed.

The fans were realistic about the limits of the club's ambitions – 'to stay in the Conference is the best we can hope for', but confident of the current team's ability to do so. Being a part-time club does have its advantages. Sean Marks, Braintree's leading scorer, had apparently been approached by other more prestigious Conference teams, but was happy to hold onto his job in Braintree and continue to play on a part-time basis.

Early in the second half, a well-worked exchange of passes on the right between Dan Holman and Sean Marks resulted in a lofted cross from the former, to the far post, where Steve Davis evaded his marker and guided a header neatly into the corner of the net. It was no more than Braintree deserved. Luton Town were singularly short of creative ideas. The only defender who appeared prepared to play the ball to the feet of his forwards was Chunky McKinlay (renamed 'The Tank' by the Braintree fans I'd been talking to). His fellow-defenders continued to loft long balls into spaces where their strikers might have been able to latch on to them, but invariably couldn't (or didn't). It's hard to understand why an ambitious side like Luton would adopt these tactics. All the more impressive Conference teams I'd seen this season have kept the ball on the ground and built up moves from the back.

After the Davis goal, Braintree sat back and let Luton come at them. They coped confidently with a long spell of Luton pressure, which led to very little in the way of scoring opportunities. Braintree's commitment was palpable; they were the first to any loose ball, well-organised at the back, and invariably had the ability to time their tackles to perfection (Dean Wells was particularly impressive in this respect). Luton never looked likely to turn the game around and, as they trudged disconsolately from the pitch, must have realised that their chances of making the play-offs had all but disappeared. They were now stranded in the safe upper-middle region of the Conference table.

Braintree Town now look likely to survive, and I hoped they would. Like Dartford and Alfreton Town, they're an example of an unfashionable team of part-timers, punching above their weight (Grimsby Town and Luton Town had both been beaten in consecutive weeks). Their average home gate is only 624 (the lowest in the Conference) but there were 1003 there tonight, courtesy of a contingent of around 200 Luton fans. The home supporters were delighted with what they saw; their Luton counterparts most unhappy (and increasingly verbally so).

The next morning I walked through Freeport on the way to its very own station. It turned out to be a 'designer outlet village', a conglomeration of large discount stores selling surplus stock at bargain prices, plus a big cinema and a couple of uninspiring pubs. At 8.30 a.m. it was totally deserted. Give me Braintree's traditional town centre any day!

# 26<sup>th</sup> February 2013 – League Table

| | Team | P | W | D | L | F | A | GD | Pt |
|---|---|---|---|---|---|---|---|---|---|
| 1 | Wrexham | 33 | 18 | 10 | 5 | 61 | 31 | 30 | 64 |
| 2 | Kidderminster Harriers | 34 | 18 | 8 | 8 | 52 | 27 | 25 | 62 |
| 3 | Grimsby Town | 32 | 17 | 10 | 5 | 53 | 24 | 29 | 61 |
| 4 | Mansfield Town | 32 | 18 | 5 | 9 | 63 | 43 | 20 | 59 |
| 5 | Newport County AFC | 31 | 18 | 5 | 8 | 66 | 47 | 19 | 59 |
| 6 | Forest Green Rovers | 34 | 16 | 8 | 10 | 53 | 35 | 18 | 56 |
| 7 | Hereford United | 32 | 13 | 9 | 10 | 50 | 47 | 3 | 48 |
| 8 | Macclesfield Town | 33 | 13 | 9 | 11 | 49 | 49 | 0 | 48 |
| 9 | Woking | 32 | 15 | 2 | 15 | 53 | 60 | -7 | 47 |
| 10 | Luton Town | 31 | 13 | 6 | 12 | 51 | 46 | 5 | 45 |
| 11 | Cambridge United | 34 | 12 | 9 | 13 | 58 | 58 | 0 | 45 |
| 12 | Dartford | 31 | 13 | 5 | 13 | 48 | 48 | 0 | 44 |
| 13 | Tamworth | 34 | 12 | 7 | 15 | 43 | 47 | -4 | 43 |
| 14 | Southport | 32 | 11 | 9 | 12 | 55 | 59 | -4 | 42 |
| 15 | Braintree Town | 31 | 12 | 5 | 14 | 42 | 53 | -11 | 41 |
| 16 | Alfreton Town | 34 | 10 | 10 | 14 | 47 | 60 | -13 | 40 |
| 17 | Stockport County | 33 | 10 | 8 | 15 | 45 | 55 | -10 | 38 |
| 18 | Hyde FC | 34 | 10 | 6 | 18 | 47 | 57 | -10 | 36 |
| 18 | Lincoln City | 33 | 9 | 9 | 15 | 47 | 57 | -10 | 36 |
| 20 | Gateshead | 30 | 8 | 10 | 12 | 35 | 39 | -4 | 34 |
| 21 | Nuneaton Town | 33 | 8 | 10 | 15 | 40 | 56 | -16 | 34 |
| 22 | Barrow | 33 | 8 | 9 | 16 | 36 | 65 | -29 | 33 |
| 23 | Ebbsfleet United | 31 | 7 | 10 | 14 | 41 | 60 | -19 | 31 |
| 24 | AFC Telford United | 35 | 5 | 15 | 15 | 44 | 56 | -12 | 30 |

# Cardinals, Robots, and a Post-Match Fracas

Woking vs Mansfield Town

Tuesday 6th March 2013

Woking was another of my 'never-been-there-before' Conference venues. The Portsmouth-bound train I boarded at Waterloo arrived in Woking a mere 25 minutes after departure. I left the station to find myself beneath an impressive large-scale station canopy, which I discovered later was built in 2007 as part of the local council's commitment to greener energy technologies. Apparently it is equipped with photovoltaic cells to collect sunlight and convert it into energy.

Woking is a town which grew with the coming of the railway. One's superficial impression, when passing through it by train, is one of opulence. The houses are large, often detached and situated in leafy environments. The industrial developments are light, clean and set in spacious surroundings. However, this impression was challenged when I wandered from the station into Chertsey Road, which I took to be part of the town centre. I passed in quick succession the 'Lickety Split Café' (closed) the RSVP Bar (closed) and the Rat and Parrot public house (also closed). There was a Wetherspoons with a group of smokers outside who looked as though they had time on their hands (it was 4.00 pm on a Wednesday). There was also, however, an inviting establishment called 'Creams' selling 'Italian Gelati and Desserts'. But other empty shops and the presence of a McDonalds outlet and (yet another) Nails establishment all contributed to a sense of decay rather than opulence. Could this be the real Woking?

## Chapter 17

It wasn't of course. The real heart of the town was not far away – a glossy new covered precinct (The Peacock Centre) linked to a slightly older example of the genre (The Wolsey Centre) grouped around a recently-constructed Town Square, which together helped explain the problems of the older shopping area I'd just visited. Chertsey Road had become the residuum for whatever couldn't afford or didn't fit in with the Peacock/Wolsey Centres, and (in several cases) had then found they couldn't survive there either.

Close to the Peacock Centre was a large metal structure which looked like a robot, and did indeed turn out to be one. 'What is a robot doing in Woking?' you may ask. Well it's because the English father of science fiction – H.G. Wells – used to live in Woking, and actually wrote one of his best-known books – 'The War of the Worlds' – whilst in residence there. Indeed the first part of the book, which deals with a Martian invasion, is set on nearby Horsell Common. By a strange twist, last week I was in Braintree, which H. G. Wells had used to raise the momentous issue of 'Braintree, Bocking and the Future of the World' and now here I was in Woking, the scene of a fictional inter-global war penned by the same author.

Approaching Woking on the train, I had noticed a mosque, set in a green suburban location. I later discovered that it was the first mosque ever to be erected in Britain (in 1890), and had resulted over the years in the growth of a significant Muslim population (mainly Pakistani) in Woking, which becomes evident when you wander around. Woking is also home to McLaren, the racing car manufacturers, to which is now attached a prestigious research and development centre. This, and other recent nice clean hi-tech developments, has changed the status of Woking from a commuter town for London, to one where there is now a good deal of inward commuting (though, as I found out the next morning, the commuter trains to Waterloo are still packed).

Woking Council is (unsurprisingly) Conservative-controlled, although for many years there was a large group of non-politically-aligned ratepayers with whom the affiliated Tories were obliged to work. But the ratepayers have disappeared over time, and the Liberal Democrats have built up a presence on the council more recently. The Woking News and Mail revealed a good deal of tension between the two parties. The co-operation which exists in the Conservative/Lib Dem coalition at Westminster doesn't appear to have been replicated in Woking. 'Angry Lib Dems snap back at Tories' was one headline. 'Living Wage row ends in defeat for Lib Dems' was another. At a budget meeting, 'disgruntled members of the Lib Dem party asked for 'rubber stamps to be made up' as temperatures plunged in the civic offices'(presumably referring to their perception of the way the Tories regarded the role of council meetings)'. Personally, I see such discord as healthy; one of the main jobs of an opposition is to oppose, isn't it?

What the council does deserve credit for is its energy policy. They've really gone to town in implementing a greener, sustainable approach which few other councils can match. There are several 'combined heat and power stations' which provide district heating and electricity (the 'Woking sustainable community energy system'). Should the public power grid fail, central Woking would continue to have an energy supply. It all goes to show how innovative local councils – even small ones like Woking – can be.

Woking has a rock music connection to match that of Dartford's link with the Rolling Stones. Paul Weller and two other members of The Jam were born and brought up here. According to Paul, his teenage experiences in Woking provided the inspiration for the band's 1982 chart-topping hit 'A Town called Malice'. One senses that Paul couldn't wait to get out of the place: 'struggle after struggle, year after year; the atmosphere's a fine blend of ice, I'm almost stone dead in a town called Malice.' And there's a bizarre reference to 'a hundred lonely housewives clutch empty milk bottles to their hearts'. Actually I thought Woking was one of the more impressive towns I'd visited; but then I wasn't raised there. Paul Weller was equally scathing about Milton Keynes (in the Style Council's 'Come to Milton Keynes') although he later admitted that he'd never actually been there!

It was time to check in at my overnight hotel, a task I approached with some trepidation. The Inn on the Broadway had appeared ideal for my needs: centrally-positioned, close to the station and 20 minutes' walk from Woking FC's ground. The name had an encouraging ring. I envisaged an old-fashioned public house, with a roaring log fire in the bar, a good range of reasonably-priced food and spacious comfortable bedrooms. But, on the day of my departure to Woking, I thought I'd better have a quick look at some TripAdvisor reviews. They were not at all encouraging. It was apparent that the place's title was a misnomer. It wasn't an inn at all. It was located above a Chinese takeaway, next door to a night club, and directly opposite the railway station. Visitors complained of a lack of heating, shower doors hanging off, bathroom floors flooding with water when the toilet was flushed, and the level of noise from the night club. One particularly irate reviewer claimed "We have stayed in a lot of B and Bs; this is by far the worst. Don't go there." The moral of the story, I guess, is to 'always check TripAdvisor before booking overnight accommodation'.

I found the Chinese takeaway, noted with some relief that the night club had ceased operations, and was confronted with a head-high (locked) iron gate at the entrance to the B&B, behind which was a closed door and an intercom. A warm welcome awaits you at the 'Inn on the Broadway! (Could I get them under the Trades Description Act?)

When I finally managed to rouse someone to let me in, I was escorted to my room by an Italian lady, handed a bunch of keys and left to get on with it. Fortunately the room seemed clean enough, the toilet flushed without flooding the bathroom, and the bed was firm.

As I walked to Woking's ground from the town centre, what struck me was the lack of terraced housing in Woking, at least on the route south. As soon as you get past the office blocks and the shops, you're into an upmarket residential area, full of large houses and blocks of superior flats. These continue all the way to the Westfield Stadium, providing an untypically middle-class setting for a football ground (rather like Southport's Haig Avenue).

The ground itself is a strange mixture. There's an impressive sizeable new stand (the Bellway Homes Stand) at one end of the ground, which rather dwarfs the rest of the stadium. This comprises of a covered terrace behind the other goal (which is where the home supporters gather), an uncovered shallow side terrace (where many of the Mansfield supporters were to be found), opposite which were two adjacent small and picturesque old stands, from one of which the teams duly emerged. There was a bar (The Cardinals) with open access (unless you were an away supporter). The programme was of high quality –full of relevant information, well-written and well-illustrated. There was an upbeat ambience about the contents; Woking FC clearly felt they were doing pretty well back in the Conference, after a period one level below.

## Chapter 17

The Westfield Stadium took my tally of Conference grounds visited to sixteen, two-thirds of the total. What a diverse and fascinating mixture they had proved to be. Three basic categories could be identified. First there were the well-established (but sometimes recently-modified) stadia of the former League clubs (Lincoln, Stockport, Wrexham), a group which also included Kidderminster's impressive Aggborough ground, although not Macclesfield's Moss Rose venue, which looked like it had always had one foot in the Conference (despite the team's fourteen year spell in the Football League). Second, there were the little grounds of the small-town clubs, some newly-constructed (Dartford, Nuneaton), some long-established (Tamworth, Braintree), and all of them well below the capacity required for League status. Third, there was an intermediate group, a varied collection including Barrow's throwback to the 1950s, Hereford's mixture of old-style terracing and cramped cantilever stands, Gateshead's athletics stadium doubling (unconvincingly) as a football venue, and Newport's rugby ground doubling (rather more effectively) in this capacity. And now Woking, where I particularly appreciated the two quaint little stands, which looked like they'd been there since the early twentieth century (and probably had).

Woking have a distinguished history in the Conference. They came up as Isthmian League champions in 1992, and stayed there until 2008, finishing as runners-up in 1995 and 1997. During their golden years, they won the FA Trophy three times (1994, 1995, 1997) the only club to have done so. Then came a decline with four years in the Conference South, before they were promoted as champions last May.

Woking had enjoyed a good season so far, and were currently placed tenth, the highest of the part-time Conference clubs. They don't draw a lot of games (only 3 out of 33 so far this season) but have won as many (15) as they have lost, including a double over Stockport County. They are a young side with a pair of prolific strikers, Betsy and Bubb (sounds like a third-rate comedy act of the 1950's).

The club is known as the Cardinals (or 'Cards' for short, as I later discovered), not because of any connection Woking has with the Vatican (it doesn't), but simply because they play in 'cardinal red'. Their manager, Garry Hill, has an impressive managerial pedigree at this level. He took Dagenham and Redbridge into the Football League in 2003, and then up to Division One the following season. He was appointed at Woking in 2011, took them to the Conference South play-offs in his first season, and then back to their customary level in 2012-13.

The visitors, Mansfield Town are known as the 'Stags' (a reference to nearby Sherwood Forest). They were currently well-established in the top five, having enjoyed a formidable run of success since the start of the year (nine wins in eleven games). Not only did a play-off place look highly likely (Forest Green Rovers appeared to be out of the running, having lost at home to Grimsby Town the previous evening) but Mansfield were well-placed to go up as champions (currently six points behind the leaders Wrexham, but with two games in hand).

Mansfield started impressively, dominating the early stages of the match with a mixture of long probing balls out of defence and more elaborate inter-passing movements. Then Woking had a spell of dominance, although it resulted in few clear-cut chances. They found it hard to make an impression on a well-organised and uncompromising Mansfield defence. The full-backs - Adam Newton and Mike Gester - both overlapped to good effect, but the final ball (from them and others) always seemed to elude the Woking strike force. Then Mansfield had another spell of

# Chapter 17

domination, which resulted in a controversial goal. Louis Briscoe sent in a high cross from the right which evaded everyone, and ended up in the net. However the linesman immediately raised his flag, apparently because another Mansfield player was offside. Derisory cheers (of relief) ensued from the Woking fans near where I was standing. But the referee decided he wanted to consult the linesman, and after a long discussion awarded the goal.

This outcome did not endear the referee to the Woking fans, who had already become critical of his tendency to give nothing (as they saw it) to their team. One particular loudmouth standing behind me unleashed a barrage of invective thereafter. The referee was a cheat, a disgrace, a stinker, a wanker, and a knobhead (amongst other choice epithets). He also wanted to know 'Are you a Turk?' a reference to the controversial sending-off of Manchester United's Nani in the European Champions League game against Real Madrid the previous evening by a Turkish referee (though with a name like Lee Swabey, it seemed unlikely). This noisy fellow was one of those characters who can't keep his mouth shut. He had to be shouting something. When the Mansfield keeper was injured and required extended attention, but then seemed to recover pretty quickly, he came up with 'It's a miracle', not just once but every time the keeper kicked the ball. I decided either he or I had to move at half-time. Conveniently he did.

A visit to the refreshment bar at half-time resulted in the discovery that there was no Bovril. No Bovril! It should be routinely available at football grounds, and usually is. At Carlisle, they ask you if you want pepper sprinkling into it.

Mansfield started the second half as dominant as they had been in the first, and a header from a defender smacked against the post. But Woking came back into the game, and in the 67th minute won a penalty, which Bradley Bubb duly converted, although Mansfield's Alan Marriott got a hand to it. The game was nicely-poised. But Mansfield continued to look more threatening, and ten minutes later defender Luke Jones found the net with a decisive header from a right-wing cross. The game then became increasingly bad-tempered, with yellow cards dished out to a succession of Mansfield players for late tackles and body checks. But their defence never looked like conceding a goal from open play, and 2-1 was how it ended. Mansfield were now three points behind Wrexham, with a game in hand.

You could see why Mansfield had reached this position. They were not a particularly attractive side, as far as the quality of their football was concerned, but defensively they were excellent, and on this, as on other recent occasions, they'd done just about enough to win. They had not been scoring many goals (apart from an 8-1 bonanza against Barrow in early February); and recent 1-0 wins against lowly-placed Hyde, Lincoln and Telford illustrated this. But they were also conceding very few (10 in the last 11 games). I would be surprised if they were not still in contention for the title in the final week or two of the season.

Meanwhile Woking, already safe, would no doubt end up with a sense of quiet satisfaction at what they'd achieved.

I survived my night at the 'Inn on the Broadway'. Train sounds ceased around 11.00 pm, and I managed around six hours of sleep, before being woken at 6.00 am by a medley of train noise, bus noise, and people-walking-along-the-uncarpeted-passage-outside-my-room noise. I don't recommend the Inn on the Broadway for anyone who's contemplating a lie-in.

When I arrived back in Kendal, and checked the match report, I was amazed to read that there had been an 'incident' after the match, whilst I was walking back to the town centre. Apparently someone had thrown a brick through the Mansfield Town dressing room, striking goalkeeper Alan Marriott on the head and showering glass everywhere. In turn, the manager, Paul Cox, was spat at (through the hole in the window, presumably). The entire team (and manager) then raced back up the tunnel and round to the back of the stand to confront those involved and there was a 'fracas', before Kingfield security staff intervened to restore order. The perpetrator of the crime was identified – a season ticket holder who was 'known to the club'. He has had his season ticket removed, and been told he is no longer welcome at the ground (what they'll do if he does show up wasn't made clear). Well, who would have thought it; violence at Woking of all places! I did wonder whether the person involved was the loudmouth who was standing behind me during the first half.

# Management by Website; the Club with 27,000 Owners

Ebbsfleet United vs Southport

Saturday March 16<sup>th</sup> 2013

Ebbsfleet United is one of only two Conference teams which doesn't feature, in their title, the names of the towns in which they are based (Forest Green Rovers is the other).

Ebbsfleet does exist, after a fashion. It's the middle-of-nowhere railway station where Eurostar trains stop. But the real towns with which Ebbsfleet United is associated are Gravesend and Northfleet, which is what the team was called in 1960, when Gravesend United and Northfleet United amalgamated, and which remained the club's name until 2008 when, as we'll see later, all sorts of the interesting developments took place.

This was the third and last of my visits to Conference venues on the fringes of south London. At Dartford, I'd passed the scene of a murder, committed only an hour or so before. At Woking I'd narrowly missed witnessing a brick thrown through the window of the visitors' dressing room, and an ensuing fracas. So it was with some trepidation that I stepped off the bus. What would Gravesend (and Northfleet) have in store? An anti-bedroom-tax riot?

I noticed Gravesend had an 'historic quarter' and a Tourist Information Office. The town clearly felt it had something to attract visitors, which can't be easy with a name like Gravesend. First prize 'a week in Gravesend', second prize two weeks….'

The origin of the name is disputed. According to the Tourist Office literature, it does not refer to the limit

## Chapter 18

reached by the Great Plague of 1665, nor does it indicate the point at which burials were considered unnecessary, and corpses were simply thrown into the Thames instead (in which case it's hard to see why that wouldn't have been equally feasible at Dartford, 8 miles upriver). The official line is much more boring (but probably true). The town was recorded as Gravesham in the Doomsday Book, which apparently could mean 'the place at the end of the grove', which later morphed into Gravesend.

Possibly Gravesend's best selling point is that it can get very hot there. It has a proud (recent) history of temperature records. In August 2003 it recorded a temperature of 38.1 Celsius (100.6 Fahrenheit) one of the highest recorded in Britain since records began. In October 2011 it reached 29.9C, the highest October temperature ever recorded in Britain. So perhaps the slogan should be 'Come to Gravesend – the hot spot of Britain – and sizzle'.

I wondered whether Gravesend's town centre would have been as equally devastated as Dartford's by the Bluewater Centre, which is only five miles away (with buses every 15 minutes) but that didn't appear to be the case. The centre was lively and boasted a range of familiar outlets (e.g. Debenhams), none of which had survived (or perhaps ever existed) in Dartford. There were a couple of precincts, one looking well past its sell-by date, but both unobtrusively tucked in behind the facades of the main street. My eye was caught by 'Lisa's Nails' and then by a further four similar establishments in quick succession. It made me wonder… what is behind the boom in nail establishments? There must be a limited number of things you do with them, apart from cutting, varnishing or artificially extending them! Still, in their absence, Gravesend would probably have had a further scattering of empty shops.

The 'historic quarter' was pleasant enough: narrow streets, old buildings, specialist shops. Its main thoroughfare – Harmer Street – ended up at the Royal Terrace Pier, which sounds impressive, but wasn't (despite recent restoration). The two empty pubs either side of the small square fronting the Pier didn't help create the right ambience. There is a passenger ferry which operates from the nearby Town Pier, between Gravesend and Tilbury (and vice versa) although it's not immediately apparent what the attractions of this journey might be. I tried to get a glimpse of the Thames, and just about managed to do so, by standing on tiptoe behind a high, sturdy and unwelcoming wall which had 'keep away' written all over it (metaphorically, of course). The Thames looked grey and uninviting but then so did everything else in the vicinity.

One of Gravesend's most famous historic figures is Charles Dickens (who lived in Higham, a nearby village, for the last fourteen years of his life). The tourist leaflet was full of suggestions that many of the familiar locations of Great Expectations were based on local landmarks. For example 'as one enters Chalk from Gravesend, the recently renovated forge along Lower Higham Road was probably the model for Joe Gargery's forge'. Along the shore at Denton is the 'Ship and Lobster', which 'is thought to be the place that appears in Great Expectations as 'The Ship'. But of course they may not have been. Still, all credit to the Tourist Office for trying.

The other notable historic figure is much more surprising. Pocahontas (everyone knows who she is, so I don't need to elaborate) is buried in the churchyard of St George's Church. Apparently she arrived in Gravesend in 1617, hoping to set sail for Virginia (after a year in England) but became seriously ill just offshore, and was hurriedly returned to land where she spent her last few hours before dying of the plague (aged 21). There's a nice statue of her in the Churchyard. But I do wonder whether the words 'probably' or 'it is thought that' should perhaps feature more prominently on the tourist literature. No-one's ever discovered her skeleton!

The Gravesend version of the Kent Messenger revealed plans for the 'world's biggest airport' on Hoo Peninsula, ten miles downriver of Gravesend. This was not some madcap scheme thought up by some local nutter with delusions of grandeur, but rather the brainchild of Lord Foster, the visionary architect. Part of the plan would be to extend Crossrail to Gravesend and then on to the airport, which is 'something the town would benefit from'. Only £1 billion of public money would apparently be needed. So that's all right then! Whatever the outcome of this project, one does sense that Gravesend enjoys certain strategic advantages, which augur well for the town's economic future.

I decided to walk the mile and a half to Ebbsfleet United's ground (via Northfleet) to familiarise myself with both of the settlements associated with the club. It was not a pleasant walk. A bitter north-westerly blew full into my face. It was still raining. On my right, on what used to be marshes, adjacent to the river, were a range of cavernous depots and storage places. A fair amount of construction work was in progress. It all looked pretty bleak, but was no doubt contributing to Gravesend's economic resilience and employment levels. There were a couple of roads leading down to the river where, for the first hundred yards or so, you could have imagined you were in Belgravia; elegant spacious terraced houses with porticos. But not for very long. The size and quality of the housing deteriorated as you went downhill.

Northfleet turned out to be much smaller than Gravesend and was unremarkable apart from a grandiose stucco-finished building that looked like it had once been a luxury hotel (in Northfleet?). It now appeared to be a nightclub.

The Stonebridge Road ground had a certain charm about it, but looked like it was in need of a makeover. The first thing that struck me was the presence across the pitch of electricity cables, slung between two pylons, one located behind the open terrace at the far end of the pitch, and the other behind the covered terrace at the side. You don't see that very often! Fortunately they were at a height which was out of range of the most lofted of clearances.

The covered terrace announced itself (in big letters) as the LIAM DAISH stand. Liam Daish is the current manager of Ebbsfleet, and has been since 2006, which makes him the longest-serving manager in the Conference (no Wenger or Ferguson equivalents at this level!). One hopes that when he leaves (or is required to depart) it will be on terms good enough to justify retaining the stand's title. Otherwise they'll just have to paint over the lettering and call it something else! Opposite the Liam Daish stand is the main stand (from which the teams, in due course, emerged). To gain access you have to pay an extra £2 (£1 for senior citizens) to a lady seated by a table at its entrance (you don't get that in the Premiership either). There were also seats in the covered terrace facing the open end which is where I decided to sit (behind which was an unused portion of terracing; closed for 'safety reasons').

Gravesend and Northfleet played in the Southern League for much of the period between their formation (1960) and the inauguration, in 1979, of the Alliance (later the Conference), of which they were founder members. They were relegated to the Conference South in 1982, moved to the Isthmian League in 1997, and were promoted back to the Conference in 2002, where they remained until 2010. Relegation in 2010 was followed by immediate promotion back (via the play-offs) in 2011. So Ebbsfleet (re-named in 2008) just about merit a classification as 'Conference stalwarts'.

But the club is unique amongst current Conference teams as a result of what happened in 2008, a momentous year for Gravesend and Northfleet. In November 2007, it was announced that the website My Football Club had agreed a deal, in principle, to take over the club (having rejected other alternatives, including Stafford Rangers). Around 27,000 website members each paid £35 to provide a takeover fund of over £700,000. All would own an equal share in the club, but would receive neither profits nor dividends. Members were to have a vote on transfers, player selection and all major decisions. The manager Liam Daish (appointed in 2006) would be retained, but redesignated as Head Coach.

In January 2008, My Football Club members were given the chance to vote on whether to proceed with the takeover. An overwhelming 90% said yes. And so a unique experiment was initiated. I remember the biggest talking point at the time was how the involvement of 27,000 members in team selection would actually work. Liam Daish, for one, was worried. 'It's not just about picking the side from the front of a laptop,' he said. 'You are dealing with human beings. Ask any manager, he runs through everything 100 times before he picks a side. I think the fans realise that.'

In fact My Football Club members never did select the team. Liam Daish needn't have worried. It would have been unworkable. Some of them expressed views and preferences, but the manager continued to select the eleven players and substitutes who turned out for each match.

After one year of ownership, a majority of members failed to renew their membership. Numbers dropped from 32,000 at the time of the takeover, to 9,000 a year later, and then to 3,500 by September 2010. I was told by one of the volunteers, working in the club shop, that membership was now down to below 1,000. 'And you won't see many of them out there today,' he added. The impression I received from him was that My Football Club had run out of steam, and although in theory it has a 75% holding in the club, in reality its involvement was currently confined to choosing playing kits or raising money. My Football Club was not really a vehicle for a takeover by genuine supporters. Most of the members had never seen their club play and were not interested in doing so. It was the website-based ownership vision which attracted them.

Oh, and in 2008 Gravesend and Northfleet changed their name to Ebbsfleet United and also won the FA Trophy, beating Torquay United 1-0 in the final at Wembley.

In 2011-12, Ebbsfleet had a reasonably satisfactory season (for a part-time club). They finished fourteenth, with identical home and away records (Won 7, Drawn 6, Lost 10). This season they had struggled, and currently looked likely (but by no means certain) relegation candidates. Their away record (Won 3, Drawn 2, Lost 12) was the worst in the conference, and their home record involved too many draws (9) to compensate. They began the season with a 5-4 win at Nuneaton, but it had been downhill ever since. The home game before my visit resulted in a commendable 1-1 draw with promotion candidates Newport, but they followed that with a 3-0 defeat at Alfreton. If they didn't win today, then relegation would become increasingly likely.

Their opponents, Southport had been pretty inconsistent since I saw them beat Gateshead in August. They had won enough games to appear safe, but had never strung together an impressive-enough sequence to emerge as play-off contenders.

# Chapter 18

I went into the Clubhouse – 'popular and friendly', according to the Blue Square Premier Football Ground Guide – or at least I thought that was what I'd done. But plates of canapés set out on a cloth-covered table didn't seem to fit with the usual Conference clubhouse ethos. I was soon accosted by a man in a suit, who asked if I was one of the sponsors' guests. I was then politely directed out of what was in effect an annexe, into the Clubhouse proper next door, which did indeed prove friendly (and popular).

By the time I took my place in the seated area behind the goal, the club mascot was on the pitch, although nobody was taking the slightest notice of him, even when he essayed a spectacular dive along the ground in the mud. It was not even clear what, or who, he was supposed to be. He was human, not animal, with a powdered wig of the type that used to be worn by carriers of sedan chairs (so perhaps Restoration period?) and he was wearing a red frock coat with white trimmings. A pilgrim father perhaps, to reflect the Pocahontas connection? Anyway, he soon lost interest, and left the pitch to widespread indifference.

Then, over the tannoy, we heard the Ebbsfleet song, no doubt specially composed for the FA Trophy final in 2008. It was difficult to hear the words, due to a distinctly sub-standard loudspeaker system, but I did manage to make out something along the lines of: 'Fleet, Fleet, we are the Fleet, we are the team that you ain't going to beat.' Oh no you're not! Prior to today's game seventeen Conference sides had done just that. I would suggest a change of lyrics to 'we are the team that gets beaten more often than not, and even when we don't are more likely to draw matches than win them'. But it doesn't quite scan, does it?

The first five minutes of the match were not encouraging: a bumpy pitch, misplaced passes galore, and lofted clearances from defence which went nowhere. Then Ebbsfleet's winger, Stefan Payne, made progress on the right and cut the ball back to the edge of the area, where unmarked midfielder Liam Bellamy hit a crisp first-time shot past the Southport keeper. Six minutes later, defender Joe Howe fended off tackles on the left and crossed for 5'10" Payne to out-jump everyone to head home. The Ebbsfleet faithful (thin on the ground today) couldn't believe it. Their credulity was stretched further two minutes later when leading scorer Mark Elder netted with a powerful close-range header, following a corner on the right. Could it get any better? It could! On the half-hour Mark Elder with another free header, glanced the ball into the path of on-loan Scunthorpe forward Matt Godden, who scored easily from close range.

What was happening? When had Ebbsfleet last scored four? I checked in the programme. Not since scoring five on the opening day at Nuneaton (and what a false dawn that proved to be!).

In his 'Members Musings' column, in the programme, My Football Club member Derek Wood had noted that Southport, in mid-table 'did not have the worry of relegation to face'. 'Hopefully they will not be at the top of their game,' he added. Prophetic words. Southport were not remotely near the top of their game. Their defence, in particular, was all over the place, allowing Ebbsfleet strikers a series of free headers, three of which had resulted in goals. Their forwards didn't seem able to get anywhere near the Ebbsfleet goal. Danny Hattersley, their on-loan signing from Stockport County, looked like he'd never played with his teammates before (which he hadn't). Towards the end of the half, Shaun Whalley was put through on the right with only the keeper to beat, but Preston Edwards (last week's hero with his penalty-save against Newport) blocked his shot confidently.

# Chapter 18

I expected Ebbsfleet to receive a standing ovation at half-time from the patrons of the main stand, but most of them had gone off for an early cup of tea (and the stand was sparsely populated anyway). Liam Daish must have wondered why his side couldn't produce this kind of display more often. Southport manager Liam Watson must have been asking himself how Southport had managed to reach the (apparent) safety of mid-table. His response was to order his players back out onto the pitch ten minutes before the second half was due to start, possibly as punishment, perhaps to work through a damage-limitation plan.

The half-time work-out had an effect, and Southport looked a different side in the second half. Liam Clancy had already hit a post, when five minutes into the half, Chris Almond scored impressively with an emphatic shot from the edge of the area. The pressure continued and had the visitors quickly scored again, I could have envisaged an increasingly nervy Ebbsfleet falling apart. But despite some near misses (including a thunderous shot from Shaun Whalley which came back out from the underside of the bar), Southport couldn't make a second breakthrough, and Ebbsfleet came back into the game, confident, after the 70-minute point, that Southport were unlikely to pull back three goals.

Two players in particular caught the eye. Stefan Payne, a recent signing from Macclesfield Town, was a lively right-side attacker for Ebbsfleet; someone who was prepared to run at and take on defenders, with a fair amount of success. For Southport, Liam Clancy had the ability to create space for himself in midfield by means of skilful twists and turns, which then enabled him to spray out accurate passes to colleagues.

The game ended without further goals. In the Non-League Paper the next day, Liam Daish was (understandably) delighted, whilst Liam Watson was 'visibly angered' by his side's performance: 'We have prepared right (for the game)' he said, 'and then to get that for the first 25 minutes is a disgrace. All I have said at half-time is stay in the game and don't make it more embarrassing than what it already was.' Well at least they succeeded in that 'damage-limitation'. 4-1 is bad enough, but 6-1 or 7-1 would have been humiliating.

So Ebbsfleet began to see a bit of daylight at the end of the tunnel, and Southport had to be a bit careful. They'd lost the last three games. Another three defeats would see them back in the relegation dogfight.

# Yarnbombing and the Birthplace of Soccer

Cambridge United vs Ebbsfleet United

Tuesday March 19th 2013

At last, a March day that was almost spring-like. It was sunny (but cool) as I walked down Euston Road to the reconstructed Kings Cross – now a worthy partner for nearby St Pancras, not least because of the spectacular curved roof which dominates its design. On the Cambridge-bound train, it struck me how quickly you can escape from built-up London on fast trains in a north-easterly direction. Within eight or nine minutes we were hurtling through Potters Bar, into the sparsely-wooded territory of Hertfordshire.

What is there to say about Cambridge that hasn't been said before? When visiting less well-known places like Alfreton, Braintree or Hyde, it's conceivable that I can tell you something you did not know. With Cambridge it's more difficult. It's a justly-famous unique historic city full of beautiful buildings. So I'll take the tourist sites as read, and just provide a few personal impressions.

I booked into my bed-and-breakfast (except that they didn't do breakfast), of which more later, and walked back into the city centre, first along the banks of the placid River Cam, where solitary scullers scuttled past from time to time, and then across Jesus Green, one of the many grassy areas surrounding or penetrating the city centre. On the edge of the centre are streets of attractive terraced houses, built of that warm mellow yellow brick with which Cambridge buildings are typically constructed (the colleges are, of course, mostly stone-built, but the colour is the same).

# Chapter 19

Picturesque narrow lanes and alleyways intersect the main thoroughfares. I discovered, close to the centre, an open space I hadn't come across before - Christ's Piece - where I watched a bloated red sun sink into a bank of cloud to the west. It was a peaceful and relaxing scene, so different from a previous visit three years previously on a hot Saturday in August, when it was difficult to progress along the pavements in the city centre because they were so crowded with tourists. Our friend – a Cambridge don – managed to get us into Kings College Chapel by a side entrance (thus avoiding the long queues). Once inside we found the aisles as packed as the pavements outside had been. That's the drawback to Cambridge: it can become uncomfortably overcrowded in summer.

I'd never been in a city where bicycles play such a major role. They're all over the place, and they come at you from all angles! When leaving the station, I narrowly avoided a collision with a (rather annoyed) cyclist, which would have been less life-threatening than my near-death experience on that road in Dartford, but which would not have been at all pleasant. Streams of traffic on the roads into Cambridge were complemented by streams of cyclists in the adjacent cycle lanes. The cycle park by the station contained more bicycles than I have ever seen before in any one place.

The headline in the local paper was the news that Astra Zeneca, the pharmaceutical giant, had chosen to relocate its London headquarters to Cambridge, investing £330 million in the city and bringing 2,000 jobs (many of them in a new global R & D centre). I did wonder whether Cambridge actually needed another 2,000 jobs. The city centre already appeared overcrowded with people and traffic, and there could not have been an unemployment problem, could there? It must already be one of the most prosperous cities in the country, with its University and its growing reputation as a site for hi-tech developments. Its socio-economic structure, skewed towards managerial and white collar occupations, reflected these distinctive characteristics. But the Cambridge News, which welcomed the proposals, claimed that 'in recent months our pages have been dominated by reports of store closures and redundancies across the business piece, creating a pall of gloom over the local economy'. So it seems that even Cambridge has been affected by the recession, in which case, the largest (and smartest) Poundland store I've ever seen will, no doubt, serve a useful purpose.

Cambridge News provided a bit of light relief in a story headlined 'Yarnbomber strikes again on dawn patrol'. The 'Yarnbomber' is a mysterious guerrilla knitter, who creates 'tree jumpers' and then goes out at the crack of dawn to dress selected trees in them! They look quite ridiculous in the accompanying photograph. I'm afraid the point of the exercise totally escapes me.

One of the problems with my Cambridge visit was that the focal points of my trip were inconveniently dispersed. The railway station is over a mile south of the city centre. The area of cheap hotels where I was to stay is another mile to its north. And the Abbey Road Stadium, home of Cambridge United is well out of the city centre to the west along the Newmarket Road. I'd walked over five miles as I approached the ground. A quick glance inside a nearby pub called 'The Wrestlers' and I decided against a visit. Instead I made my way to the Cambridge United Supporters Club bar, where I knew I could gain entrance on payment of a £1.50 visitor's fee.

Inside the bar I met a couple of visiting Ebbsfleet fans and congratulated them on their team's performance (4-1 against Southport) the previous Saturday. I then got into a fascinating conversation with two long-term Cambridge

## Chapter 19

supporters (Dave and Ross), one of whom (Dave) had followed the team for fifty years. I asked them why Cambridge United, who should be one of the big-hitters in the Conference, on the basis of their recent history in the Football League, were having such an indifferent season. They argued that lack of finance was at the root of the problem. Cambridge fans, they claimed, were a fickle bunch, who would turn out in large numbers (well 4-5,000) if the team were doing well, but who were much less inclined if they were not (the average home attendance this season was a mere 2,200).

There was also the problem that, in previous years, money had been invested in several downwardly-mobile players from the Football League who had invariably failed to deliver. They felt, however, that the club was now on the up, with a young team that was beginning to gel as a unit. Next season, I was assured, Cambridge would be up there with the promotion contenders (although I would anticipate a similar expectation in around two-thirds of the Conference supporters' club bars).

The openness and friendliness of the bar was typical of my recent experiences at similar venues (Newport, Woking, Braintree, Dartford), and are amongst the most endearing features of the Conference. Many of these bars are open to all (in a few cases, visiting supporters are excluded, but if you kept quiet about your identity, and hid your club scarf in your coat pocket, you'd probably get in). In some cases there is a small membership fee. In all of them there is a lively buzz of pre-match conversation, and it is relatively easy to engage with home supporters, from which many insights into the state and current performance of the club can be gleaned. Again there is a striking contrast with the Football League. Even at Morecambe, who were until recently a Conference club, and still feel like one, visiting supporters can't get anywhere near the club bar. But here at Cambridge, home and visiting fans were mingling freely and unproblematically.

The club's director of football (previously its manager) Jez George discussed the financial challenges of running a Conference club in his long and informative column in the programme. He made an interesting distinction between the kind of budget available to pay players in the better-off Conference clubs (£1 million) and the less well-off (£500,000), the category into which Cambridge United currently fitted. For £500,000, if you wanted a squad of 20 players, you could only pay them £475 a week which, George claims, is 'under par for good players in this league.' So do you settle for 15 players and pay them £600-£700 a week? Or do you pay a higher rate (£800-£900 – the average rate for the top clubs such as Luton Town) in which case you can only afford 11 players, which is clearly not an adequately-sized squad. What do Cambridge United do? Look out for bargains in the lower-middle price ranges, or push the wages budget up, thereby threatening the club's financial stability? George doesn't provide an answer (though he'll need to develop a strategy in the close season) but it's certainly an illuminating analysis.

Cambridge United were originally Abbey United (Abbey is a suburb of Cambridge). In 1949 Abbey United turned professional and in 1951 changed their name to Cambridge United. The club prospered, reaching the Premier Division of the Southern League in 1961. After winning two consecutive Southern League titles, Cambridge United were elected to the Football League in 1970, replacing Bradford Park Avenue. They were only the third non-league side to break the stronghold of the 'old pals' re-election syndrome in the lower reaches of Division Four (Peterborough United were the first, in 1960, followed by Oxford United in 1962).

# Chapter 19

The club's thirty-five years in the Football League were eventful. Over this period they experienced six promotions, seven relegations and one (successful) application for re-election. They spent a total of fourteen years in Division 2 (later 1), ten in Division 3 (later 2), and eleven in Division 4 (later 3). Life was rarely dull at the Abbey Stadium.

This history of instability on the pitch was accompanied by frequent managerial changes. Eighteen managers were employed (three of them on a caretaker basis) over their time in the Football League, an average job tenure of just under two years. There were some illustrious occupants of this hot seat. Ron Atkinson, having played for Oxford, cut his managerial teeth at Cambridge, where he took them from Division 4 to Division 2 over a four-year period, before moving on to greater things at West Bromwich Albion. Roy McFarland took the club back up to Division 1 during his sojourn there in the early 2000s, although they were struggling when he left, and were relegated the following year.

Cambridge's most successful season (1991-92) was under the managership of John Beck, famous (or notorious, depending on how you look at it) for his adherence to a no-frills direct route long-ball game, not particularly pretty to watch, but extremely effective, at least for a couple of seasons. In 1992, Cambridge United finished in fifth position in Division Two. Had they been successful in the play-offs, they would have been one of the founder members of the Premiership. In the event, they were thrashed 6-1 by Leicester City in the semi-finals.

My informants, Dave and Russ, both singled out Chris Turner (manager between 1986 and 1990) with particular affection, as a neglected but hugely important figure in the club's recent history. He arrived the season Cambridge were at rock bottom, having just suffered the indignity of having to submit a re-election application. Over the next four years, he rebuilt the side to the point (when he left) where they finished sixth in Division Four, and were at take-off point for their achievements in the two seasons under John Beck which followed. A key figure during this period was Dion Dublin who, according to Dave and Russ, was outstanding when at Cambridge, before moving to Manchester United.

Cambridge were eventually relegated to the Conference in 2005. The eight subsequent years there have been mixed. They reached the play-off final in 2008 and 2009, but lost in each case to Devonian clubs Exeter City and Torquay United. Subsequently, persistent financial troubles, boardroom squabbles, and managerial shortcomings, have hindered progress towards a return to the Football League.

2012-13 had proved a disappointment to date: Cambridge had never been in danger of relegation, but neither had they ever looked like serious play-off contenders (seventh was the highest position they'd reached, in early January). They had proved incapable of stringing a series of good results together and there was really very little for them to play for now (apart from pride and renewals of contracts).

So, this was a golden opportunity for Ebbsfleet, who I had seen the previous Saturday, to make further progress to (possible) safety. But their away record remained the worst in the Conference (won 3, drawn 2, lost 12) and they'd lost their last seven away games in succession. Could they reproduce their performance on Saturday against Southport whom they ripped apart in the first half? Or would there be a repeat of the 3-0 defeat at Alfreton from the previous week?

Abbey Stadium, as you'd expect from a club that not long ago played in the Championship, is one of the better grounds in the Conference, although not quite the same class as Aggborough, Sincil Bank or Edgeley Park. There's a traditional Main Stand, opposite which is a covered standing area (half of which was currently 'closed for repair'). The habitat of the vociferous home fans was a similar covered standing area, adjacent to the Supporters' Club Bar. Opposite it was the newest and most impressive structure in the ground: the Marstons Smith South Stand which is reserved for away supporters. The fifty diehards who'd travelled from Ebbsfleet looked lost amongst the yellow seats in one corner of the structure, although (in due course) they certainly made plenty of noise. The rest of the stand was totally empty, which seems an unnecessary under-use of a valuable resource.

The game took time to settle into a pattern. In the first fifteen minutes there were no clear-cut goal opportunities for either side. Both defences looked solid. Cambridge's central defender Charlie Wassmer dealt calmly with everything required of him and distributed the ball thoughtfully. His tall opposite number, Phil Walsh, sought out and won everything at head height that came anywhere near him. Cambridge displayed some fluent approach work, and had the greater share of possession, but lacked penetration. Ebbsfleet counter-attacked intermittently but with an equal lack of impact. Certainly they hadn't looked remotely like replicating their four-goal bonanza of the previous Saturday. At half-time it was still goalless, and I couldn't recall that either keeper had needed to make a serious save.

The second half continued in the same vein as the first. As the match wore on (and 'wore' is appropriate: the football was distinctly uninspiring) it became apparent that despite head coach Richard Money's commitment to a 'high tempo passing game' (highlighted in the programme), several of his players didn't share it. There were too many unproductive high balls lofted in the general direction of 6' 4" striker Tom Elliott. Not that Ebbsfleet were any better. But their manager hadn't announced any similar intention to play pretty football, had he!

Halfway through the second period, Ebbsfleet began to look the more threatening side, and created (and missed) a couple of reasonable opportunities. The Cambridge fans were proving remarkably patient with their team, who continued to misplace passes and rely on ineffective upfield punts. Then, in the 70th minute, the previously-immaculate Charlie Wassmer failed to prevent Ebbsfleet's Matt Godden from breaking clear in the Cambridge penalty area, where he slotted the ball neatly past the advancing keeper, to the delight of the travelling Ebbsfleet contingent, who had a bird's eye view of the goal. The groans and mutterings increased in frequency and volume amongst the home supporters. But a degree of urgency did then develop in Cambridge's game. Overlapping full-backs began to make it to the goal-line and put in dangerous crosses, which Phil Walsh or keeper Preston Edwards dealt with confidently enough, until the 80th minute when a free-kick on the right led to a goal-bound header and a goal-line clearance from an Ebbsfleet defender. The clearance fell to the feet of a midfielder, with the unlikely name of Harrison Dunk, who drove the ball first-time into the roof of the net.

In the time that remained, Ebbsfleet looked the more likely to score again. Matt Godden had a good opportunity which was not taken, a miss that may cost them dear, come the end of the season. It would have been an injustice had Ebbsfleet lost; but they really needed a win to boost their slender chances of avoiding relegation.

I walked back to my bed-and-no-breakfast along a, now freezing, Newmarket Road. It proved to be unimpressive, although not as dire as two of the contributors to Trip

## Chapter 19

Advisor had claimed ('Terrible-don't go there' and 'Beware Colditz'!).

On the way back to the station the next morning, I made a detour to an area of open land just to the south of the city centre, known as 'Parkers Piece' (Cambridge is full of 'pieces'). Parkers Piece has great significance in the historical development of association football. In 1848, members of Cambridge University had drawn up the first codified set of rules to regulate the fast developing game of soccer, and the first game ever played under these rules took place on Parkers Piece. Twenty years later, the first set of Football Association rules, which were greatly influenced by the 1848 version, were drawn up, and again the first ever game under this code was played on Parkers Piece. So I guess Cambridge United have more reason than most of the ex-Football League clubs now languishing in the Conference to feel that the League is where they rightfully belong. After all they represent a city where the game as we know it today actually 'kicked off'.

# Accommodating Publicans and Phantom Bus Stations

Mansfield Town vs Nuneaton Town

Tuesday 26<sup>th</sup> March 2013

It was another bitterly cold day. An unseasonal blizzard, the previous weekend (22-23 March), had caused a further spate of postponements, including Mansfield's home game against Macclesfield Town. On the Monday before the match there were four inches of snow covering Field Mill, but a team of fifty assorted volunteers (including members of the armed forces and Mansfield's youth team) had spent nearly five hours clearing the pitch. There were two pitch inspections earlier the next day (when the game was scheduled), with the referee finally giving the go-ahead at lunchtime.

I drove across the Pennines along roads which were like canyons carved out of snow. The road surfaces were clear, but there was up to three feet of snow at the side, with smooth walls created by snow ploughs, which had later refrozen. There were some spectacular snow sculptures close to the road created in the drifts that had resulted from the swirling easterly wind, which had accompanied the weekend blizzard.

The pile-up of snow was an appropriate metaphor for the pile-up of fixtures in the Conference, which had reached alarming proportions. Despite protestations from several of those most affected, the season had to end on April 20<sup>th</sup>, which was now a mere 25 days away. The play-off final, to be staged at Wembley had been earmarked for May 4<sup>th</sup> and apparently could not be rescheduled, because there was an international game due to be played on May 18<sup>th</sup>, and (for some obscure reason) the Wembley pitch had to rest undisturbed for two weeks beforehand. This meant the home and away play-off semi-finals had to be played between April 20$^{th}$ and May 4$^{th}$, which, in turn, precluded any shift from April 20$^{th}$. Why it wasn't possible to reschedule the play-off final at one of the many suitable alternative Premiership grounds was never addressed by the FA, who remained unmovable. This obduracy had generated a critical outburst from Newport County's manager, Justin Edinburgh (Mr Angry), who argued (with some justification) that the decision would be likely to have adverse effects on Newport's chances of automatic promotion.

Newport had ten games left to play, which meant one every two-and-a-half days. Braintree Town were even worse off; they had eleven fixtures to fulfil. There were six clubs (including Mansfield Town) who had nine games left. And the weather forecast (more snow next weekend) made further postponements a distinct possibility. Would Braintree Town (or Newport County) end up playing games on consecutive days, I wondered? Well, there are historical precedents for that. Until the 1960s, Football League clubs were expected to play on Christmas Day and Boxing Day, and then on Good Friday and Easter Saturday. It was going to be a frenetic end to the 2012-13 Conference Season.

Mansfield is at the centre of what was once a coal-mining area. All the mines have gone of course, but the haphazard pattern of development that is the legacy of coal-mining remains. Groups of terraced houses can be seen around the places where the collieries used to be. The approach to Mansfield from the west is not pretty. Nor is Mansfield when you arrive. When I got out of the car I noticed a trace of sulphur in the air; maybe from the same coal-burning installation which caused a similar (but stronger) odour in Alfreton.

The town centre is grim, with one or two redeeming features. There's the usual concrete-constructed covered shopping precinct (The Four Seasons), built in the 1970s, but already aging prematurely. The surrounding streets contain the familiar mix of charity shops, money lenders, amusement halls, pizza and kebab takeaways, and vacant premises. But there is an impressive railway viaduct, which straddles the town centre, and a pleasant-enough market place with a 'Buttercross' in the centre, and old Court House (now a Wetherspoons establishment) adjacent to it. Oh, and there was not a nails establishment in sight. Well done Mansfield for bucking the trend!

The advice in the excellent 'guide to Conference grounds' was to avoid pubs in Mansfield's town centre, so I did. The problem was that there was a total dearth of restaurants; eating out in Mansfield is clearly not what the locals do. I moved away from the town centre towards the ground, looking for inspiration (of the food and drink variety). En route I found myself walking past a gleaming new bus station, largely constructed of glass, which was totally deserted, despite the fact that all the bays advertised details of destinations and bus numbers.

I learned later that the bus station was to be officially opened the very next Monday (April 1$^{st}$) by the Secretary of State for Transport, Patrick McLoughlin. The source of my information was the local paper – the Mansfield Chad – which I purchased from WH Smith in the town centre. I asked the assistant why the paper was called the Chad but she had no idea. In fact, the dictionary definition of 'chad' is 'a piece of waste material removed from card or tape by punching'. Sadly, as I later discovered, the origins of this unusual name were much more mundane. There used to be

# Chapter 20

two weekly Mansfield papers – the Chronicle and the Advertiser – which in due course amalgamated and became the Chad. No doubt it seemed like a good idea at the time!

The new bus station seemed to have divided local public opinion. Some welcomed it as a much-needed replacement for the existing bus station (inconvenient, cold, and inhospitable). Others felt that the resources spent on it could have been put to much better alternative uses. Liam Mango Jackson (now there's an impressive name for you) had this to say, when interviewed for a feature in the Mansfield Chad.

> 'They should be investing in things that are needed, and a new bus station – costing a million – is not. I mean, Mansfield – not exactly the tourist capital of the Midlands is it, with all our lovely hotels and amazing boarded-up high street?'

After an hour or so wandering around the town centre on a cold March evening, I could see his point. Indeed, it should be noted that in Channel Four's 'Best and Worst Places to live in Britain' programme, Mansfield was rated sixth worst in 2005 and ninth worst in 2007 (which shows some improvement I suppose). But some Mansfield notables clearly see the town in a different light. Mansfield made a bid for city status in 2009, along with several other hopefuls. Unsurprisingly it was absent from the short list drawn up in 2012. It may be the second biggest settlement in Nottinghamshire, but a city? I don't think so.

Mansfield's elected mayor, Tony Egginton, was much more enthusiastic about the new bus station than Liam Mango Jackson had been. He saw it as "a significant development and focal point that we can be proud of for many years to come." Pride in a focal point? A strange concept indeed!

Who is elected mayor Tony Egginton, you may be asking? Well, Mansfield is one of the few areas which have opted for a directly-elected mayor, and he was the successful candidate in 2001. Both the previous Labour government and the current Conservative-led coalition have encouraged councils to introduce elected mayors. David Cameron recently enthused about the prospect of 'a Boris in every large city'. Probably not a well-judged soundbite with the benefit of hindsight! Boris Johnson (the elected mayor of Greater London since 2008) has proved a controversial figure – much-loved and much-detested. Indeed the elected mayors (of which there are currently sixteen) are a mixed bunch. The elected mayor of Hartlepool, Stuart Drummond, was the mascot of Hartlepool United FC, where he appeared at home games dressed in a monkey suit. One of his election promises was 'free bananas for every child in Hartlepool'. Amazingly, he won the election in 2001 (much to the disbelief and consternation of Peter Mandelson, the town's MP) and was then re-elected in 2005 and 2009. But the good people of Hartlepool have since reconsidered their initial enthusiasm for an elected mayor and in a 2012 referendum, voted to scrap the idea. Let's hope there's still a job at Hartlepool United for Stuart!

Having crossed the busy ring road, I noticed a pub which claimed to serve food, looked reasonable, and which was sparsely populated. I ordered a pint of Hobgoblin and asked if they were still serving food. 'I'm sorry,' said the young woman who served me 'We stop doing food at four.' Her attention was then caught by a rather older lady sitting at a nearby table, as a result of which I was then informed that she (the landlady) was prepared to provide some food for me. I was greatly impressed at a further example of people putting themselves out for me on my Conference visits. There was the free ticket at Lincoln, the free programme at Cambridge, the steward who fetched me a programme and brought it to my seat at Hereford, and now this readiness to serve me a meal outside specified hours. Heartwarming!

There was no problem locating Mansfield's ground, now called the 'One-Call Stadium' (in honour of the club's sponsors), but still widely known as 'Field Mill' by local supporters. The tall floodlight pylons towered above east Mansfield.

My approach was on a path alongside an ascending row of terraced houses, most of which had smoke billowing from their chimneys; an evocative, traditional football ground environment. Field Mill, itself, turned out to be an impressive, large-scale (by Conference standards) ground, with one shortcoming. The old Bishop Street stand on one side of the pitch is unused (safety reasons again; it's made of wood) which adversely affected the ambience of the stadium. However the main stand (The Ian Greaves Stand) would grace a major Football League ground. It replaced a much-loved construction (the West Stand) which had a roof similar in design to the old East Stand at Highbury, and had been purchased in its entirety from Hurst Park racecourse in Surrey for £30,000 in 1959. Simon Inglis describes it as a gem which "looks like a plastic kit, like an artist's impression from an old soccer annual of what a modern stand should resemble." (The Football Ground of Britain, p148). Sadly it is no longer with us.

I located myself in the Quarry Lane Stand, at one end of the pitch (the identical stand opposite is reserved for away supporters). I asked the bloke sitting next to me why he thought Mansfield's season had taken off only after Christmas. On Boxing Day, Mansfield lost 1-2 at home to Alfreton Town and languished twelfth in the table. Since then they had won 14 of the 16 Conference games played and were second in the table, with games in hand over the leaders, Kidderminster. He reminded me that exactly the same thing had happened the previous year (2011-12). Mansfield had been mid-table at Christmas and then stormed up to third position (with 89 points) by the end of the season, but were beaten in the play offs by York City. What the manager, Paul Cox, does, he said, is to try out various combinations of his squad in the first half of the season, then he decides on the best line-up, and plays them (injuries permitting) for the rest of the campaign. So it was last season, so it is this.

Mansfield Town never set the Football League alight after they were elected to it in 1931. They were moved between Division Three North and South from 1931 until 1958, when they made it to the new Division Three, after a season in which they scored 100 goals, but conceded 92.

Between 1958 and 2008 they alternated between the third and fourth levels, with one memorable season in Division Two (now the Championship), after finishing as Division Three champions in 1976-77. Their history is pretty similar to that of other ex-league sides now in the Conference (such as Wrexham, Lincoln City, Grimsby Town and Stockport County). They had rarely made the headlines in their seventy years in the League, but feel that is where they belong.

After three or four bleak seasons, Mansfield Town were relegated in 2008 to the Conference. By then serious financial problems had developed, and the owner, Keith Haslam, was becoming increasingly unpopular. In 2006-07, an organisation was formed called 'Stags Fans for Change' whose primary aim was the removal of Haslam from the club. They achieved this goal in 2010, when local millionaire John Radford bought the club, and purchased the ground

## Chapter 20

from the obdurate previous owner. Above the directors' box in the Main Stand, there's a hoarding proclaiming 'In John Radford we trust.' With good reason, it would appear. At least so far.

Since John Radford took over, things have also improved on the pitch. After three mediocre seasons in the Conference, punctuated by an FA Trophy final at Wembley in 2011 (where Mansfield lost 1-0 to Darlington), Paul Cox was appointed manager, having worked miracles at Eastwood Town (sadly, not sustained since he left). Under his guidance Mansfield finished third last season. They now had the look of potential champions.

Mansfield had featured in the news (beyond the pages of the Non-League Paper) on two occasions this season. First, they were drawn against Liverpool, at home, in the third round of the FA Cup, where they gave a very good account of themselves, losing 1-2 as the result of a controversial goal from Luis Suarez, who looked like he had handled the ball before scoring (and looked like he knew he had!). Second, they had appointed a young photogenic chief executive, Carolyn Radford, who just happens to have recently married the club's owner. The fact that she was engaged to him was apparently not known or revealed at the time of the interviews, but of course she was the best person for the job, wasn't she.

Nuneaton Town, today's opponents, were struggling to stay in the Conference, having been promoted via the play-offs last season. They were certainly not giving up without a fight, though. Prior to tonight's match they had enjoyed an eight-game unbeaten run, including a 1-0 win over promotion candidates Grimsby Town.

Mansfield dominated the early stages of the contest. Within two minutes Tony James (who'd scored the winner at

Woking) had hit the post with a header. Mansfield's football wasn't particularly elegant, but they were creating numerous opportunities. Lindon Meikle was lively on the right, and on several occasions crossed dangerous balls into the Nuneaton penalty area, where their young keeper, Lee Burge, was performing heroically to keep Mansfield at bay. It looked only a matter of time before they scored. But Nuneaton's well-organised defence continued to hold firm, and gradually the frequency of the home side's goal-scoring attempts began to diminish.

The pitch was uneven which was, no doubt, why Mansfield were favouring a long-ball game, although when they did keep the ball on the ground they looked more impressive. Nuneaton rarely progressed as far as the Mansfield penalty area. Towards the end of the first half, there was a frenetic scramble deep in the Nuneaton box, but somehow the visitors managed to get the ball clear. It had not been a particularly distinguished half, but Mansfield had certainly dominated it.

I'd expected Mansfield, after the interval, to continue where they'd left off, and for a while they did. But Nuneaton were coming into the game more, and much of their approach play was of a higher quality than you might expect from a side locked in a relegation battle. It began to look like they might get something from the game, and so end Mansfield's run of nine straight wins. Mansfield's formidable defence was performing with its customary panache, but began to look vulnerable. Was I about to witness one of the upsets of the season?

But then Mansfield were deservedly awarded a penalty. I was seated directly behind the incident, and it was hard to imagine a more blatant push than that administered by Nuneaton's Gavin Cowan on substitute Matt Rhead, who had only been on the field for two minutes. Rhead was

# Chapter 20

Mansfield's 'secret weapon', according to the supporter sitting next to me. He was overweight, and rarely started games ('there's no way he could last ninety minutes') but had scored some crucial goals as a second- half substitute. He would have made an ideal sparring partner for Luton's Chunky McKinlay!

Leading scorer Matt Green stepped up to take the kick, but was dismayed to see Lee Burge make an excellent diving save to his right. The crowd were becoming increasingly restless; was it going to be 'one of those nights'? Their fears were allayed in the 74$^{th}$ minute, though, when Mansfield at last achieved a breakthrough. There was an element of good fortune about the goal. Louis Briscoe hit a free kick from just outside the area, which took a deflection from someone in the wall, totally wrong-footing Lee Burge, who made a gesture of despair to his colleagues ('you can't blame me for that') before he retrieved the ball from the net.

After that Mansfield could easily have increased their lead. Burge pulled off another excellent save from Matt Green, who did eventually find the net with a close-range header, but was adjudged (perhaps mistakenly) to have been offside. The crowd were beginning to turn against the referee, although they would have done well to remember that the game was being played only because he had been prepared to give the pitch the benefit of the doubt, after two earlier inspections. Nuneaton continued to threaten in breakaways, but couldn't manage an equaliser. Ten minutes before the end, they brought on leading scorer Andy Brown for the not particularly impressive loan-signing from Northampton Town, Louis Moult. They might have done better to start with him, for a crucial game such as this. But maybe they were saving him for Woking (Thursday) and Telford (Saturday). The game ended with Mansfield having extended their run of wins to ten. In the programme, the

## Accommodating Publicans and Phantom Bus Stations

Chairman, John Radford, had made a point of wishing the best of luck to Woking in their game at Mansfield's promotion rivals Kidderminster. He would have been pleased that Woking came away with a 2-2 draw, leaving Mansfield only one point behind Kidderminster with three games in hand. The Stags now seemed clear favourites for the title.

# 26<sup>th</sup> March 2013 – League Table

| | Team | P | W | D | L | F | A | GD | Pt |
|---|---|---|---|---|---|---|---|---|---|
| 1 | Kidderminster Harriers | 41 | 23 | 9 | 9 | 69 | 37 | 32 | 78 |
| 2 | Mansfield Town | 38 | 24 | 5 | 9 | 75 | 46 | 29 | 77 |
| 3 | Wrexham | 38 | 20 | 12 | 6 | 69 | 36 | 33 | 72 |
| 4 | Newport County AFC | 37 | 21 | 6 | 10 | 74 | 53 | 21 | 69 |
| 5 | Grimsby Town | 38 | 18 | 11 | 9 | 56 | 32 | 24 | 65 |
| 6 | Forest Green Rovers | 39 | 17 | 10 | 12 | 57 | 40 | 17 | 61 |
| 7 | Macclesfield Town | 37 | 16 | 10 | 11 | 55 | 51 | 4 | 58 |
| 8 | Hereford United | 39 | 15 | 11 | 13 | 59 | 57 | 2 | 56 |
| 9 | Luton Town | 38 | 15 | 10 | 13 | 55 | 49 | 6 | 55 |
| 10 | Woking | 39 | 16 | 6 | 17 | 63 | 69 | -6 | 54 |
| 11 | Cambridge United | 40 | 14 | 11 | 15 | 63 | 63 | 0 | 53 |
| 12 | Dartford | 38 | 15 | 7 | 16 | 56 | 57 | -1 | 52 |
| 13 | Braintree Town | 36 | 14 | 7 | 15 | 50 | 61 | -11 | 49 |
| 14 | Hyde FC | 40 | 14 | 6 | 20 | 56 | 64 | -8 | 48 |
| 15 | Tamworth | 39 | 13 | 9 | 17 | 47 | 55 | -8 | 48 |
| 16 | Alfreton Town | 38 | 12 | 12 | 14 | 55 | 64 | -9 | 48 |
| 17 | Lincoln City | 40 | 12 | 10 | 18 | 57 | 65 | -8 | 46 |
| 18 | Southport | 40 | 12 | 10 | 18 | 63 | 76 | -13 | 46 |
| 19 | Gateshead | 38 | 11 | 12 | 15 | 47 | 50 | -3 | 45 |
| 20 | Stockport County | 40 | 12 | 9 | 19 | 51 | 65 | -14 | 45 |
| 21 | Nuneaton Town | 39 | 10 | 13 | 16 | 44 | 59 | -15 | 43 |
| 22 | Barrow | 38 | 10 | 10 | 18 | 41 | 70 | -29 | 40 |
| 23 | Ebbsfleet United | 37 | 8 | 12 | 17 | 50 | 73 | -23 | 36 |
| 24 | AFC Telford United | 41 | 5 | 16 | 20 | 49 | 69 | -20 | 31 |

# It's not the Despair I can't handle, it's the Hope

AFC Telford United vs Nuneaton Town

Saturday March 30th 2013

I nearly didn't make it to Telford. In the morning we went to collect our new(ish) car, in plenty of time for me to drive it the 140 miles to Telford. The paperwork took far longer than we'd anticipated, but finally we were installed in our Vauxhall Zafira. I turned the ignition key. Nothing happened. Karen tried it, with the same result. We summoned the salesman. He tried it. Nothing doing. He called over a mechanic, who quickly diagnosed a flat battery, which he attempted to recharge, without success (it must have been a very flat battery!), so he went to look for a replacement. Meanwhile it was an hour later than my planned departure time.

By the time a new battery had been installed, and we were able to drive off, I'd decided to postpone today's visit and reschedule the remaining four games I had left to cover. But when we got home, it transpired that rescheduling wasn't possible, unless Grimsby Town could be guaranteed to reach the play-offs, which, on their current form, they couldn't. So I set off down the M6, uncertain whether I would make it to Telford for kick-off.

In the event, it was a straightforward journey. I arrived with forty minutes to spare, and parked close to the New Bucks Stadium. Wellington town centre was a mile away, so I decided to leave that until after the game. I should explain that AFC Telford United used to be Wellington Town, in the days before Telford New Town was conceived and

built. At this time the largest place in the vicinity was
Wellington, a traditional Shropshire market town.

Wellington Town prospered in the Cheshire County League
and had several notable giant-killing acts to their name. In
1969 they were re-named Telford United (by then the New
Town was beginning to become a reality) and joined the
Southern League. Finishing third in the Southern League in
1978 led to membership of the Conference (then the
Alliance) in its first season, which is where they have spent
most of their time since (further details below). But the
ground is still in Wellington, and given the club's roots in
that vicinity, it was only right that I should explore
Wellington after the match, rather than Telford's town
centre, three miles to the east.

In fact I know the new centre of Telford well. I've done a
good deal of work, over the years, for Telford and Wrekin
Council, whose offices are situated there. It is one of those
purpose-built covered shopping developments, where you
can buy everything you could possibly want, under one
roof. It is surrounded by a sea of car parks (in which it's
easy to forget where you actually parked your vehicle) and
bizarrely, it closes every day at 5.30 pm. When I first stayed
at a nearby hotel, I thought I'd have a wander around after
checking in, and found that at 6.00 pm I couldn't get into
the shopping centre! What kind of a place is that? Okay,
there is a cinema on the periphery, plus a couple of
unprepossessing-looking pubs. But that doesn't compensate
for a town centre that only operates on a 9.00 – 5.30 basis.

The area covered by Telford and Wrekin Council is steeped
in history. To the south is an area which the tourist
literature claims is the 'Birthplace of the Industrial
Revolution', no less! (a disputed claim, but one with a
degree of credibility). In Coalbrookdale, in the late
eighteenth century, Abraham Darby pioneered the

technique of smelting iron with coke, which facilitated the much cheaper production of iron. In nearby Ironbridge, he masterminded the construction of the first bridge fabricated from cast iron, which spans the Severn gorge and has survived until the present day. It is a potent tangible symbol of the dawn of the industrial revolution (whatever other claimants might say). There is another bridge across the Severn at nearby Buildwas, designed by Thomas Telford. Hence the name chosen for the New Town.

Famous sons and daughters of Telford are otherwise thin on the ground. Well, I suppose it's not been there that long. Just across the river from Ironbridge is a village called Broseley, which is the birthplace of Billy Wright the legendary captain of Wolves and England (who married one of the Beverley Sisters). Broseley is technically in Bridgnorth Council's area, but I think Telford can reasonably claim it. Links between Wolverhampton and Telford have become increasingly strong, and those employed in Wolverhampton have taken advantage of the fact that you can get there from Telford in only sixteen minutes by train.

Telford's ground (New Bucks Head) was built a dozen years ago, at a time when the team was achieving mid-table respectability in the Conference on a regular basis. It is on the site of their previous ground which, by all accounts, was in serious need of attention by 2001. It is integrated with a hotel development which is located in one corner, but extends its premises into the area at the back of the main stand, where you can book conference space, if you're so inclined. I decided to stand on the end-terrace reserved for home supporters (£11 concession).

The stadium is impressive: a well-designed and spacious main stand, flanked by two similar covered terraces. Opposite the main stand is a narrow open terrace with an AFC Telford Learning Centre behind it. I bought a pint of

## Chapter 21

Banks' excellent bitter, and looked for someone with whom I could discuss the decline in Telford's fortunes. When I'd seen them at Alfreton in October, they were sitting comfortably in the upper-middle reaches of the table, with five wins and only four defeats to their name (but a good number of drawn games). Who would have thought (certainly not me) that the 1-1 draw deservedly earned there would turn out to be the second in a sequence of 27 games without a win in the Conference, which was still unbroken. They had moved inexorably down the table from eighth (on October 27th) to bottom (by the end of February).What had gone wrong? I approached a trio of middle-aged supporters, one of whom referred me to his son, who was standing next to the bar.

His son was indeed both knowledgeable and helpful. He explained that after Telford had been promoted from the Conference North in 2011, they played with most of the same squad from their promotion-winning season. They'd struggled, but done well enough to avoid relegation. The quality of the players was such, he said, that this was the best they could have hoped to achieve, but at least they knew one another's game, and played as a team, and that was enough to keep them up. This season, despite the reasonable start, the manager, Andy Sinton, wanted to strengthen the squad, and brought in new players on a regular basis. ('It felt like there were one or two new signings making their debut every week'). Many of these newcomers seemed not to be committed to Telford ('It looked like they thought they were doing us a favour turning out for us'). Gradually the continuity of a settled team was undermined, and performances deteriorated. Manager Andy Sinton was sacked (after what I thought was a creditable 1-0 defeat at high-flying Kidderminster) which was the signal for a further bout of instability. Two successive managers came and went in the space of three months. The caretaker manager John Psaras would no doubt survive until the end of the season, but probably not beyond it.

Although Telford seemed doomed – if they lost today they would be relegated, and even if they didn't, relegation wouldn't be long delayed – Nuneaton were fighting for their life. In a sense they were in a similar position to Telford in the 2011-12 season. Nuneaton had stayed with the group of players who won promotion for them last season, and although they have struggled, they have turned in some impressive performances and have a good chance of survival. I saw them draw 3-3 with high-flying (at the time) Macclesfield Town in October, lose narrowly to Stockport County early in February, and turn in a creditable performance at Mansfield earlier in the week. In each case the quality of the teamwork was apparent. The players were used to one another, and that makes a big difference at this level (Dartford and Braintree provide two further examples). Coincidentally three of them – Andy Brown, Gavin Cowan and Simon Forsdick – used to be Telford regulars.

We discussed other Conference topics. Most impressive team seen this season? He said Kidderminster; I agreed. Worst ground in the Conference? He thought Alfreton, and although I could see his point, I felt Barrow's Holker Street deserved this accolade. I thanked him for his help and moved to the Snack Bar for a much needed intake of sustenance.

AFC Telford United are known as the Bucks. So when they play Mansfield Town, it's the Bucks versus the Stags. A buck-headed mascot made a brief appearance before the kick-off, but never reappeared thereafter. Until 2004, Telford United (as it then was) was the only club left in the

# Chapter 21

Conference to have been there ever since its inception in 1979: twenty-five consecutive seasons. During this time, they rarely challenged for promotion; but equally they were rarely faced with relegation. Only Woking (1992-2007), Kidderminster Harriers (1983-2000) and Forest Green Rovers (1998-2013) have approached this consistency of membership. Telford United have also won the FA Trophy three times (1971, 1983, and 1989). Until 2004, they were the quintessential Conference club; then everything went wrong, not on the football field, but financially. Telford United, having typically finished in a respectable mid-table position, went bust. Fortunately (as things turned out) they had, by then, the asset of an impressive new stadium which for several seasons thereafter played host to the likes of Kendal Town. Telford United were reinvented as AFC Telford United (you have to change your name, in such circumstances, as Nuneaton Borough discovered a few years later). The club was taken over by a Supporters' Club Trust, and were demoted four levels to the Northern Premier League Division One. Gradually they worked their way back up the pyramid, finally making it back to the Conference in 2011, after beating Gainsborough Trinity in the play-off final. As noted earlier, they survived their first season back, finishing one place above relegated Hayes and Yeading.

Of the current members of the Conference, only Nuneaton, Barrow and Ebbsfleet (then Gravesend and Northfleet) were there with Telford in their inaugural season (1979-80). There has been an extensive turnover of clubs throughout the Conference's thirty-three year history. Of its founder members, only Barnet and Yeovil Town are now in the Football League. The remainder (with the exception of the four survivors) are now to be found in the lower levels of the pyramid; five (including Altrincham, Worcester City and

Bath City) at level two, and the rest (including one-time non-league giants such as Weymouth, Northwich Victoria, Stafford Rangers and Scarborough) at level three or below. Yet, as far as I can ascertain, few if any of the teams who have played in the Conference have totally disappeared from the football scene. Even Runcorn - the conference champions in 1982 - who fell apart in 2006, are now to be found (resurrected as Runcorn Linnets) in the North-West Counties League Division One. Enfield, also previous champions in 1983 and 1986, hit major financial problems thereafter, co-existing acrimoniously with a newer local club Enfield Town (who on several occasions proposed a merger but were always turned down). The original Enfield do now seem to have sunk without trace, but Enfield Town are to be found in the Rymans Premier League.

There are now many examples of so-called 'phoenix' clubs, which have risen from the ashes of their failed predecessors. Both AFC Telford United, and today's opponents Nuneaton Town are cases in point, but probably the most notable example is AFC Rushden and Diamonds, successors to their once-proud predecessors of the same name (minus the AFC). What an inspired piece of labelling! The word 'phoenix' suggests something you would be proud of, rather than the fall-out from financial collapse. But in a sense, the name is appropriate; it epitomises the commitment and spirit of supporters who refuse to accept the demise of their beloved clubs.

The match began, and Nuneaton started as though they intended to condemn Telford to relegation within the first ten minutes of the game. The home side couldn't get out of their own half. Telford legend Ryan Young saved well from Louis Moult, and Andy Brown (ex Telford) sent a header wide when he should have scored. But Telford somehow weathered the storm and could have scored themselves when James Spray latched onto a loose back pass from Gavin Cowan. But his shot was blocked by Nuneaton's Lee Burge (who looked like he was fresh out of school). On one occasion, Andy Brown was put through on the left, but overran the ball as he surged past Ryan Young, from whom he received a consolatory smile and pat on the shoulder as he disconsolately turned away – a nice gesture, I thought, from a former team-mate.

Ten minutes before half-time Nuneaton broke the deadlock. Defender Aaron Phillips outpaced Ryan Valentine on the left and beat Ryan Young neatly. There followed an angry exchange of words between Telford defender Louis Briscoe and a group of home supporters behind the goal. I couldn't hear what was shouted, but the incident marred what had so far been a benign atmosphere.

There was a sense that this was the game's decisive moment and Telford were not going to delay relegation until Easter Monday (when they were away to play-off contenders Forest Green Rovers). Nuneaton nearly added to their lead before half-time, and then four minutes into the second half did so, when Wes York surged past a Telford defender on the right and put over a low cross which Andy Brown stabbed home.

From this point onwards, it became clear why Telford were where they were. They became unable to put together a coherent attacking move. Their pair of strikers – James Spray and Steven Leslie – six goals between them in 67 appearances – looked utterly incapable of adding to that meagre tally. Passes were misplaced with monotonous regularity whilst Nuneaton were well-organised and penetrative with Wes York creating havoc down the right flank. A third goal came in the 67th minute when Andy Brown headed home after a goalmouth scramble. The linesman had raised his flag, but the referee overruled him.

### It's not the Despair I can't handle, it's the Hope

Even if he hadn't, it wouldn't have mattered. The game was effectively over long before then. Andy Brown's two goals here (plus the two at Stockport, and the one against Macclesfield) meant I'd seen him score five in three games. He was clearly going to be the leading scorer of my Conference season.

Nuneaton could well have scored more. They had produced a creditable team performance, and on the basis of this game (and the one at Mansfield) did not deserve to go down. Their travelling fans (190 in number) applauded them off the field. Telford too received sympathetic applause. There was probably some relief, amongst their supporters, that relegation had finally become certain. As Brian Stimpson (the headmaster memorably portrayed by John Cleese in the film *Clockwise*) said, 'It's not the despair, Laura, I can take the despair. It's the hope I can't stand.'

It was time to explore Wellington. Parking was free, which was welcome, but also a warning sign as to the viability of the area. If it were well-used, you can bet your life there would have been parking charges. Walking into the centre was like walking onto a film set. It was totally pedestrianized; no buses, cycles or traffic of any kind. There was hardly anyone around, which at 4.50 on a Saturday afternoon was worrying. It soon became clear that this was yet another clapped-out town centre; come quickly, Mary Portas we need you! Quite apart from the usual mix of charity shops, money lenders and amusement arcades, there was a dispiriting mix of building styles. There were a handful of nice old half-timbered buildings and some of traditional Shropshire red brick, but they were juxtaposed with a lot of infill from the 1960's and 70's, when design standards were uninspiring. Fifty years ago, I guess Wellington must have been a pleasant vibrant traditional Shropshire town. It had totally lost that ambience, and was

# Chapter 21

now a dispiriting place. The poverty of the environment was matched by the poverty (in so far as one could tell) of its few patrons. It looked like a place the middle-classes were now steering well clear of. There was a branch of Bon Marche, which I understand is a relatively classy clothes shop, but it looked totally out-of-place surrounded by betting shops, money-lenders and cut-price stores.

I later learned later that there was a big retail park just down the road, which would help explain the plight of Wellington's centre. Also Telford town centre itself, which was only three miles away, is where Telford and Wrekin Council (and its predecessor the New Town Development Corporation) had concentrated investment ever since the 1960s. Wellington had been neglected, and was very put out by the fact that it had been. It was now the poor relation; the once prosperous uncle who had fallen on hard times.

During my wanderings around Wellington, I looked in at an (otherwise uninviting) pub which I noticed had the football scores on a screen. I needed to find out what kind of result Stockport County had achieved. Much had happened since I'd seen them beat Nuneaton Town in January. Their new manager, Darije Kalezic, the only foreign import in the Conference, had lasted only ten weeks. After three successive defeats in March, including a 3-1 home reverse to Braintree Town (the last straw?) he had been sacked, and replaced by Ian Bogie, formerly Gateshead's manager. In his first game in charge, County had beaten highly-placed Newport County 1-0 at Edgeley Park. This was his second game. I waited with bated breath for the Conference scores. Macclesfield Town 1 Stockport County 1. So they were still hanging on in there, with the other seven or eight relegation candidates.

It's not the despair I can't cope with, it's the hope...

# Badger Pasties and Taiji Wuxigong

Forest Green Rovers vs Southport

Saturday 13<sup>th</sup> April 2013

Second only to my nostalgic return to Stockport and Edgeley Park, the visit to Forest Green Rovers was the one I had been most eagerly anticipating. What are a team with a name like that doing in the Conference? Shouldn't they be in the Sydenhams Wessex League, the Cherry Red Combined Counties League, or some such rural confederation? They sound like a village team and, in one sense, they are.

Forest Green is a suburb of a small town called Nailsworth (population 6,600) which lies in a valley in the Cotswolds, four miles south of Stroud. How could a club like this compete with the likes of Luton Town (population 204,000), Newport County (170,000) or AFC Telford (145,000)? But they can, and indeed have been doing so since 1998, when they first made it to the Conference. Their record of fifteen consecutive seasons is way ahead of any of the other current Conference clubs.

In so many ways, Forest Green Rovers is the most idiosyncratic club in the Conference. Its chairman and principal benefactor is a multi-millionaire - Dale Vince. But unlike his wealthy counterparts at Mansfield and Newport (John Radford and Les Scadding) Dale Vince has made his money through green, sustainable and organic enterprises. A new age traveller in earlier life, he founded the green energy company Ecotricity in 2004, and in October 2010 he became Forest Green's club chairman. His distinctive vision and principles have since been applied to almost every

# Chapter 22

aspect of the club's operations. For example, in February 2011, Forest Green Rovers players were banned from eating red meat, for health reasons (I bet that went down well!). Shortly afterwards, a ban on all meat products was introduced in the pub which had been built into the main stand, and all the other food outlets in the ground. I couldn't wait to visit this unique venue.

I travelled to Forest Green with my friend Christine. The last match she'd been to was at Anfield in 1978, when she was pregnant with her first child, and where she fainted. I was hopeful that thirty-four years on, in the much calmer atmosphere of the New Lawn, and a crowd unlikely to exceed a thousand, the experience would not be repeated.

Outside the ground is a board with a kind of manifesto; a statement of the practices which put Dale Vince's green principles into operation. It's an impressive list, which includes electric-car charging facilities (available in the car park); the use of solar-powered electricity generators; the conservation of habitats for wildlife in and around the stadium; a 'fully organic' playing pitch, and an Etesia robot mower (or Mowbot for short) which uses GPS technology to guide it automatically around the pitch without human intervention (it gathers its power from the stadium's solar panels, of course). And the board also contains a justification for the meat-free menu in the food outlets. Is there anywhere like this in the football world?

We had lunch in the Green Man, the pub at the corner of the ground, which is accessible to all (i.e. you don't have to enter the stadium first). I was fascinated to see what would be on the menu, given the ban on meat products. There were 'Badger Pasties' available, which didn't contain minced badger (surprise, surprise) - the main constituent of which was tofu. If you didn't fancy one of those, there were Red Veg Burgers or Red Veg Falafel Wraps, which was my choice, and which proved very tasty. The pub also served excellent organic real ale from the nearby Stroud Brewery.

Over lunch, I got talking to a Southport supporter, in his late fifties I would guess, who had been to every Southport game, home and away, this season. We compared notes on fixtures we'd both seen: the fortuitous early season 2-1 home win against Gateshead and the more recent ignominious 4-1 away defeat at lowly Ebbsfleet. We also discussed the players who'd impressed us: Shaun Whalley (destined for an upward move, it would appear) and cultured midfielder Sean Clancy. His enthusiasm was transparent and his knowledge of the Conference formidable. People like him inspire a real affection for the Conference. I told him that I hoped Southport would avoid relegation, and actually meant it, despite the fact that they were competing with Stockport County to do so.

The programme notes were full of hurt at Forest Green's failure to reach the play-offs, an outcome which was sealed by their 1-0 home defeat against Hereford the previous Tuesday. Until mid-February, Forest Green Rovers had looked virtual play-off certainties, but their last eleven games had yielded only two wins and seven points. Dave Hockaday, the manager, sounded inconsolable. 'To have been so forceful and powerful in the first three-quarters of the season, and then to tail off in the final quarter goes far beyond frustration… not to be in the mix at the end of the season is devastating to us all.' You shouldn't worry, Dave, at least you'll still be in the Conference next season! It's the Southports and Stockports my heart goes out to, at the present time. And the likelihood that Forest Green will finish just outside the play-off positions is not bad for a 'village club'.

The reality, of course, is that with a multi-millionaire chairman Forest Green are not really a village club anymore;

financially they are on an equal footing with the Mansfields and Newports, and one of the few full-time sides in the Conference who aren't a former league club.

Their switch to full-time status is a recent innovation, following Dale Vince's takeover in 2010. Prior to that, Forest Green Rovers had typically graced the lower-middle reaches of the Conference. Indeed the movement into the upper levels of the non-league pyramid is itself fairly recent.

Formed in 1890 by a local church minister as 'Nailsworth and Forest Green FC', the club spent most of their time in the Gloucestershire County League, until they were promoted to the Hellenic League in 1975, and then to the Southern League (Midland Division), in 1982. Under the guidance of chairman Trevor Horsley, the club then reached the heights of the Southern League in 1998 and, at the end of the 1997-98 season, were promoted (as champions) into the Conference.

Until Dale Vince arrived, Forest Green Rovers had struggled to survive in the Conference. Twice they'd finished in relegation positions (2005 and 2010) and twice been reprieved by the expulsion or resignation of clubs higher up the table for financial reasons. They owe a big debt to Salisbury City in 2010 for conveniently going bankrupt after finishing ninth. The club's best position was eighth in 2008, under the managership of Jim Harvey, who had previously spent ten years with Morecambe, where he had guided them up the table to become regular promotion candidates. But typically, Forest Green Rovers would end the season hovering just above the relegation zone. Last season they finished a respectable tenth. This year they were expected to better that.

We were in our seats in the attractive East Stand by 2.40 (as instructed) to watch a parade of the Forest Green Rovers youth and ladies teams. Youth development is another of the impressive (and unusual) features of the club. The scheme is tailored to produce locally-based players, and four of the current senior squad have graduated through the youth ranks. But it is not just about that. In the programme it is argued that '…children participate in football to have fun. We never forget that football is just that – a game. It's not about how many wins and losses are accumulated. [I suspect the first team is excluded from this commendable principle!] It's all about enjoying the game and learning and developing football and life skills.' Amen to that!

First out were the Boys under 7's (who don't participate in a league), followed by ten sides from under-8 to under-18, all of whom do. The younger they were, the more delighted they appeared, to be on show before a large and appreciative crowd. Then came the Ladies under-14s (recent winners of the Gloucestershire County Cup) and under-16s, several of whom looked like they'd rather be somewhere else, and who had to be vocally encouraged to smile by the announcer. Christine noticed that the Christian names of several of the girls would have been equally applicable to boys; Sam, Sammy, Charlie, Cally, Jamie. What does that tell us about Nailsworth? A frustrated preference for male offspring? But the boys' names did provide clues to the social characteristics of the Nailsworth area. Theo, Lucien, Oliver, Colby, Blake, Harvey and Oscar were all amongst the youth team ranks. These names do have a distinctly middle-class feel about them. And we noted only two or three black youngsters.

The view that Forest Green/Nailsworth is the most upmarket location of all Conference teams was strengthened by a quick scan of the occupants of the main stand (where 80% of the entire crowd was congregated). There was a profusion of dapper, elderly gents, well-turned-

out couples, and smartly-dressed family groups (many of
whom were no doubt there to watch their offspring in the
pre-match parade). It reminded me of my visit to Southport,
where the main stand had a similar ambience.

The village feel of Forest Green Rovers was bolstered by
the view from the main stand. There wasn't a building in
sight. Across from the stand was a shallow open terrace
(four or five steps only); behind it was a grassy hillside. On
the right was a covered standing area (the 'Sustainability in
Sport' Terrace), which was sparsely populated. On the left
was a smaller stand, on one side of which were gathered the
130 or so Southport fans who had made the journey to
Gloucestershire. They were making a lot of noise. The
home fans were not (as yet).

Fortified by falafel wraps and badger pasties, the Forest
Green faithful, who had turned up today in substantial
numbers, sat back in anticipation of seeing their team end
their run of disappointing results with a win against
struggling Southport. In the early stages, the home side
certainly dominated. They wove pretty patterns of short-
range inter-passing, which then tended to break down as
Southport's penalty area was approached. Forest Green
seemed incapable of delivering a decisive final ball so they
rarely looked threatening, for all their intricate approach
work. Indeed it was Southport, on their infrequent counter
attacks, who looked more likely to score. Karl Ledsham's
in-swinging free-kick just skidded past Danny Hattersley's
outstretched boot in the ninth minute, and later Andy
Owens' cross-cum-shot came back off the far post with
Forest Green's keeper Sam Russell well beaten.

The home crowd were remarkably patient in the face of an
increasingly lacklustre display from their team. Forest Green
lacked penetration, and hardly had a shot on target
throughout the half. Time after time their bouts of inter-

passing ended up at the feet of grateful Southport defenders, who then hit long balls in the general direction of strikers Chris Almond or Danny Hattersley. I attributed their patience to their middle-class upbringing. The parents of the Sebastians, Tobys, Elliots, Theos and Olivers, whose sons had paraded around the ground before the game, weren't the kind of people to howl abuse when witnessing an inept display, littered with errors, from their local team. Just keep calm and wait for things to improve!

During half-time, we talked to a couple sitting in front, who provided us with delicious pecan tarts (which seemed very much in keeping with the culinary ambience of the club; sausage rolls would have been inappropriate!) I asked why Forest Green's form had declined so drastically in recent weeks. 'It's difficult to put your finger on it,' we were told. The pretty football which had been a feature of the team's game all season, had lost its edge, and had recently resulted in few scoring opportunities. The goals had dried up. The team had been chopped and changed too much. There had been injuries (but wasn't that the case throughout the Conference?). Some of the recent signings had proved disappointing, including Yemi Odubade, who'd impressed me, when playing for Gateshead earlier in the season. The first half we'd just seen was, one man told me, typical of recent weeks. Pretty but punchless.

Would we see an improvement in the second half? No. Forest Green's performance got even worse, with bursts of inter-passing often ending with the ball booted back to their keeper, to the increasing frustration of the crowd. A 0-0 draw seemed likely, but if any side was going to win it, it was Southport. I couldn't recall Forest Green having had a single serious shot at goal. Southport's Shaun Whalley, meanwhile, squirmed and barged his way past a succession of defenders on the right, but no-one could connect with his cross. Then the same player hit a powerful free-kick from way out on the left which Sam Russell just managed to tip over the bar. Karl Ledsham's subsequent corner skimmed off the head of home defender Chris Stokes and sailed into the corner of the net to an ecstatic response from the 130 Southport fans seated behind the goal.

The Southport fans had been brilliant throughout. Despite being outnumbered ten-to-one, they'd outshouted and outsung the home fans by a big margin. I realised that, as befits a middle-class club, almost all the home supporters were in the main stand. In the 'Sustainability in Sport' terrace, at one end of the ground (opposite to the Southport supporters enclosure), where you'd expect the home fans to be, there was a large banner with the wording 'Green Army'! Scattered haphazardly around it were at most 50-60 occupants who remained largely silent. Occasional strangled cries of 'Green Army' came from individuals in the stand, but there was no evidence of the knot of 80 or so vociferous home supporters who had been present at all my other visits (even at Braintree, Ebbsfleet and Alfreton). That was what was missing at Forest Green; its absence helped explain why their home record was less impressive than their away performances.

Southport played out time without looking remotely stretched. When the final whistle went, all eleven of their players, the manager, and the other occupants of the bench rushed to where their supporters were congregated, and celebrated with them. Many joyful embraces between players and supporters took place. I found it quite moving, and symbolic of all that was good about the Conference. A team of part-timers (competing in a predominantly full-time league) visit full-time, bankrolled Forest Green and win a game which secures their survival in the Conference. 130 fans make a long trip with them and provide vocal support out of all proportion to their numbers. Team managers and supporters celebrate together at the end. Mission accomplished.

There was a totally different reaction in the Main Stand, of course, although this being Forest Green, it was all very low key. There was a sporadic outburst of booing as Dave Hockaday turned to wave (apologetically) at the crowd, before gathering his players together in a huddle in the middle of the pitch. It wasn't clear what the purpose of this was; perhaps it was: 'You were crap, weren't you', 'Yes boss, we know we were.' Almost anywhere else in the Conference, after a display of such ineptitude, home supporters would have given the team and manager a much rougher reception with cries of 'You're not fit to wear the shirt' or 'Resign!' But not at Forest Green.

The bizarre choice for man-of-the-match was Forest Green's Chris Stokes, unfortunate scorer of the own-goal which won it for Southport. I'm sure the entire Southport team and bench were very happy with that choice.

Then came the moment when the other Conference results were announced. Surely Stockport had beaten Dartford at home? But they hadn't; they'd lost 0-1. Elsewhere Nuneaton had beaten Hyde; Gateshead had drawn at Hereford, and it was announced that Lincoln had drawn at home to Tamworth (actually they hadn't; it later emerged that they'd won 2-1). How could Stockport do this to me (and the 6,000 fans who had actually turned up on the day)? I began to hope that they would lose at fellow-strugglers Gateshead on Tuesday, and put us all out of our misery!

We'd been told by our half-time acquaintances that Nailsworth was a 'pretty village' which we'd enjoy exploring. Unfortunately the reality did not match the recommendation. Nailsworth is actually a small town rather than a village. The main problem was that it lacked focus. There were two parallel 'main streets'. One contained a sizeable car parking area, a small bus station, a Tesco Express Store and a modest-sized Co-op. Almost all the buildings were relatively new. It wasn't remotely picturesque! It was called 'Old Market Place' but there was no indication that a market still operated there. Parallel was Fountain Street, which did contain a more interesting-looking group of shops in attractive old buildings. On closer inspection they turned out to comprise a mixture of the twee and the esoteric, with a few upmarket charity shops and cafes thrown in. It was clear that the 'alternative' ethos of Forest Green Rovers was also prevalent in Nailsworth itself (and, for all I know, throughout the Cotswolds). In Fountain Street there were hardly any 'normal' shops; instead there were organic health food stores (including 'Shiny Goodness'), antique shops, 'Jacaranda Flowers', and the recently opened Number 28 café ('Passionate about coffee, James has made every effort to create a lovely space to relax, read the paper, chat to all and sundry and even bring your own music to put on in the background'). If this strikes you as a touch pretentious, have a look at what else is available in Nailsworth[*]. You can join a 'Mindfulness Group' and learn simple techniques to reduce stress, increase concentration, and enrich your personal and professional life. You can make a positive change in your life by giving 'solution-focused hypnotherapy' a try. You can party yourself into shape by joining a 'Latin-inspired easy-to-follow calorie-burning dance fitness party'. You can enrol for classes in 'Awareness through Movement', Tae-Kwan-Do, Buddhist meditation, Taiji Wuxigong (!) Taiji and Qi Gong (!!), Lightwaves Shintaido, or 'Nia Dance'; and that's

---

[*] Information from April 2013 issue of the 'Nailsworth News'

only a small selection of the delights available in and around the town. Is there anywhere else in the country, of comparative size, where there is such a mind-blowing range of 'alternative' activities available? Personally, I felt more relaxed in the town centres of Alfreton and Tamworth, for all their limitations.

There was much to admire about Forest Green Rovers. It stands out in the Conference as a club with a distinctive vision, who have put that vision into practice. They are clearly ambitious for Football League status, and with Dale Vince bankrolling them, why wouldn't they be? But they need to be aware of the track record of 'little clubs' like themselves, who have attracted wealthy backers and achieved promotion from the Conference. It's been fine whilst the benefactors have stayed with them, but much more problematic when, for various reasons, they've backed out, and taken their chequebooks elsewhere. A trawl through the list of Conference champions over the years reveals some examples of sustained success (Wycombe Wanderers, Cheltenham Town, Yeovil Town, and more recently, Crawley and Fleetwood). But there have also been some spectacular falls from grace. Boston United, champions in 2004, fell out of the Football League in 2009, went into receivership, were demoted to level five of the pyramid, and have only recently made it back to the Blue Square Bet North. Maidstone United's problems have already been discussed in the Dartford chapter (moral of the story: it's a mistake to sell your local ground and move elsewhere in a push to reach the League. Your supporters will not want to travel to Dartford, or at least, not enough of them will). And who now remembers Rushden and Diamonds, purchased by the owner of Doc Martens Shoes, who financed the building of a new stadium, and bankrolled the club into the Football League in 2002? By 2006 he had left, the club had gone bankrupt, and it now languishes in the United Counties League Division One (level six of the pyramid) in its resurrected form of AFC Rushden and Diamonds. Scarborough (champions in 1988) provides a further cautionary tale (they currently play in a level five league).

It would be sad if Forest Green Rovers were to overreach themselves, and end up back in the Hellenic League, which is where they were when the Conference was launched in 1979.

# What do you think of it so far...?

Luton Town vs Newport County

Tuesday April 16<sup>th</sup> 2013

Luton was my penultimate destination. I travelled down by train on the Tuesday of the last week of the Conference season, for what seemed a relatively meaningless fixture between Luton Town and Newport County. The latter were already assured of third place, but couldn't realistically hope to win the title (Kidderminster Harriers would have to lose 5-0 at home to Stockport County in the final game of the season, to give Newport any chance of doing so, and that wasn't going to happen, was it?). Luton had blown their play-off chances during their cup run, during which memorable cup victories (1-0 away to Norwich) were interspersed with inexplicable league defeats (1-0 at Barrow). I walked from Euston to St Pancras, to catch my train to Luton, where I enjoyed listening to some bravura performances on the pianos in the station concourse, which someone had helpfully, and imaginatively, made available for passers-by to use casually.

It had been a long time since I'd last been in Luton – thirty years or so. I remembered a busy high street and wondered whether it was still there. Or had it been superseded by a bright purpose-built new centre? It had indeed. What was once the High Street was now a gigantic linear concrete structure called 'The Mall'. Why would anyone want to shop there? (The reality, I suppose, is that they have little choice).

There was a scattering of more down-market establishments in the streets around 'The Mall'. One in particular caught my eye, 'Julia's Wigs', the shop window of which contained row upon row of the heads of smiling women decked in an amazing variety of wigs. The effect was a bit like the front cover of the Beatles classic album 'A Hard Day's Night'. Either there's a chronic problem of hair loss amongst women in Luton, or wig shops are the next big thing, and Julia is ahead of the game. There may be scope for a coming-together with nails. Lisa's Wigs and Nails perhaps?

It was clear from my meanderings around Luton's depressing town centre that the town was the most multi-racial of the places I'd so far visited. I later discovered that Luton is one of three sizeable towns where the white population is now in a minority (the others are Leicester and Slough).

I caught a bus along the Dunstable Road to my Travelodge destination, three miles out. Adjacent to the road was an almost completed 'fast track' dedicated bus route, next to which could be seen the back of one of the stands of Kenilworth Road, Luton Town's ground, which I would be visiting later. The Travelodge was not amongst the better examples of the species. It looked more like a factory than a hotel, and was situated alongside the junction from which you left the M1 for Luton town centre. My spartan room had double-glazed windows, though quadruple-glazing might have been more appropriate. But I'd coped with the noise level at the Inn on the Broadway in Woking, so ought to be able to rise to this new challenge.

The bus back towards Kenilworth Road deposited me near the ground in a shopping area dominated by Asian food stores, clothes shops and other outlets. It reminded me of the Belgrave area in Leicester, where I'd once lodged, and where I once found myself the only white man in an otherwise Asian-dominated pub (I was made very welcome and given free samosas). The area was so much more vibrant and interesting than Luton's town centre. It was just about warm enough for people to stand around on the pavements chatting, or to sit outside the cafes. There were several stalls outside the shops, or in the side streets, selling fruit and vegetables. If there was any racial tension in Luton, it certainly wasn't apparent here.

That perception was not, however, confirmed by what I later discovered. I'd forgotten that Luton was where the four London bombers boarded a train on 7 July 2005, although (to be fair to Luton) they had travelled down earlier from West Yorkshire. In a powerful and deeply-felt article in the Guardian (13 December 2010), journalist Sarfraz Manzoor, who was born and brought up in Luton, argued that, today, Luton has come to embody the failure of multiculturalism and community relations. Not only is there the link with the 7/7 bombers, but the town is also where the far-right English Defence League was born. It was they who invited Pastor Terry James, the American anti-Muslim extremist, to address a meeting.[*] Abdulwhab-al-Abduly who, in 2010, detonated two bombs in Stockholm, the second of which killed him, had been studying in Luton before his self-inflicted death. There had been several arrests of suspected terrorists in Luton since then. Manzoor identified three reasons for the deterioration in community relations. First there are now schools (and streets) in Luton which are 'ominously monocultural'. The school he attended is now 96% Asian. 'Living in such bubbles', he argued, 'can breed ignorance which spills over into intolerance.' Secondly, until 2002, Vauxhall was by far the largest employer in the working-class town. 'You would get workers from different communities all together, and that,' he wrote, 'had a positive impact on community cohesion.' Vauxhall was the glue which held the town together, and

---

[*] The Home Office wisely refused to grant him a visa

with its demise, it had come unstuck.' Thirdly the white working class in Luton had been ignored, and into the subsequent void had stepped the English Defence League, whose extremism has been fuelled by the (equally unrepresentative) groups of Muslims who took to the streets to scream at returning British soldiers in 2010.

As noted by Manzoor, Luton, like Barrow, was for a large part of the twentieth century a company town. In 1907, Vauxhall opened its first factory in Luton and began car production. At its peak, the factory employed more than 30,000 workers. But the decline of car manufacturing in Britain, in the 1980s and 1990s, hit Luton as it did so many other sites, and in 2000, Vauxhall announced that it was to cease car production here. In 2002 the last car rolled off the production line, and although commercial vehicles are still manufactured in Luton, the current number of employees is only just over 1,000. In the circumstances, it is a minor miracle that the unemployment rate in Luton is only 5%. The town has managed to reinvent itself as a service centre, thanks to its proximity to the M1.

I'd been to Kenilworth Road once before, in the late 1970's. The ground hadn't changed much. As Simon Inglis points out, however 'cramped' you think your team's ground is, wait until you visit Kenilworth Road! It is hemmed in to the north east and west by row upon row of terraced houses, the occupants of which must have dreaded Saturdays in the days when football hooliganism was at its height. To the south, what used to be a railway (soon to become the new fast-track bus route) runs close to the ground.

What was new was the row of executive boxes, replacing what used to be the Bobbers Stand opposite the Main Stand. But otherwise, Kenilworth Road proved to be an unreconstructed delight to rival Barrow's Holker Street. Luton Town have been intending to move for the past thirty-five years, at one time to Milton Keynes, more recently to a new stadium on the edge of Luton. But their intentions have been frustrated (thanks to indignant supporters and unhelpful local councils), and Kenilworth Road is where they remain. In these circumstances, the club has not seen fit to invest in the ground, so, as with Holker Street, it's like walking back into the 1950s. The stadium is now all-seater (remember Luton Town were in the Championship as recently as 2006) but it has remained virtually unchanged in almost every other respect.

There are three clubs in the Conference who have played a hundred or more seasons in the Football League: Grimsby Town (108), Lincoln City (102) and Stockport County (100). All could reasonably be regarded as 'fallen giants' but the club with the best claim to be the biggest fallen giant of them all is surely Luton Town. They entered the League later than the other three, and hence have fewer years of League experience (84) but Luton have played more seasons at the top level (fifteen in total, including a long spell there as recently as 1982-92), compared with Grimsby's twelve, the last of which was as long ago as 1948. And Luton have a much more impressive honours board; League Cup winners in 1988 when they famously beat Arsenal 3-2; FA Cup finalists in 1959; League Cup finalists in 1989. They received public attention for another reason, in the mid-1980s, when their chairman David Evans proved a rare enthusiastic supporter of Margaret Thatcher's crackpot scheme to introduce identity cards to regulate access to Football League grounds.

From 2006, it has been downhill all the way, with relegation from the Championship in 2007, followed by another downward move in 2008, after a season in which all manner of financial irregularities were exposed, and the club went into receivership. If that was bad enough, then being

# Chapter 23

obliged to start the 2008-09 season in Division Two with a 30-point penalty was worse. Despite a reasonably successful season on the pitch, a handicap of this magnitude could not be overcome, and Luton were relegated to the Conference. Since then they had reached the play-offs each season, losing the final in the last two to AFC Wimbledon (on penalties) and York City (1-2) respectively.

I noticed an Eric Morecambe bar, commemorating Luton's most famous supporter of recent times. Eric Morecambe lived for many years in nearby Harpenden, and became a director (and focus of attention whenever he attended a match). It's said that half-way through many a first half in which Luton had fallen behind, fans would turn to him and shout 'what do you think of it so far, Eric?' To which, of course, he would reply 'rubbish!' A celebrity link of sorts continues, in that Luton Town's current chairman is Nick Owen, the veteran newsreader. In his 'From the Boardroom' column, he shared his disappointment at Luton's campaign.

> 'The best way to describe the season as
> far as I'm concerned is wretched. I have
> been following the Town for 55 years
> now, and I have to say this has been the
> worst… some results have been
> inexplicable… I promise you we have
> found it as gut-wrenching as you have…'

There was also a Nick Owen bar, where I spoke to a couple of supporters who echoed their chairman's sentiments, but who were perhaps less gut-wrenched than he might have forecast. There had been problems with injuries, they said. A couple of the pre-season 'big signings', Danny Spiller and Garry Richards, had not kicked a ball for the first team. The cup run, exciting though it was at the time, led to a lack of motivation in bread-and-butter league games (e.g. at

Dartford, Braintree and Barrow). There had been too much chopping and changing of personnel. Stuart Fleetwood, who was top of the Conference goalscoring table by the end of September, had fallen out of form and favour since. I asked them if they thought Paul Buckle would have survived as manager had he not resigned for 'personal reasons' in February. They thought he could have been given another season to prove himself, but they were happy with the recent improvement in the team's performances under the (highly-paid) new manager John Still, whom they expected to initiate a major clear-out at the end of the season.

I took my place in an uncomfortable tip-up plastic seat in the Main Stand. Despite the previous disappointments, Luton received a warm reception from the biggest crowd I'd been in all season. So did the eight-year-old mascot, as he trotted off the field just before kick-off. What a joyous experience that must have been for a young lad; something he'll cherish for the rest of his life.

It was hard to believe that this was, for both sides, a relatively meaningless end-of-season fixture. The football flowed right from the start, with both sides committed to an attacking game, and both creating early chances. The atmosphere was infectious, helped by the sense of enclosure at the ground, and the presence of a reasonable contingent of Newport supporters. Luton were playing what the manager later described as a 'fluid 4-3-3 formation', with Alex Lawless positioned between, and just behind, the two principal strikers Andre Gray and Jon Shaw. Dave Martin (ex-Dartford) looked confident and dangerous on the left.

After 11 minutes, the home side went ahead when Andre Gray neatly slotted a loose ball in the area into the bottom right-hand corner of the net. After half-an-hour the same player was put clean through and attempted a delicate chip over Newport's Lenny Pidgeley, which just cleared the bar. Minutes later Jon Shaw lined himself up for a long-range shot just outside the area, and was unlucky to see it bounce back from the angle of the crossbar and post. But Newport were also creating chances, as the ball switched from end-to-end in what was probably the best 45 minutes I'd seen all season, despite the uneven surface of the pitch.

The only sour notes in an otherwise excellent half were the monkey noises directed by a handful of home supporters at Newport's leading scorer Aaron O'Connor, who had, a season or so ago, played for Luton. Why he was singled out was difficult to understand. There were several other black players in both the home and away sides, and you'd expect those who were minded to behave in this brainless and prejudiced manner, to do it consistently! O'Connor was substituted at half-time and replaced by Christian Jolley (also black) who was mercifully spared the jungle noises.

The second half proved just as entertaining as the first. It was not long before Newport deservedly equalised, as Jolley slotted the ball neatly past Luton's Dean Brill. They then looked more likely to take the lead than Luton. Lee Minshull in midfield was a dominant figure, winning or receiving the ball on countless occasions and invariably using it creatively. However, it was Luton who regained the lead in the 78th minute when the impressive Andre Gray received the ball just inside the area from substitute Matt Robinson and hit a thunderous first-time drive past Lenny Pidgeley. Game over? Indeed no. Newport rallied, counter-attacked and in the 83rd minute Christian Jolley (again) equalised with a neatly-taken header from a right-wing cross at the far post. Either side could subsequently have won it. The cracking pace and end-to-end football continued right through to the end. Andre Gray was deservedly awarded the man-of-the-match honour. The Luton fans departed in a reasonably positive frame-of-mind, disappointed at another home draw (one of many over the season) but pleased about the quality of the football. A 2-2 draw was a fair result, I thought. It would have been unjust if Newport had come away with nothing. I will be seeing them again at Grimsby on the last day of the season, when it will be interesting to see if they field as strong a side as they did today, and if they play with the same commitment. Today's results mean Newport will definitely finish third, whatever they (or anyone else) does next Saturday.

As the 5,125 crowd dispersed into the streets of terraced houses surrounding the ground, it was apparent that the ethnic balance of the town was not reflected in the make-up of the club's supporters, who were predominantly white (and male), with a fair sprinkling of youngsters. This was a pity; mutual support for a football team is another way in which community cohesion can be strengthened. Now that the Vauxhall plant has become a shadow of its former self, one wonders what other large-scale shared experiences there are in Luton for the different ethnic groups.

Still I was left with a feeling of exhilaration after witnessing the best game of football I had seen all season, in an atmospheric 'old-style' football stadium, set in the traditional environment of streets and terraced houses. Over the year my view of Luton Town had changed. I had been impressed by their early season victory at Hyde and seen them as possible champions and certainly play-off contenders. I'd then witnessed lacklustre performances at Dartford and Braintree, and relished the fact that the 'moneybags' club of the Conference (where Luton Town are the equivalent of Chelsea or Manchester City) could be defeated by unfashionable part-timers. But now I'd been to Kenilworth Road and observed the fervour of their supporters, I began to hope that their determination to

## Chapter 23

regain their Football League status was successful. After all they'd only lost it (in 2009) when an uncompromisingly severe 30-point penalty was imposed on them. Whilst it is fair enough that clubs who are guilty of financial irregularities should be penalised (after all, the purchase of players they couldn't really afford may well be involved) the penalty imposed on Luton was out of all proportion to those meted out before or since.

I walked the two miles back to the Travelodge, stopping off at an almost deserted modern pub, to check on the Stockport result. They had drawn 1-1 at Gateshead. A win would have given them a reasonable chance of survival. The draw meant that they would have to win at promotion-seeking Kidderminster to have any hope. It didn't look good.

# Sing when we're fishing...

Grimsby Town vs Newport County

Saturday 20<sup>th</sup> April 2013

Grimsby: the end of the journey that commenced back on August 11<sup>th</sup> 2012 in Barrow.

April 20<sup>th</sup> 2013 was sunny and warm, as it had been on August 11<sup>th</sup>. In the interim we had experienced the coldest winter for fifty years with numerous Conference match postponements due to snow, frozen or flooded pitches, and one coach journey that never made it to the destination (Grimsby Town failed to reach Macclesfield on Friday February 22<sup>nd</sup> for a TV-relayed fixture, as a result of a long traffic delay on the M62).

Grimsby was an appropriate place to end my journey, because there are a number of parallels between Barrow and Grimsby. Both are coastal towns (two of only three in the Conference). Both are out on a limb, not on the way to anywhere else, the end of the road, the end of the line. Both have seen their economic base decline over the past thirty years; Barrow with the decline of the shipbuilding workforce at Vickers (now BAE systems), Grimsby with the virtual disappearance of the fishing industry.

However, Grimsby has an appendage which Barrow lacks. To the south of the town and contiguous with it lies rundown Cleethorpes, which is struggling to maintain its identity as a holiday resort. Cleethorpes is where Grimsby Town's ground, Blundell Park, is located, giving rise to the 'trick question' (when Grimsby were in the Football League) of 'which football club plays all its fixtures away from home'? In fact they share this distinction with Manchester United, whose ground is outside the boundaries of

# Chapter 24

Manchester, in Stretford, and Nottingham Forest whose ground is (just) outside the City of Nottingham.

I travelled by car, mainly because the kick-off time was 5.15 pm for all the final day Conference fixtures, to enable one of the key games to be televised (Mansfield Town versus Wrexham, as it turned out). It is possible to get from Kendal to Grimsby by train (via Manchester) but it takes forever, and with the match not finishing until 7.15 pm, it would not have been possible to get back home that night. To be honest, I didn't relish an overnight stop in Grimsby (or Cleethorpes for that matter). My experiences in Newport, Cambridge and Woking had made me doubtful of my ability to judge the suitability of accommodation! So it was that, on a sunny April afternoon, I found myself driving across the flatlands of South Yorkshire and North Lincolnshire on motorways (M18 and M180) that were virtually deserted.

Lincolnshire is one of the most rural of English counties, with one of the lowest county population densities. Certainly rurality dominates, until you pass south of Scunthorpe and move towards Grimsby, where the estuarial coast, south of the Humber, is dominated by industrial developments including a large chemical works north of Immingham. As you get closer to the town, there's a belt of shed-like units, many of which, I guessed, housed examples of the five hundred food-related companies which are located in Grimsby.

Food-processing has turned out to be a key factor in the economic survival of Grimsby. The town, until the 1980's, was dominated by fishing. In the 1950's it was reputedly the largest fishing port in the world. I remember visiting Grimsby in the early 1970's and seeing masses of trawlers in the docks, which were surrounded by sheds for processing the catches. Then came the Cod War, and the spectacular decline of the industry. By the 1990's only a handful of trawlers still operated. Large numbers of skilled trawlermen became redundant, and struggled to find work ashore.

Grimsby continues to house a fish market of European importance (the largest in the UK), but most of what is sold is now brought overland from other ports (or Iceland) via containerisation. In partnership with Immingham, it remains the UKs largest port by tonnage.

As mentioned above, food processing - not just fish but also vegetables – has become a major industry in the area, drawing on the agriculture of the surrounding countryside. The Ross group, Findus, and Youngs, are all based in Grimsby, which now markets itself as 'Europe's Food Town'.

But food processing is not likely to prove an acceptable alternative to redundant trawlerman. Traditionally it's an occupation dominated by women, many of them operating on a part-time basis. Some of the grizzled old timers I passed in the town centre were, I suspect, disenchanted ex-fishermen.

On entering the town on the A180 the sign tells you it's 'Great Grimsby'. This is not, as you might suspect, an attempt at local self-aggrandisement, but rather a legitimate way of distinguishing the town from Little Grimsby, a tiny hamlet some fourteen miles inland. In fact, the local authority which contains Grimsby is called 'North East Lincolnshire' which doesn't exactly inspire feelings of local identity.

The first building that you notice on entering Grimsby is the tall, slender Dock Tower, built in 1852. Having admired it (a 'focal point' which puts the new Mansfield bus station in its place) I drove into what I took to be the town centre. Having parked the car near a building called 'Central Hall',

and wandered along Freeman Street, I quickly concluded
that it wasn't. It reminded me very much of Gateshead
High Street, not least because of its seedy, sinister ambience.
Overweight men with shaved heads stood in public house
doorways. Youths with hoodies loitered outside boarded-up
shops like they were 'waiting for the man' (or looking for
trouble). I passed 'The Angel' which proclaimed itself a
'Traditional Pub of Character since 1867' and which assured
passers-by that there was 'always a warm and friendly
welcome'. It was closed. After passing a tattoo parlour and a
pawnbroker, I began to worry about the vulnerability of my
car, parked in a side street. Would the tyres have been
slashed? No, they were fine, I was just being paranoid! But I
was glad to drive away from Freeman Street.

The real town centre, when I found it, was not as I dimly
remembered it from the 1970s. It was dominated by the
usual large-scale precinct, the Freshney Place Shopping
Centre. There seemed precious little left of Grimsby's
traditional town centre, with its narrow winding streets, and
quaint specialist shops. I later learned that the construction
of the new precinct had involved the wholesale demolition
of much of the old town, including the historic Bull Ring
and East St Mary's Gate (of which no trace remains). No
wonder it seemed unfamiliar. I didn't linger long.

There is a profoundly depressing feel about the area
surrounding Grimsby's town centre. It's not that there are
large areas of dereliction and decay (although there are some
pockets), but rather that the quality of the buildings is so
uninspiring: large superstores surrounded by seas of car
parks: the utilitarian sheds used for storage or food
processing purposes: the intrusive road system: and the run-
down fringe shopping areas such as Freeman Street.

The headline in the Grimsby Telegraph suggested that
respect for the monarchy is not part of the town's culture.

'Kate was a Cheap Date' referred to a recent visit of the Duchess of Cambridge, and the response to a 'Freedom of Information' enquiry as to how much the visit cost the town. The answer was £3,856, spent mainly on the elimination of graffiti and a 'jet wash and sand block paving outside the Fishing Heritage Centre'. An indignant council leader told the Telegraph that 'the work we did to prepare for the visit needed to be done anyway. We just brought it forward a little, so that Grimsby looked its best while the world's eyes were watching.' Oh yes?

I drove the two miles to Cleethorpes. The floodlight towers of Blundell Park soon came into view on my left. I parked the car on a street parallel to the beach (which you couldn't reach because the railway line was in the way). There was seventy-five minutes before kick-off, and I had plenty of time to explore.

Blundell Park is situated a couple of miles north of Cleethorpes town centre, in a small traditional shopping area, which was packed with fans, even an hour or so before kick-off. There were two pubs, both heaving. Outside the Imperial, there was some raucous singing under way. Apparently Grimsby fans are still prone to bursts of 'Sing when we're fishing'. Determined to enjoy my customary pre-match pint, I walked into an establishment called the 'New Imperial Club' expecting to be challenged by someone on the door. But challenge there was none, and I was served a (mediocre) pint of fizzy Bass without any questioning of my club membership (or lack of it).

Of the numerous 'sleeping giants' in the Conference, Grimsby Town would come second only to Luton Town in terms of status. Like Luton, they have graced the highest level of the Football League, albeit well before any of today's players were born. They were there between 1901 and 1903, and then 1929-32 and 1934-39. Having survived for a further couple of seasons after the war, they were relegated in 1948, never to return. Grimsby's league history goes back further than Luton's, having first played in Division Two in 1892 (with Luton it was 1897).

Since they departed Division One in 1948, Grimsby Town have moved up and down the Leagues on a regular basis. They've had spells in the Championship (or its previous incarnations) including one as recently as 1998-2003. They've had brief spells in Division 2 (or its predecessors) including a period between 1968 and 1972 which involved an application for re-election. Following relegation to that division in 2004, the club struggled on the pitch (never higher than the lower-middle of the table) and off it (financial problems, frequent changes of management) until, in 2010, they were relegated to the Conference, after an unbroken run of 118 years (and 108 seasons) in the Football League. Grimsby Town's decline had finally caught up with the decline of Grimsby as a fishing port.

Grimsby Town have, since the war, been managed by one very famous manager, one fairly famous one, and one less well-known, but arguably the most successful of the three. After a brief managerial debut at Carlisle United (well they've all got to start somewhere!) the legendary Bill Shankly spent two years with Grimsby, nearly but not quite lifting them out of Division Three North (they finished second in1951-52) before moving on to Workington and eventually (in 1959) Liverpool. Lawrie McMenemy had a spell at Grimsby between 1971 and 1973, taking them up from Division Four to Division Three, before departing for Southampton. But equally venerated in Grimsby is Alan Buckley, who had three successful managerial spells with the club (1984-1988, 1997-2000 and 2006-08) inspiring promotions in each of the first two spells, and a Wembley appearance in the Johnstones Paint Trophy (or whatever it was called then) in 2007. Sadly, he could not halt the long-term decline of the club, and he was sacked (for the second time) in 2008.

The club found it hard to adjust to life in the Conference, finishing eleventh in both 2010-11 and 2011-12. This season, under the supervision of joint managers Rob Scott and Paul Hurst, they have done much better, heading the table for a period of 10 weeks in mid-season, and always looking likely (apart from a brief recent wobble) to reach the play-offs.

Blundell Park has a traditional feel; not so much the interior of the stadium, but rather the way it dominates the area of terraced housing in which it is situated. In particular the Findus Stand (where I sat) towers above its surroundings. It was opened in 1982, and now houses the administrative offices, and the changing rooms, which had previously been located in the old Main Stand opposite. At the time the Findus Stand was built, the club put seats where once there had been a paddock, in front of the old Main Stand, and discovered that the oldest section of the stand, built in 1901, had simply been plonked onto the ground without any foundations.[*] As Simon Inglis suggested, it's remarkable that it had survived in this state for so long.

The ground has the ambience of one that is accustomed to Football League status and expects to return there before long (there are, for example 14 executive boxes between the upper and lower tiers of the Findus Stand). Like Luton's Kenilworth Road, there's a sense of enclosure, and a good atmosphere, helped by the size of the crowds Grimsby attract (over 4,500 there today).

---

[*] Simon Inglis; The Football Grounds of Britain, 1983 p107

# Chapter 24

The match was likely to prove a dress rehearsal for a play-off semi-final between the two sides. Newport County were firmly entrenched in third place, and Grimsby would finish fourth, unless they lost to Newport, and Wrexham won at Mansfield. Newport's relative indifference to the outcome became clear when the teams were announced. Several key players, including Aaron O'Connor, Christian Jolley, Lee Minshull and David Pipe were being rested. Their team-sheet bore a passing resemblance to Newport Reserves.

Grimsby had also 'rested' one or two regulars, including leading scorer Ross Hannah, and Andy Cook, but were fielding a closer approximation to their first team. Nonetheless it was Newport who looked more threatening in the early stages, with Connor Washington twice testing the home keeper Greg Fleming. Then, after 18 minutes, Grimsby were awarded a free-kick way out on the left. Jamie Devitt curled a long-range shot into the far corner of the net – either a piece of inspiration or a total fluke (on balance I'd give him the benefit of the doubt). Six minutes later a shot from midfielder Andi Thanag from outside the area took a deflection and arced over a helpless Alan Julian. Newport began to lose interest and although they continued to mount attacks, it was never with much conviction. Grimsby, however, were playing really well, moving the ball around purposefully and looking dangerous every time they approached their opponent's penalty area. Jamie Devitt impressed as an old-fashioned 'tricky winger' jinking and body-swerving his way past defenders. It's good that tricky wingers are not (quite) yet a dying race! Five minutes before half-time, there was a moment for celebration. Liam Hearn, who last season was Grimsby's leading scorer, had only recently returned to the side after a season-long problem with a ruptured Achilles tendon. Receiving the ball in the box, he swivelled superbly and fired an unstoppable shot past the helpless Newport keeper. The home crowd, who had kept up an impressive volume of vocal support throughout the half, rose to him. Liam is back!

My seat was in a crowded part of the main stand, and at half-time, the men on either side of me had questions to ask. 'What's in your bag?' asked the supporter to my left, in a friendly rather than a suspicious way. 'Nothing of interest', I responded, 'my lunch, amongst other things.' The supporter on my right, who was there with his teenage son, had noticed I'd been taking notes throughout the first half, and wanted to know why. I explained about the book. He was genuinely interested (as indeed most of the supporters I've told about it on my various visits have been). I also mentioned my attachment to Stockport County. He shook his head sympathetically. The half-time score at Kidderminster was 0-0, as it was at Gateshead. Tamworth were also drawing 1-1. So there was still hope. But not much!

During the interval, a large ferry sailed down the estuary, clearly visible from the Upper Findus Stand. 'Where else in the country could you see that from a football ground?' he asked, expecting the answer 'nowhere' which is probably right (Arbroath? Dunfermline Athletic? Greenock Morton?) We agreed that the stadium deserved better than the Conference, and that the vocal intensity of the home support deserved better than a play-off place. From early December to mid-February, Grimsby had been top of the league. Currently they were fifth. Why had there been a decline?' I asked him. 'It was Wembley, wasn't it,' was his response. Wembley? When had Grimsby last been to Wembley? And then I remembered: Grimsby had played (and lost) to Wrexham in the FA Trophy final at Wembley four weeks previously. I checked their record around that time in the programme. Four consecutive league defeats in

# Chapter 24

the run-up to the final; two draws against lowly-placed sides in the anticlimactic aftermath. If they'd won three of those six games they'd still be up there with Kidderminster and Mansfield. Temporary celebrity status (appearing at Wembley) and financial gain (the proceeds from a 20,000 crowd) are all very well, but I bet Grimsby would have preferred automatic promotion back to the League. If they failed to achieve promotion via the play-offs, they could commiserate with Luton Town, whose promotion ambitions were similarly scuppered by a high-profile run in the FA Cup.

The second half was a non-event. Newport weren't going to pull three goals back, and were playing like they didn't expect to, or particularly want to. Grimsby, no doubt with next Wednesday's play-off first leg in mind, were content to go through the motions, although they had opportunities to add to their lead. Five minutes before the end, the bloke with whom I'd shared a half-time conversation, nudged me. He'd asked his son to check the score at Kidderminster. Stockport were losing 1-0. What I didn't know at the time was that the game had been delayed for half-an-hour following a pitch invasion by a handful of Stockport fans after Kidderminster had scored their first goal. They went on to win 4-0.

So in a sense, Stockport had gone down fighting! We exchanged rueful smiles. This was it, the end of the road for the club whose promotion prospects had inspired me to undertake the succession of journeys to places like Grimsby. I left the stadium, walked back to the car, and departed past the dock tower, past the multiple industrial units, through the fields of rural Lincolnshire, back towards home.

# 21st April 2013 – League Table

| | Team | P | W | D | L | F | A | GD | Pt |
|---|---|---|---|---|---|---|---|---|---|
| 1 | Mansfield Town | 46 | 30 | 5 | 11 | 92 | 52 | 40 | 95 |
| 2 | Kidderminster Harriers | 46 | 28 | 9 | 9 | 82 | 40 | 42 | 93 |
| 3 | Newport County AFC | 46 | 25 | 10 | 11 | 85 | 60 | 25 | 85 |
| 4 | Grimsby Town | 46 | 23 | 14 | 9 | 70 | 38 | 32 | 83 |
| 5 | Wrexham | 46 | 22 | 14 | 10 | 74 | 45 | 29 | 80 |
| 6 | Hereford United | 46 | 19 | 13 | 14 | 73 | 63 | 10 | 70 |
| 7 | Luton Town | 46 | 18 | 13 | 15 | 70 | 62 | 8 | 67 |
| 8 | Dartford | 46 | 19 | 9 | 18 | 67 | 63 | 4 | 66 |
| 9 | Braintree Town | 46 | 19 | 9 | 18 | 63 | 72 | -9 | 66 |
| 10 | Forest Green Rovers | 46 | 18 | 11 | 17 | 63 | 49 | 14 | 65 |
| 11 | Macclesfield Town | 46 | 17 | 12 | 17 | 65 | 70 | -5 | 63 |
| 12 | Woking | 46 | 18 | 8 | 20 | 73 | 81 | -8 | 62 |
| 13 | Alfreton Town | 46 | 16 | 12 | 18 | 69 | 74 | -5 | 60 |
| 14 | Cambridge United | 46 | 15 | 14 | 17 | 68 | 69 | -1 | 59 |
| 15 | Nuneaton Town | 46 | 14 | 15 | 17 | 55 | 63 | -8 | 57 |
| 16 | Lincoln City | 46 | 15 | 11 | 20 | 66 | 73 | -7 | 56 |
| 17 | Gateshead | 46 | 13 | 16 | 17 | 58 | 61 | -3 | 55 |
| 18 | Hyde FC | 46 | 16 | 7 | 23 | 63 | 75 | -12 | 55 |
| 19 | Tamworth | 46 | 15 | 10 | 21 | 55 | 69 | -14 | 55 |
| 20 | Southport | 46 | 14 | 12 | 20 | 72 | 86 | -14 | 54 |
| 21 | Stockport County | 46 | 13 | 11 | 22 | 57 | 76 | -19 | 50 |
| 22 | Barrow | 46 | 11 | 13 | 22 | 45 | 83 | -38 | 46 |
| 23 | Ebbsfleet United | 46 | 8 | 15 | 23 | 55 | 89 | -34 | 39 |
| 24 | AFC Telford United | 46 | 6 | 17 | 23 | 52 | 79 | -27 | 35 |

# Reflections

May 6th 2013. The Conference season was over. It was a time for recollection and reflection.

It had been an exciting season, full of uncertainty as to the ultimate outcomes. Automatic promotion was not decided until the final day of the season, when Mansfield Town became champions, two points ahead of Kidderminster Harriers. The final relegation place was also decided on the last day; unfortunately it went to Stockport County. The play-off final between Newport County and Wrexham was won 2-0 by Newport, who returned to the Football League after an absence of 25 years.

Discounting the twelve-match 'settling-in' period up to the end of September, six different teams had occupied the leadership position of the Conference, and the leadership changed hands on twelve occasions. Contrast this with the increasingly predictable Premiership, where the comparative figures are one and none respectively. Manchester United dominated throughout the season.

I noted earlier that this was a league where anyone could beat anyone, and often did! It was only after Christmas that two clubs - Mansfield and Kidderminster - rarely got beaten by anyone. Both clubs illustrate the fact that a poor or mediocre start to the season is no barrier to ultimate success. After ten games, Kidderminster were bottom of the table with 5 points, having played 10, drawn 5 and lost 5. Of their remaining 36 games, they won 28, drew 4 and lost only 4. They would have finished as champions, had it not been for an even more impressive sequence of results from Mansfield Town. At the end of 2012, they were stranded in mid-table with 32 points, and a record which read 'played

**Reflections**

21, won 9, drawn 5, lost 7. Of the remaining 25 games, they won 21 and lost only 4, finishing just ahead of Kidderminster, who then lost to fifth-placed Wrexham in the play-offs. There's a lot to be said for the play-off system, but it does sometimes carry with it a sense of injustice.

On Saturday, April 6th, two weeks before the end of the season, there were still eleven clubs vulnerable to relegation. AFC Telford United's fate had been sealed the previous weekend, but the other three places were not decided until the last week of the season, when Telford were joined by Ebbsfleet United, Barrow, and (eventually) Stockport County.

It had been a season of contrasts, as far as my 24 visits had been concerned. At several grounds – Lincoln, Grimsby, Stockport, Wrexham, Luton – it was like being back in the Football League. At others – Tamworth, Alfreton, Braintree, Hyde – you could imagine you were down in the Blue Square Bet North Division. One of the delights of the Conference is the contrast between the big (ex-league) clubs and the little clubs, who've never been in the League and wouldn't realistically expect to get there, with their part-time players. I particularly enjoyed the examples I witnessed of the latter taking on, and beating, the former (Dartford 1 Luton Town 0; Braintree Town 2 Luton Town 0; Forest Green Rovers 0 Southport 1). The part-timers Woking, Braintree and Dartford all finished in respectable mid-table positions, and Hyde, Nuneaton and Alfreton all survived, against the odds. Well done and good luck to all of them. Having said that, the top nine places in the Conference were all filled by the more affluent full-time clubs, of which all but one (Forest Green Rovers) had, within the past ten years, played in the Football League.

The quality of football I witnessed varied. At its best, as in the draws between Luton Town and Newport County (2-2),

Newport County and Wrexham (1-1) and Nuneaton Town
and Macclesfield Town (3-3), it was as good as anything
you'd see in Division 2 of the Football League. Many of the
teams promoted from the Conference in recent years have
prospered (Crawley Town, Stevenage Borough, Burton
Albion). I'd also seen a quota of more mundane games, but
there are plenty of those in Division Two as well. The sides
which I thought played the most attractive football were
Kidderminster Harriers, Newport County and, at least in the
earlier stages of the season, Gateshead and Macclesfield
Town. Amongst those in the lower reaches, Nuneaton
Town impressed me most. They, Braintree and Dartford all
benefited from playing settled teams, with players who
actually knew one another's game. What they lacked in
individual skill, they made up for in teamwork. Mansfield
Town were not a particularly attractive footballing side but
they were extremely effective. In the two games I saw,
(away to Woking, home to Nuneaton Town) they did
enough to win, but little more. They were not a side which
inspired affection.

I warmed to the friendliness of the Conference, particularly
amongst its smaller outposts. I liked the fact that, in the
smaller venues, segregating the visiting fans was not felt to
be necessary, and how they were usually welcome in the
bars of the home teams' supporters or social clubs. But
even in the bigger ex-league venues, people were happy to
talk to me and answer my questions. I experienced several
examples of the kindness of strangers: the bloke who gifted
me a stand ticket at Lincoln; the steward at Hereford who
went away to procure a programme for me at half-time and
brought it to my seat; the Cambridge supporter who gave
me his programme with his e-mail address on it, so I could
send him details of the book's publication; and the

## Reflections

Mansfield pub landlady who provided food for me a couple of hours after they'd officially stopped serving it.

There were many other memorable moments: the banter between Jimmy Dack, Newport's assistant manager and a section of the home supporters at Macclesfield; the friendly pat on the back for Nuneaton's Andy Brown from former colleague Ryan Young, the Telford keeper when the striker had missed a good opportunity; the older couple I sat next to at Stockport, with whom I exchanged memories of the town and the football club; the exceptional quality of the cheese and onion pies at Kidderminster; and the Lowryesque procession of homeward-bound fans at Wrexham seen in the fading light on the railway bridge above Wrexham General Station.

As far as football-specific memories are concerned, there was Macclesfield's Mathew Barnes-Homer's spectacular goal from an overhead kick at Gateshead; Ryan Donaldson's long-range dipper at Wrexham; the euphoria of Jon Nolan's winning goal for Stockport against Nuneaton; Steve Davis's neatly-taken headed goal for Braintree which gave them a 2-0 lead, and which heralded a deserved win against 'big-time' opposition; and the mutual celebrations of Southport players and fans at Forest Green, following a 1-0 victory which virtually guaranteed their safety.

I was impressed by the achievements of Forest Green Rovers (in particular) and Dartford in building new stadia which were refreshingly different, in both cases displaying an imaginative approach to energy conservation and sustainability. The most atmospheric stadia were the Racecourse Ground at Wrexham, Kenilworth Road (Luton) and Blundell Park (Grimsby). The most subdued were the Lamb Stadium (Tamworth), Gateshead's International Stadium, Alfreton's Impact Arena and the New Lawn at Forest Green (where the home supporters were particularly unsupportive). The most ramshackle ground was Barrow's Holker Street, closely followed by Luton's Kenilworth Road, which (unlike Barrow) was compensated for by the highly-charged atmosphere generated by the enthusiasm of the crowd.

My experience of the Conference was free of violence, with one unlikely exception. Woking was arguably one of the more affluent of the Conference towns I visited, but it was there that a post-match fracas took place between Mansfield Town players and a group of Woking supporters, following the smashing of a window in the visitors' dressing room.

There were several follow-ups to events I described in my pen-pictures of the towns visited, which are worth recording. Soon after my visit to Hyde (see Chapter 2) the town hit the national headlines (again) when two policewomen were shot dead on the Hattersley estate. In North Wales, a new enquiry was instigated into the prevalence of abuse at children's homes in the area, at which large numbers of witnesses came forward, many of them former residents of the Bryn-Estyn home near Wrexham (see Chapter 8). After November, Gateshead (see Chapter 5) never played another game at the International Stadium. The pitch developed serious drainage problems, aggravated by heavy rainfall, and has not yet become playable again. Gateshead played their remaining home fixtures at the grounds of Hartlepool United, Blyth Spartans, Carlisle United, Boston United (180 miles away, this one) and for the final face-saving game, Middlesbrough. Ebbsfleet United's relationship with My Football Club, which had become increasingly untenable, was finally terminated in April 2013, with the club needing to raise £70,000 to buy out My FC's stake (see Chapter 17); so Liam Daish can now pick his teams untrammelled by unwanted advice from My FC members (or could have done if he hadn't resigned in May). The use made of the £79,000 Mary Portas grant in Dartford to rejuvenate its disintegrating town centre (see Chapter 14) attracted further ridicule when it was revealed that a chunk of its grant had been spent on visits not just from Peppa Pig, but also Fireman Sam and Mike the Knight!

There have been further managerial changes too. Liam Watson resigned (amicably) after eight impressive seasons with Southport. Macclesfield's Steve King was relieved of his duties a few weeks before the end of the season. Being a Conference manager can be as precarious as managing a Premiership side! Into the Conference next season will come Barnet and Aldershot, down from Division Two, both of whom will know what to expect, having been there in the not-too-distant past. Up from the next level down will come Chester (back on the road to the League?), FC Halifax (likewise?), Welling (an occasional Conference presence since 1979), and Salisbury City.

So the season was over; a season of 24 trips to 24 different towns (or in four cases, cities). It started with a visit to Barrow, a place as distinctive as you could hope to find; an isolated shipbuilding town with a unique history and culture. It ended with a trip to Grimsby, the food processing capital of Europe (or so it claimed). Some of the towns I really warmed to, in particular Southport, Macclesfield, Braintree and Wrexham. In others there was something about the ambience of the place I found less appealing, in particular Newport, Nuneaton, Luton and Nailsworth. But they were all distinctive, interesting and collectively they greatly enhanced my experience and knowledge of the medium-sized towns of middle England and Wales.

But, as I'm sure has become apparent from the content of the last four or five chapters, the journey has not been without its anguish. You may (or may not) recall from the introduction that the main motivation of my journey and the book was relief at the survival in the Conference last season, of a club I have supported since 1956 – Stockport County. I expressed the hope and expectation that the implementation of my project would coincide with the promotion of Stockport back into their rightful place in the Football League. How unfounded this confidence turned out to be! Not only did Stockport not make it back to the Football League, but they ended up travelling in the reverse direction. Next season will be spent in the Blue Square Bet North League, with the likes of North Ferriby United, Gainsborough Trinity, and Vauxhall Motors.

The last few weeks of the season, during which I visited Telford, Forest Green, Luton and Grimsby, I will recall as much for my nervous anticipation of the Stockport County results, as for the games witnessed and the towns visited. How could they do this to me?! Would it have been any different if they hadn't sacked Jim Gannon in February? Can the third manager of the season, Ian Bogie, turn the club round? Are they right to become a part-time outfit next season? Can I stop tormenting myself with these unanswerable questions?

But it doesn't really matter does it? It's only a game. When there's widespread starvation in Africa, untold suffering in Syria, and increasing numbers of poorer families in Britain hit by the unjust welfare reforms (including the iniquitous bedroom tax), how can anyone of sound mind get too upset about the relegation to Blue Square Bet North of Stockport County (who 15 years ago finished 8th in the Championship), or too ecstatic about the promotion of Mansfield Town into the Football League.

Well, in comparison with all these much weightier issues, it doesn't really matter. But in another sense, if you attach importance to local communities, it does. 6,000 Stockport

## Reflections

residents turned out on an April afternoon to watch
Stockport play Dartford, in a game which would have
almost certainly guaranteed survival if they'd won. But they
lost 1-0 to one of the successful part-time outfits in the
Conference. No doubt many left Edgeley Park in tears, or if
not then, certainly when they learned of, or witnessed, the
4-0 defeat at Kidderminster on the last day of the season
which sentenced them to relegation (it's no consolation that
even if they'd won they'd still have been relegated).

Football is a wonderful game, based on the importance of
collective teamwork as much as individual brilliance. It is no
coincidence that it has captured the imagination of millions
of people who turn out on a regular basis to support their
local team, or even if they don't, check and care about the
result. The commitment and local significance operates at all
levels; as much in Alfreton and Nailsworth as it does in
Manchester and Liverpool. The link between a sense of
identification with the places where we live and support for
the local football team is important. We all need a sense of
place and a sense of belonging to a local community, and
football teams are the best vehicle I know for symbolising
and expressing these qualities.

For the many supporters, like me, whose sense of identity
with a local club developed in childhood, there is a further
way in which football becomes ingrained in one's persona.
Experiences of watching your local team become
intertwined with landmarks in one's personal history. I'd
just moved to Stockport in 1957, when I saw County defeat
Luton Town (then fourth in Division One) in the third
round of the FA Cup. I had recently started my first job as a
(very) junior planning officer in Chester in 1969, when
County held the mighty Liverpool to a one-all draw at
Anfield (third round again; they lost the replay 0-2).When
my father died in 1984, I went to Edgeley Park for the first

time in ten years, and felt, in a strange way, comforted.
Soon after I started work at De Montfort University in
Leicester in 1996, I travelled to Chesterfield and saw County
win one-nil and secure promotion to the Championship in
the penultimate game of the season. And I took my first son
Callum to his first big football match in 2000 (a two-all
draw against Bristol City in the Championship)So of course
it matters to me that next season County will have fallen
into a league where the average home attendance is around
four or five hundred. The town of Stockport and Stockport
County have become embedded within me, with key
matches acting as milestones in the trajectory of my life.

I will take comfort from the club motto of Hereford United
– 'Our greatest glory lies not in never having fallen but in
rising when we fall'. But I remain profoundly saddened by
the gulf between the great days in Stockport's (recent)
history, and where they are now bound for. But as
Stockport County go down, they will pass Chester FC and
FC Halifax coming up. Further down the pyramid are
Darlington 1883, with several levels yet to ascend to League
status (but they'll get there in the end). County can also
console themselves with the recent return of Accrington
Stanley (the club that refused to die) to the Football League,
and of Aldershot (who nearly did) although Aldershot are
now back down in the Conference. And Newport County,
who were expelled from the Conference in 1988 for failing
to fulfil their fixtures, made it back to the Football League,
which provides another encouraging precedent. Clubs with
histories like Stockport's rarely die. They'll be back, and
hopefully it will be whilst I'm still alive to celebrate. And
next season I fully intend to travel to places like Altrincham,
Stalybridge and Guiseley (if I can locate it) to lend my
support on the first stage of the journey back.

## Small Time: A Life in the Football Wilderness by Justin Bryant

In 1988, 23-year-old American goalkeeper Justin Bryant thought a glorious career in professional football awaited him. He had just saved two penalties for his American club - the Orlando Lions - against Scotland's Dunfermline Athletic, to help claim the first piece of silverware in their history. He was young, strong, healthy, and confident.

Small Time is the story of a life spent mostly in the backwaters of the game. As Justin negotiated the Non-League pitches of the Vauxhall-Opel League, and the many failed professional leagues of the U.S. in the 1980s and 90s - Football, he learned, is 95% blood, sweat, and tears; but if you love it enough, the other 5% makes up for it.

## José Mourinho: The Rise of the Translator by Ciaran Kelly

From Porto to Chelsea, and Inter to Real Madrid – the Mourinho story is as intriguing as the man himself. Now, a new challenge awaits at Stamford Bridge. Covering the Mourinho story to October 2013 and featuring numerous exclusive interviews with figures not synonymous with the traditional Mourinho narrative.

"Enlightening interviews with those who really know José Mourinho" – Simon Kuper, Financial Times.

"Superb read from a terrific writer" – Ger McCarthy, Irish Examiner

### Graduation: Life Lessons of a Professional Footballer by Richard Lee

The 2010/11 season will go down as a memorable one for Goalkeeper Richard Lee. Cup wins, penalty saves, hypnotherapy and injury would follow, but these things only tell a small part of the tale. Filled with anecdotes, insights, humour and honesty - Graduation uncovers Richard's campaign to take back the number one spot, save a lot of penalties, and overcome new challenges. What we see is a transformation - beautifully encapsulated in this extraordinary season.

### Saturday Afternoon Fever: A Year On The Road For Soccer Saturday by Johnny Phillips

You might already know Johnny Phillips. He is a football reporter for Sky Sports' Soccer Saturday programme and a man who gets beamed into the homes of fans across the country every weekend.

For the 2012/13 season, Johnny decided to do something different. He wanted to look beneath the veneer of household-name superstars and back-page glamour to chronicle a different side to our national sport. As Johnny travelled the country, he found a game that he loved even more, where unheralded stars were driven by a desire to succeed, often telling stories of bravery and overcoming adversity. People who were plucked from obscurity, placed in the spotlight and, sometimes, dropped back into obscurity again. Football stories that rarely see the limelight but which have a value all fans can readily identify with.

Printed by BoD™in Norderstedt, Germany